THE HIDDEN PLACES OF THE

DORSET, HAMPSHIRE & THE ISLE OF WIGHT

By Peter Long

Regional Hidden Places

Cornwall
Devon
Dorset, Hants & Isle of Wight
East Anglia
Lake District & Cumbria
Lancashire & Cheshire
Northumberland & Durham
Peak District and Derbyshire
Yorkshire

National Hidden Places

England
Ireland
Scotland
Wales

Country Living Rural Guides

East Anglia
Heart of England
Ireland
North East of England
North West of England
Scotland
South
South East
Wales
West Country

Other Guides

Off the Motorway
Garden Centres and Nurseries of Britain

Published by: Travel Publishing Ltd, Airport Business Centre, 10 Thornbury Road, Estover, Plymouth, Devon PL6 7PP

ISBN13 9781904434825

First published 1990, second edition 1994, third edition 1997, fourth edition 1999, fifth edition 2001, sixth edition 2003, seventh edition 2005, eighth edition 2009

Printing by: Latimer Trend, Plymouth

Maps by: ©MAPS IN MINUTES/Collins Bartholomew (2009)

Editor: Peter Long

Cover Design: Lines and Words, Aldermaston

Cover Photograph: Godshill Village, Isle of Wight
© www.picturesofbritain.co.uk

Text Photographs: © Bob Brooks, Weston-super-Mare
www.britainhistoricsites.co.uk

Foreword

This is the 8th edition of the ***Hidden Places of Dorset, Hampshire and The Isle of Wight***. The guide has been fully updated and in this respect we would like to thank the Tourist Information Centres in Dorset, Hampshire and The Isle of Wight for helping us update the editorial content. The guide is packed with information on the many interesting places to visit in the area. In addition, you will find details of places of interest and advertisers of places to stay, eat and drink included under each village, town or city, which are cross referenced to more detailed information contained in a separate, easy-to-use section to the rear of the book. This section is also available as a free supplement from the local Tourist Information Offices.

Dorset is a beautiful county with rolling chalk downs, dark heathland (so beloved of Thomas Hardy), the long ridge of the Purbeck Hills and an incomparable coastline with its wealth of magnificent rock formations sculptured by the sea. *Hampshire and the Isle of Wight* offer the visitor a wonderful combination of seafaring tradition in the many coastal towns and villages and wonderful countryside epitomized by the New Forest and the rolling hills of northeast Hampshire.

Hidden Places of Dorset, Hampshire and The Isle of Wight contains a wealth of interesting information on the history, the countryside, the towns and villages and the more established places of interest. But it also promotes the more secluded and little known visitor attractions and places to stay, eat and drink many of which are easy to miss unless you know exactly where you are going.

We include hotels, bed & breakfasts, restaurants, pubs, bars, teashops and cafes as well as historic houses, museums, gardens and many other attractions throughout the area, all of which are comprehensively indexed. Many places are accompanied by an attractive photograph and are easily located by using the map at the beginning of each chapter. We do not award merit marks or rankings but concentrate on describing the more interesting, unusual or unique features of each place with the aim of making the reader's stay in the local area an enjoyable and stimulating experience.

Whether you are travelling around the area on business or for pleasure we do hope that you enjoy reading and using this book. We are always interested in what readers think of places covered (or not covered) in our guides so please do not hesitate to use the reader reaction form provided to give us your considered comments. We also welcome any general comments which will help us improve the guides themselves. Finally if you are planning to visit any other corner of the British Isles we would like to refer you to the list of other ***Hidden Places*** titles to be found to the rear of the book and to the Travel Publishing website.

Travel Publishing

Location Map

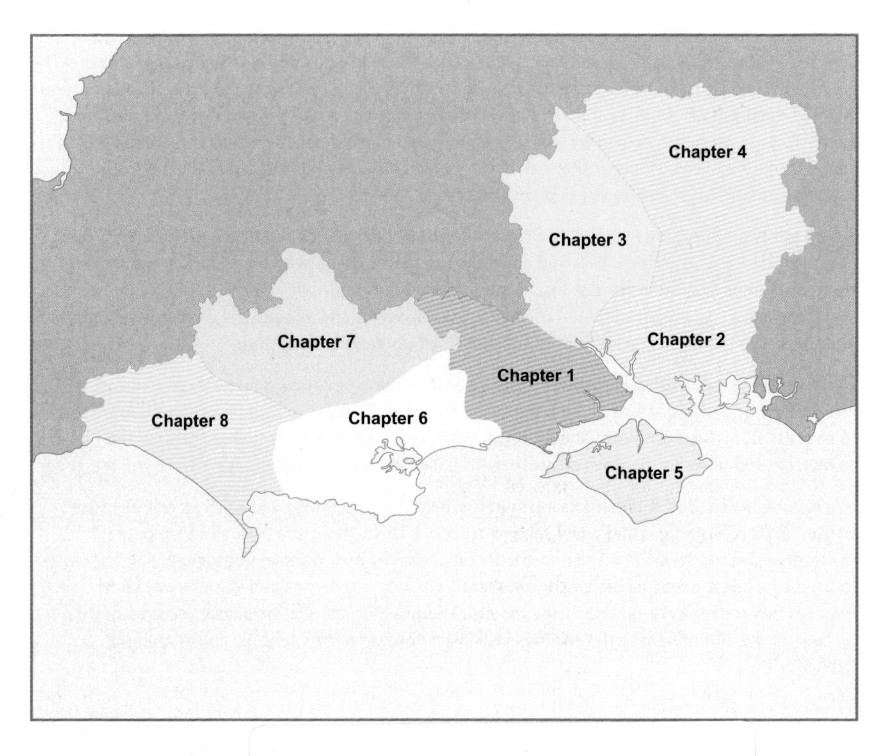

Contents

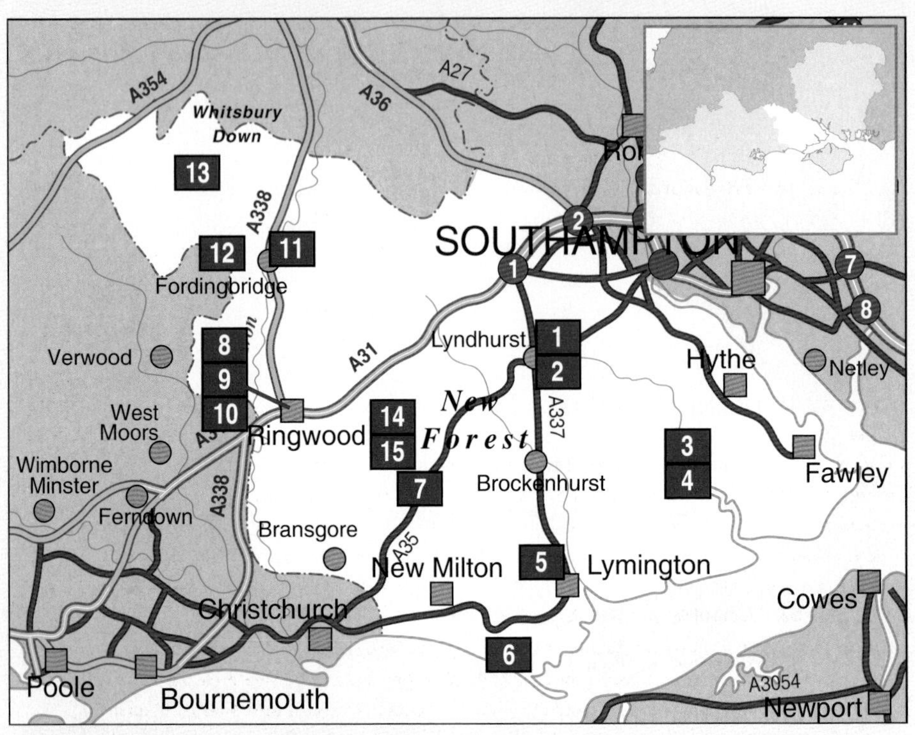

ACCOMMODATION

8	The Lamb Inn, Ringwood	p 12, 136
11	New Farm Cottage, South Gorley, nr Fordingbridge	p 13, 138
12	Alderholt Mill, Alderholt, nr Fordingbridge	p 14, 137
14	Wayside Cottage, Burley, nr Ringwood	p 15, 139

FOOD & DRINK

1	Under The Greenwood Tree, Lyndhurst	p 4, 132
2	Café Parisian, Lyndhurst	p 4, 132
3	The Royal Oak, Beaulieu	p 7, 133
5	Fisherman's Rest, Lymington	p 9, 134
6	Polly's Pantry, Milford-on-Sea, nr Lymington	p 10, 134
7	Station House At Holmsley, Holmsley, nr Ringwood	p 11, 135
8	The Lamb Inn, Ringwood	p 12, 136
9	White Hart Inn, Ringwood	p 12, 136
12	Alderholt Mill, Alderholt, nr Fordingbridge	p 14, 137
13	Rose & Thistle, Rockbourne, nr Fordingbridge	p 14, 138
15	The Old Farmhouse Restaurant & Tea Room, Burley, nr Ringwood	p 15, 140

PLACES OF INTEREST

4	Beaulieu National Motor Museum, Beaulieu	p 7, 133
10	Bettles Gallery, Ringwood	p 12, 136

The New Forest

Designated a National Park in 2004, the New Forest, as is the way with many English place-names, is neither New nor a Forest, although much of it is attractively wooded. Some historians believe that 'Forest' is a corruption of an ancient British word, *gores* or *gorest,* meaning waste or open ground. 'Gorse' comes from the same root word. The term 'New Forest' came into use after William the Conqueror proclaimed the area a royal hunting ground, seized some 15,000 acres that Saxon farmers had laboriously reclaimed from the heathland, and began a programme of planting thousands of trees. To preserve wildlife for his sport, (the deer especially), William adopted all the rigorous venery laws of his Saxon royal predecessors and added some harsh measures of his own. Anyone who killed a deer would himself be killed. If someone shot at a beast and missed, his hands were cut off. And, perhaps most ruthless of all, anyone who disturbed a deer during the breeding season had his eyes put out.

There are still plenty of wild deer roaming the 145 square miles of the Forest Park, confined within its boundaries by cattle grids, (known to Americans as Texas Gates). You are much more likely though to see the famous New Forest ponies, free-wandering creatures which nevertheless are all privately owned. They are also something of a hazard for drivers, so do take care, especially at night.

The largest wild area in lowland Britain, the forest is ideal walking country with vast tracts virtually unpopulated but criss-crossed by a cat's cradle of footpaths and bridle-ways. The Forestry Commission has also established a network of waymarked cycle routes which make the most of the scenic attractions and are also designed to help protect the special nature of the forest. A map detailing the cycle network is available, along with a vast amount of other information about the area, from the **New Forest Museum and Visitor Centre** in Lyndhurst. Visitors can watch an audio visual show, see life-sized models of forest characters, make use of its Resource Centre and Library, and explore a gift shop specialising in locally made forest crafts. The only town of any size within the New Forest, Lyndhurst is generally regarded as its 'capital', a good place then to begin a tour of the area.

1 UNDER THE GREENWOOD TREE

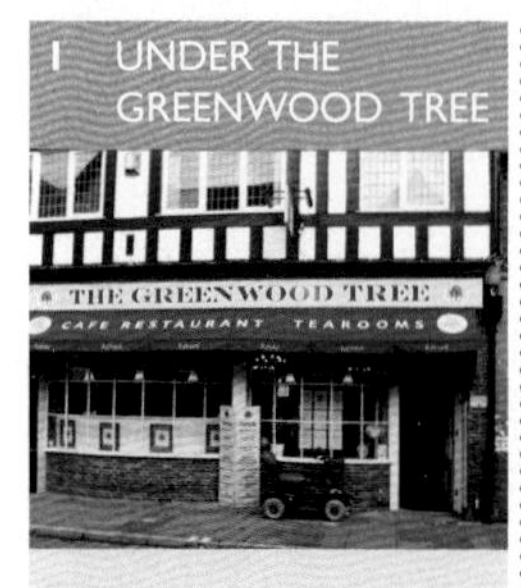

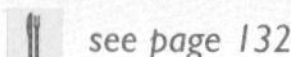

Lyndhurst

This quaint café in Lyndhurst is the perfect spot for lunch during an activity packed day in the New Forest.

see page 132

2 CAFÉ PARISIAN

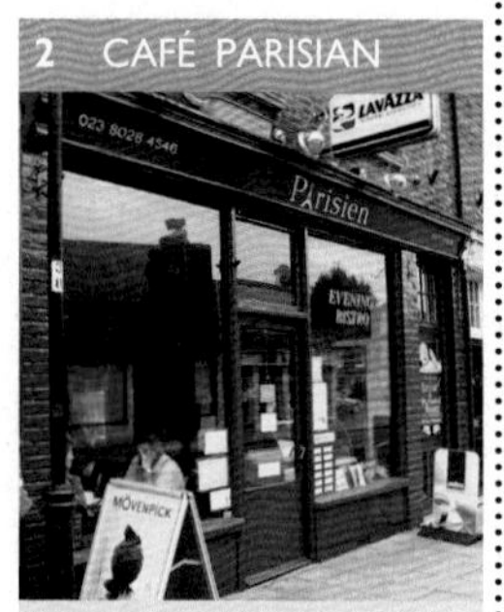

Lyndhurst

The quality food and drink, great service and warm welcome all create a wonderful place to escape the daily race.

see page 132

LYNDHURST

The most striking building in this compact little town is the **Church of St Michael**, rebuilt in mid-Victorian times in what John Betjeman described as "the most fanciful, fantastic Gothic style that I ever have seen". The rebuilding coincided with the heyday of the Pre-Raphaelite movement so the church contains some fine stained glass by Burne-Jones, produced by the firm of William Morris, as well as a splendidly lush painting by Lord Leighton of *The Wise and Foolish Virgins*.

In St Michael's churchyard is the **Grave of Alice Liddell** who, as a young girl, was the inspiration for Lewis Carroll's *Alice in Wonderland*. As Mrs Reginald Hargreaves, Alice lived all her married life in Lyndhurst and was very active in local affairs.

Next to the church is the **Queen's House** which rather confusingly is re-named the King's House whenever the reigning sovereign is male. Originally built as a royal hunting lodge, its medieval and Tudor elements are still visible. Many kings and queens have lodged here and the last monarch to stay, George III, graciously allowed loyal villagers to watch through the window as he ate dinner. Queen's House is now the headquarters of the Forestry Commission and is also home to the **Verderer's Court**, an institution dating back to Norman times which still deals with matters concerning the forest's ancient commoning rights. The verderers (forest officials) still sit in public ten times a year and work closely with the Commission in managing the forest. They also appoint agisters, or stockmen, who are responsible for the day-to-day supervision of the 5000 ponies and cattle roaming the forest.

At the **New Forest Museum and Visitor Centre**, in the heart of the town, visitors can learn about the history and the wide variety of plants and animal life that the forest supports. Interactive displays, activities and quizzes add to the appeal for younger visitors. There's also an exhibit exploring the mysterious death in 1100 of William Rufus, son of William the Conqueror, who was killed by an arrow whilst out hunting. It was officially described as an accident but some believe that it was murder.

This little town is noted for its variety of small shops where you can find "anything from fresh food to Ferraris!" Many are located in the High Street, an attractive thoroughfare of mostly Edwardian buildings, which gently slopes down the hill to **Bolton's Bench**, a tree-crowned knoll where grazing ponies can usually be found. The spot enjoys excellent views over Lyndhurst and the surrounding forest. At the other end of the town, **Swan Green**, surrounded by picturesque thatched cottages, provides a much-photographed setting where cricket matches are held in summer.

AROUND LYNDHURST

MINSTEAD

2 miles NW of Lyndhurst off the A337

The village of Minstead offers two interesting attractions, one of which is the unusual seating arrangement in the **Church of All Saints.** During the 18th century, the gentry and squirearchy of Minstead seem to have regarded church attendance as a necessary duty which, nevertheless, should be made as agreeable as possible. Three of the village's most affluent residents paid to have the church fabric altered so that they could each have their own entrance door leading to a private "parlour", complete with open fireplace and comfortable chairs. The squire of Minstead even installed a sofa on which he could doze during the sermon (delivered from an unusual 3-decker pulpit). It's easy to understand his concern since these sermons were normally expected to last for at least an hour; star preachers seem to have thought they were short-changing their flock if they didn't prate for at least twice that long. It was around this time that churches began introducing benches for the congregation.

Admirers of the creator of Sherlock Holmes, Sir Arthur Conan Doyle, will want to pay their respects at his grave in the churchyard here. He loved the New Forest and a few years before he died he bought a house at Bignell Wood near Minstead. The lettering at the base of the cross describes Sir Arthur as a 'patriot, physician and man of letters'. Minstead's other main attraction is **Furzey Gardens,** eight acres of delightful, informal woodland gardens designed by Hew Dalrymple in the 1920s and enjoying extensive views over the New Forest towards the Isle of Wight. Beautiful banks of azaleas and rhododendrons, heathers and ferns surround an attractive water garden, and amongst the notable species growing here are incandescent Chilean Fire Trees and the strange 'Bottle Brush Tree'. To the northwest of Minstead stands the **Rufus Stone**, said to mark the spot where King William II (William Rufus) was killed by an arrow while out hunting. His body was carried on the cart of Purkis, a charcoal burner, to Winchester, where William's brother Henry, who had also been hunting elsewhere in the Forest and had soon got wind of the accident, had already arrived to proclaim himself King. William had not been a popular monarch and his funeral in the Cathedral at Winchester was conducted with little ceremony and even less mourning. The fatal arrow was fired by a Norman knight, Sir Walter Tyrrel, who was aiming at a deer that had broken cover.

Rufus Stone, Minstead

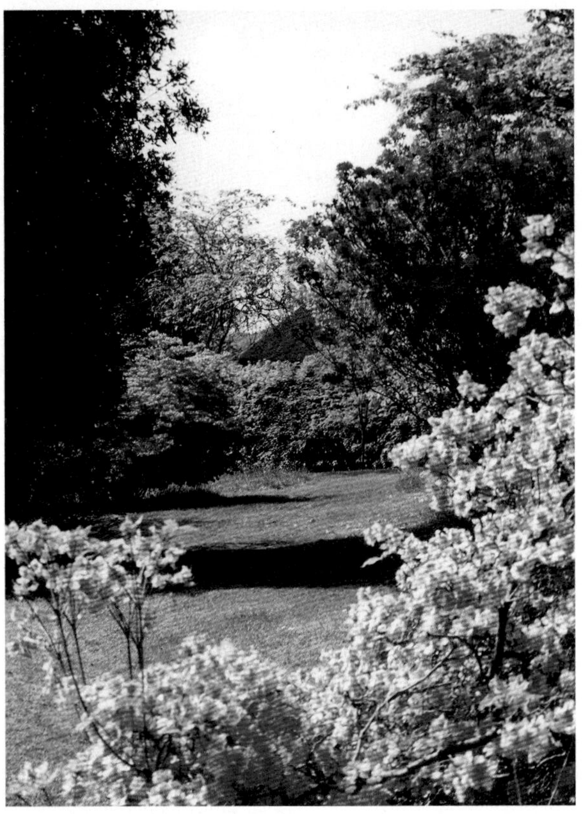

Furzey Gardens, Minstead

He missed the deer and the arrow bounced off a tree and hit William. Tyrrel escaped across the Avon at a point that has become known as Tyrrel's Ford.

ASHURST

3 miles NE of Lyndhurst on the A35

Just to the east of Ashurst, in 25 acres of ancient woodland, is the **New Forest Otter, Owl and Wildlife Conservation Park**, home to the largest gathering in Europe of multi-specied otters, owls and other indigenous wildlife. Conservation is the key word here. The park has an ongoing breeding programme for otters and barn owls, both of which are endangered species. Visitors can meander along woodland trails and encounter the otters and owls in their enclosures along with other native mammals such as deer, wild boar, foxes and badgers.

A popular family attraction, **Longdown Activity Farm** offers hands-on activities every day, including small animal handling and bottle-feeding calves and kids. There's an outdoor play and picnic area; indoor trampolines; tearoom and gift shop.

ELING

5 miles NE of Lyndhurst off the A35

Standing at the head of Southampton Water, Eling is notable for its working **Tide Mill,** the only one left in Britain. Naturally, its operation depends on the tides so if you want to see the mill working, call 023 8086 9575. The mill is on the old quay, close to the Totton & Eling Heritage Centre (free); there are pleasant walks from here along the reed-lined river.

HYTHE

8 miles E of Lyndhurst off the A326

A small town with a pleasant pedestrianised Georgian high street, Hythe is one of the very best places to watch the comings and goings of the big ships on Southampton Water. No visit here is complete without taking a ride along the pier on the quaint little electric train, the oldest electric pier train in the world. From the end of the pier, a ferry plies the short route across to Southampton. Hythe is the birthplace of the Hovercraft – its inventor Sir Christopher Cockerell lived in the town. In the 1930s Hythe was the home of the British Powerboat Company and of TE Lawrence (Lawrence of Arabia) while he was testing the RAF 200 series powerboats.

BEAULIEU

7 miles SE of Lyndhurst on the B3056

The ruins of a 13th century Cistercian Abbey, a stately home which grew up around the abbey's imposing gatehouse, and the **National Motor Museum** sited in its grounds are three good reasons why the village of Beaulieu has become one of the county's major visitor attractions. When Lord Montagu of Beaulieu first opened his family home to the public in the 1950s, he organised a display of a few vintage motor vehicles in homage to his father who had been a pioneer of motoring in Britain. That modest clutch of cars has now expanded to include some 250 of the oldest, newest, slowest and fastest motorcars and bikes in British motoring history, plus some rare oddities in the Weird Cars display. The motoring theme is continued in fun features such as Go Karts, Miniature Motors, and 'Fast Trax' which is promoted as the 'best in virtual racing simulators'.

Montagu family treasures are on display in **Palace House**, formerly the gatehouse of the Abbey, and visitors can meet characters from Victorian days who will talk about their lives in service.

It was an ancestor of Lord Montagu, the 2nd Duke of Montagu, who created the picturesque riverside village of **Buckler's Hard** in the early 1700s. It was designed as an inland port to receive and refine sugar from the duke's West Indian estates and His Grace planned his model village on a grand scale: the streets, for example, were to be 80feet wide. Unfortunately, the enterprise failed and only a single street was built. That 18th century street remains intact and unspoiled, and one of its buildings has been converted into a **Maritime Museum** reflecting the subsequent history of the village when it became a ship-building centre. More than 50 naval ships were built at Buckler's Hard, amongst them one of Nelson's favourite ships, the *Agamemnon.* Displays include models of ships, among them *Victory*, *Agamemnon* and the yacht *Bluebottle*, which Prince Philip raced with success. A special display recounts the exploits of Sir Francis Chichester, who sailed round the world in *Gypsy Moth* from his home port of Bucklers Hard.

A lovely riverside walk passes through **Bailey's Hard**, a former brickworks where the first naval vessel built on the river was completed in 1698. Henry Adams, the most distinguished of a family of shipbuilders, lived in the village

3 THE ROYAL OAK

Beaulieu

Fine old traditional hostelry with excellent cuisine; large beer garden

see page 133

4 BEAULIEU NATIONAL MOTOR MUSEUM

Beaulieu

The motor museum contains a superb collection of vehicles covering all aspects of motoring. The house is also open and together make a great day out for all the family.

see page 133

Beaulieu Abbey, Beaulieu

in what is now the Master Builders Hotel. In the summer, half-hour cruises on *Swiftsure* depart from the pier at Buckler's Hard.

EXBURY

10 miles SE of Lyndhurst off the B3054

Created by Lionel de Rothschild in the 1920s and still run by members of the family, **Exbury Gardens** fully justify the reaction of one visitor, who described them as 'Heaven with the gates open'. One hundred and fifty gardeners and workmen took 10 years to create the gardens, and Rothschild sent expeditions to the Himalayas to find the seeds he wanted. He himself bred hundreds of varieties of plants and the displays of rhododendrons, camellias and azaleas which he planted are renowned the world over. The 200-acre grounds are a delight to visit in spring, summer or autumn, with May perhaps the best time of all. A leisurely way of seeing the gardens is by taking a trip on the narrow-gauge Steam Railway. Many varieties of the Exbury specialities are on sale in the plant centre, where there's also a gift shop, tea room and restaurant – there is free entry to all of these.

Exbury's **Church of St Catherine** is best known for its moving, lifelike bronze memorial to two brothers who were killed in action in World War l. The work was commissioned by the brothers' parents and executed by Cecil Thomas, a gifted young sculptor who was a friend of the brothers. The area around Exbury and Lepe is featured in Nevil Shute's sad story *Requiem for a Wren*, which describes the preparations made in the New Forest for the D-Day landings. Shute himself was an aero-engineer as well as a writer, and for a time worked here on a top-secret pilotless plane.

FAWLEY

12 miles SE of Lyndhurst on the A326

Oil is king here, and the terminals and refineries of what is probably the largest oil plant in Europe create a science fiction landscape; standing bravely apart is the village church, a link with earlier days, looking out over Southampton Water. Fawley is where some islanders from Tristan da Cunha settled after fleeing a volcano that threatened their island in 1961; a model of one of the boats they used for their escape can be seen in the chapel. Also of note in Fawley is **Cadland House**, whose 8-acre garden overlooking the Solent was designed for the banker Robert Drummond by Capability Brown. It houses the national collection of leptospermums and also features a splendid kitchen garden and a modern walled garden. Beyond the refineries a road leads off the B3053 Calshot road to **Ashlett Creek** and another world, the natural, unrefined world of creeks, mud flats and bird-haunted marshland.

CALSHOT

14 miles SE of Lyndhurst on the B3053

The RAF was based in both World Wars at Calshot, where seaplanes were prepared and tested for the Schneider Trophy races. The hangars once used by the RAF are now the Calshot Activity Centre, whose many activities include an artificial ski slope. At the very end of a shingle spit stands one of Henry VIII's coastal defence castles. This is **Calshot Castle**, which is now restored as a pre-World War I garrison. Visitors can admire the view from the roof of the keep, walk round the barrack room that looks as it did before World War I and see the exhibition of the Schneider air races. A little way to the west is **Lepe**, one of the major embarkation points for the 1944 D-Day invasion. The area at the top of the cliffs at Lepe is now a country park, and there's safe swimming off the beach.

BROCKENHURST

3 miles S of Lyndhurst on the A337

A large village in a lovely setting in the heart of the New Forest. Forest ponies are frequent visitors to the main street and the village green (they naturally have right of way!) The **Church of St Nicholas** has a vast graveyard with a yew tree that is probably the oldest tree in the whole region. In the graveyard lie many soldiers, many of them from New Zealand, who had died of their injuries in a nearby military hospital. But the best known grave is that of Harry Mills, known as 'Brusher' Mills, who brushed the New Forest cricket pitch and followed the occupation of snake-catcher. His tombstone states that his 'pursuit and the primitive way in which he lived caused him to be an object of interest to many'.

LYMINGTON

An ancient seaport and market town, Lymington was once of greater importance than Portsmouth. It was also once a major manufacturer of salt, with hundreds of salt pans stretching between the quay and the tip of the promontory at Hurst Castle. There are some great walks along the tidal salt marshes which are designated a

5 FISHERMANS REST

Lymington

A traditional pub that welcomes many visitors to Lymington and its marinas. Tasty food and thirst quenching drinks on offer.

see page 134

Hurst Castle, Lymington

6 POLLY'S PANTRY

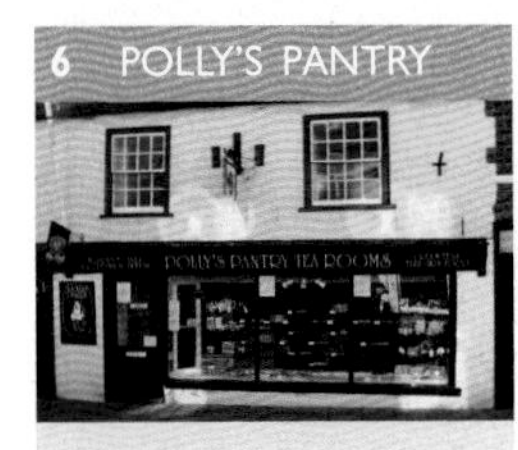

Milford-on-Sea

Nick and Jan provide a warm welcome, traditional cream teas and good food at reasonable prices.

see page 134

Site of Special Scientific Interest. The town itself is very appealing with narrow streets lined with period cottages and houses, and a high street leading down to the busy quay and marina where fresh fish is sold.

St Barbe Museum, in New Street, tells the story of the area between the New Forest and the Solent, with special reference to the salt industry, boatbuilding, smuggling and the area at war. There is also a changing exhibition of the work of artists both local and world-renowned – the gallery has in the past hosted works by artists as diverse as David Hockney and Goya. The broad High Street leading up from the quay is a hive of activity on Saturday, when the market established in the 13th century is held. A 4-mile railway linking Brockenhurst with Lymington was opened in 1858 as a rival to the already established route to the Isle of Wight via Portsmouth. The line was extended to the harbour in 1884; it survived the Beeching axe and was electrified in 1967. The Isle of Wight ferry runs from Walhampton, just outside Lymington, where a notable building is the Neale Obelisk, a memorial to Admiral Neale erected in 1840.

AROUND LYMINGTON

BOLDRE

2 miles N of Lymington, on the A337

"The village is here, there, and everywhere" wrote Arthur Mee in the 1930s, struggling to give some literary shape to an agglomeration of hamlets – Portmore, Pilley and Sandy Down, which together make up the parish of Boldre. Mee approved of the medieval church, with its squat square tower, standing isolated on a hill-top, and also paid due tribute to its 18th century rector, the Revd William Gilpin, whose books describing travels around Britain achieved cult status during his lifetime and even received a mention in Jane Austen's novel, *Sense and Sensibility*. Summing up his view of the village, Mee declared that "The quaint simplicity of Boldre is altogether charming". Some seventy years later, there's little reason to dispute his description.

In School Lane, on a slope overlooking the Lymington valley, **Spinners** is a charming, informal woodland garden with a national collection of trilliums.

MILFORD-ON-SEA

3 miles SW of Lymington on the B3058

This sizeable coastal village is notable for its fine, remarkably well-preserved 13th century **Church of All Saints;** its grand views across Christchurch Bay to the Needles; its excellent Shorefield Country Park and the odd-looking construction called **Hurst Castle.** At the centre of Hurst Castle is a squat fort built by Henry VIII to guard the Solent entrance against incursions by the French. Its tower is flanked by two long low wings added in the 1860s for gun emplacements, the square openings making them look rather like shopping arcades. The castle was used as a garrison right up until World War II but is now in the care of English Heritage which has an on-site exhibition explaining its history.

Hurst Castle stands at the tip of a long gravel spit which stretches out across the Solent to within three quarters of a mile of the Isle of Wight coast. It can only be reached by a 1.5 mile walk along the shingle beach or, in the summer months, by ferries operating from Keyhaven Quay, one mile east of Milford-on-Sea. The excursion makes a pleasant day or half-day trip since in addition to the castle itself there's safe bathing north of the lighthouse, good fishing off the southern tip of the spit, and spectacular views of the Needles as well as of huge ships making their way up the Solent.

To the north of Milford, **Braxton Gardens** are set around the red-brick barns of a Victorian farmyard. There are actually three individual gardens here: the Courtyard Garden with its pool and fountain; the Walled Herb Garden which features a knot garden planted with germander and lavender; and the Rose Garden with more than 100 varieties of roses.

NEW MILTON

5 miles W of Lymington on the A337

If you were allowed to see only one visitor attraction in New Milton, you would have a difficult choice. One option is the town's splendid **Water Tower** of 1900. Late-Victorian providers of water services seem to have enjoyed pretending that their storage towers and sewage treatment plants were really castles of the Middle Ages. They built these mock-medieval structures all around the country, but the one at New Milton is particularly striking. Three storeys high, with a castellated parapet, the octagonal building has tall, narrow windows.

If you are more interested in the arts, you'll be pleased to hear about **Forest Arts** in New Milton. Music of all kinds is on offer, from jazz, salsa and blues, to traditional and classical matinée concerts. Performances are conveniently timed so that you can arrive after picking up the kids from school. Other daytime events include slide talks by experts on a wide range of topics. Forest Arts also hosts some of the best contemporary dance companies around, ensembles who have performed at The Place in London and indeed all over the world. And if you enjoy the buzz and excitement of seeing new, vibrant theatre, the type of theatre which is on offer at the Edinburgh Fringe Festival for example, Forest Arts provides that as well.

SWAY

3 miles NW of Lymington off the A337

This rural village and the surrounding countryside were the setting for much of Captain Marryatt's *Children of the New Forest*, an exciting tale set in the time of the Civil War and written a year before Marryatt died in 1848.

In Station Road, **Artsway** is a visual arts centre that was originally

7 STATION HOUSE AT HOLMSLEY

Holmsley

A real 'Oasis in the Forest'; superb fresh food, award winning cream teas and an atmosphere to complement the stunning surroundings.

see page 135

Devotees of vintage motorcycles will make for a very different attraction. The Sammy Miller Museum, to the west of New Milton, is widely regarded as one of the best motorcycle museums in the world. Sammy Miller is a legend in his own lifetime, still winning competitions almost half a century after his first racing victory. More than 300 rare and exotic motorcycles are on display here. Also within the museum complex are a craft shop, tea rooms and a children's play area.

8 LAMB INN

Ringwood

Right next to the New Forest and not far from the coast, this comfortable Inn is in an ideal location.

see page 136

9 WHITE HART INN

Ringwood

This 350 year old Inn offers character in droves to go with its homely atmosphere, good food and great beer.

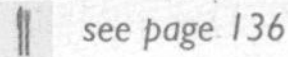
see page 136

10 BETTLES GALLERY

Ringwood

With a reputation for the quality of the work on display, this gallery specialises in British studio ceramics and contemporary paintings.

see page 136

a coach house; the site contains a garden and a gallery. South of the village is a famous 220feet folly called **Peterson's Tower**. This curiosity was built by a retired judge, Andrew Peterson, in honour of his late wife and as proof of the efficacy of concrete. The tower was originally topped by a light that could be seen for many miles, but it was removed on the orders of Trinity House as a potential source of confusion to shipping. The judge's ashes were buried at the base of his folly but were later moved to be next to his wife in the churchyard at Sway.

RINGWOOD

Wednesday morning is a good time to visit Ringwood since that is when its market square is filled with a notable variety of colourful stalls. The town has expanded greatly in recent years but its centre still boasts a large number of elegant Georgian houses, both large and small. **Ringwood Meeting House**, built in 1727 and now a museum, is an outstanding example of an early Nonconformist chapel, complete with the original, rather austere, fittings. **Monmouth House** is of about the same period and stands on the site of an earlier house in which the luckless Duke of Monmouth was confined after his unsuccessful uprising against James II. The duke had been discovered hiding in a ditch just outside the town and, despite his abject pleas to the king to spare his life, he was beheaded at Tower Hill a few days later.

Ringwood developed around a crossing point of the River Avon. Visitors can learn all about the town's history at the **Ringwood Heritage Museum** where the exhibits are specially designed to let you feel that you are there in the past – not just viewing it as an academic exercise. The extremely varied displays include a 'timewarp journey' that takes in the earliest settlements, Roman occupation, smugglers, Victorian life and the coming of the railway. A visit can be pleasantly concluded by taking refreshment in the 1940s-style tea room. The Museum is part of the Ringwood Town & Country Experience comprising 30,000 square feet of exhibition space.

The town still boasts its own brewery: at the **Ringwood Brewery Store** you can purchase its highly regarded Jug & Bottle draught beers, available in 4-pint 'pottles' up to 72-pint casks. On Wednesday afternoons during the summer, tours of the brewhouse are available during which visitors can taste the different malted barleys, see the fermentations bubbling and sample the beers.

A mile or so south-east of Ringwood, in the hamlet of Crow, the **Liberty's Raptor & Reptile Centre** is named after its impressive American Bald Eagle. 'Liberty' has plenty of companions – the Centre is home to the largest collection of owls in Europe. There are flying displays, both inside and out, daily lectures to entertain visitors of all ages, a café and shop.

This is also rescue centre, and in the hospital units Bruce Berry, founder of the sanctuary, and his dedicated staff have prepared hundreds of birds for release back into the world. As well as the owls, eagles and vultures Liberty's is home to giant rabbits, giant tortoises, snails, snakes, lizards and many other creatures. The Sanctuary is open daily from March to October and at weekends only during the winter.

Five miles west of the town stretch the great expanses of Ringwood Forest, which includes the **Moors Valley Country Park** at Ashley Heath. One of the most popular attractions here is the **Moors Valley Railway**, a delightful narrow gauge steam railway with rails just 7¼ inches apart. The railway has eleven locomotives, all in different liveries, and 33 passenger vehicles. The signal box at Kingsmere, the main station, was purpose-built but all the equipment inside comes from old redundant signal boxes – the main signal lever frame for example came from the Becton Gas Works in East London. At Kingsmere Station, in addition to the ticket office and the engine and carriage sheds, there's also a Railway Shop, buffet and Model Railway Shop.

AROUND RINGWOOD

ROCKBOURNE

3 miles NW of Fordingbridge off the B3078

One of the prettiest villages in the region, Rockbourne lies by a gentle stream at the bottom of a valley. An attraction that brings in visitors by the thousand is **Rockbourne Roman Villa,** the largest of its kind in the region. It was discovered in 1942 when oyster shells and tiles were found by a farmer as he was digging out a ferret. Excavations of the site, which is set in idyllic surroundings, have revealed superb mosaics, part of the amazing underfloor heating system and the outline of the great villa's 40 rooms. Many of the hundreds of objects unearthed are on display in the site's museum and souvenirs are on sale in the well-stocked museum shop.

A mile or so beyond the Roman Villa, looking out on to the downs, is the little village of **Whitsbury**, a major centre for the breeding and training of racehorses.

FORDINGBRIDGE

7 miles N of Ringwood, on the A338

The painter Augustus John (1878-1961) loved Fordingbridge, a pleasant riverside town with a graceful medieval 7-arched bridge spanning the River Avon. He spent much of the last thirty years of his life at Fryern Court, a rather austere Georgian house just north of the town (not open to the public, but visible from the road). Scandalous stories of the Bohemian life-style he indulged in there circulated around the town but didn't deter the townspeople from erecting a strikingly vigorous statue of him in a park near the bridge. John is also remembered

•

Within Moors Valley Country Park to the west of Ringwood, Go Ape! is an absolute must for those with a sense of adventure. The experience includes a high wire aerial assault course of extreme rope bridges, Tarzan swings and zip slides (age and height restrictions apply - call 0870 444 5562)

•

11 NEW FARM COTTAGE

South Gorley

Two quality self-catering properties located in the New Forest National Park.

see page 138

12 ALDERHOLT MILL

Alderholt

Picturesque working Water Mill in lovely surroundings offering both B&B and self-catering accommodation.

 see page 137

13 ROSE & THISTLE

Rockbourne

Quintessential English country pub in idyllic village close to the New Forest.

see page 138

with a special exhibit in the **Fordingbridge Museum**.

Branksome China Works is well worth a visit. Visitors can see how the firm, established in 1945, makes its fine porcelain tableware and famous animal studies.

On the edge of the town, there's a special treat for anyone who savours daft public notices. As a prime example of useless information, it would be hard to beat the trim little 18th century milepost which informs the traveller: "Fordingbridge: 0".

Two miles west of Fordingbridge off the B3078 - follow the signposts - is **Alderholt Mill** (see panel), a restored working water-powered corn mill standing on Ashford Water, a tributary of the Hampshire Avon. The site includes an arts and crafts shop and a place for the sale of refreshments and baking from the mill's own flour.

BREAMORE

10 miles N of Fordingbridge on the A338

Breamore is a lovely and largely unspoilt 17th century village with a very interesting little church with Saxon windows and other artefacts. Most notable, in the south porch, is a Saxon rood, or crucifixion scene.

Breamore House, set above the village overlooking the Avon Valley, was built in 1583 and contains some fine paintings, including works of the 17th and 18th century Dutch School; a unique set of 14 Mexican ethnological paintings; superb period furniture in oak, walnut and mahogany; a very rare James I carpet and many other items of historical and family interest. The house has been the home of the Hulse family for well over 250 years, having been purchased in the early 18th century by Sir Edward Hulse, Physician in Ordinary at the Courts of Queen Anne, George I and George II. In the grounds of the house, the **Countryside Museum** is a reconstructed Tudor village with a wealth of rural implements and machinery, replicas of a farm worker's cottage, smithy, dairy, brewery, saddler's shop, cobbler's shop, general store, laundry and school. Amenities for visitors include a tea shop and a children's adventure play area close to the Great British Maze. Children also love seeing 'Rye' – one of the estate's Flemish rabbits which are amongst the largest in the world. The museum's Millennium project was the restoration of an extremely rare Bavarian four-train turret clock of the 16th century, a fascinating piece of horological wizardry.

Mizmaze, Breamore

On **Breamore Down** is one of those oddities whose origins and purpose remain a mystery: this is a mizmaze, a circular maze cut in the turf down as far as the chalk. Further north can be seen part of Grim's Ditch, built in late-Roman times as a defence against the Saxons.

BURLEY

4 miles SE of Ringwood off the A31

At Burley, it's very clear that you are in the heart of the New Forest, with woodland running right through the village. A pleasant way to experience the peacefulness of the surrounding forest is to take a trip with **Burley Wagon Rides** which run from the centre of the village. Rides in the open wagons last from 20 minutes to one hour and are available from Easter to October. This lovely, unspoilt village with its picturesque thatched cottages, is also home to **New Forest Cider** where farmhouse cider is still made the old-fashioned way from local orchard apples and cider fruit. Visitors can taste and buy draught cider from barrels stored in the former cowshed. The centre is open most times throughout the year although ideally you should time your visit to coincide with pressing time when the grand old cider press is in operation.

14 WAYSIDE COTTAGE

Burley

This charming Edwardian cottage is the perfect base for exploring everything the New Forest has to offer.

see page 139

15 THE OLD FARMHOUSE RESTAURANT & TEA ROOM

Burley

The Old Farmhouse has a long tradition of quality food, friendly service and value for money.

see page 140

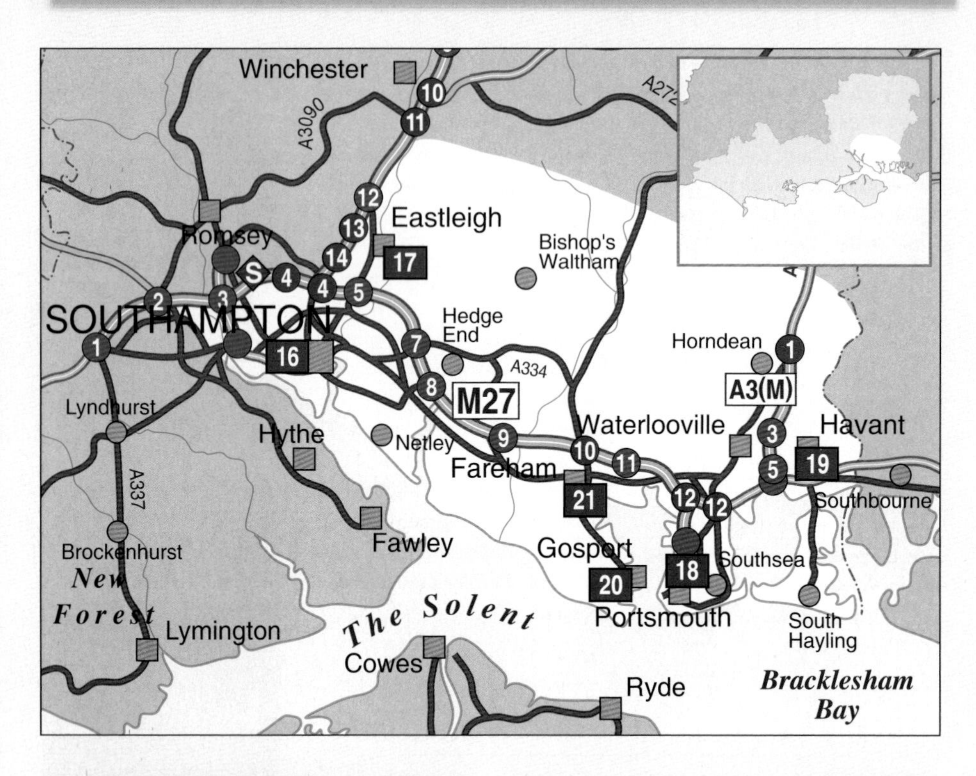

FOOD & DRINK

19	The Robin Hood, Havant	p 28, 142
21	The Crofton, Hill Head, nr Fareham	p 31, 143

PLACES OF INTEREST

16	Southampton City Art Gallery, Southampton	p 19, 140
17	Eastleigh Museum, Eastleigh	p 21, 142
18	Portsmouth Historic Dockyard, Portsmouth	p 26, 141
20	Explosion! The Museum of Naval Firepower, Gosport	p 30, 142

Southeast Hampshire

With a population of 1.2 million, Hampshire is the 5th most populous county in England. A goodly proportion of those 1.2 million people live along the coastal crescent that stretches from Southampton through Fareham and Portsmouth to Havant. Inland, though, there are parts of the South Downs as peaceful and scenic as anywhere in the country.

Southampton boasts one of the finest natural harbours in the world and has been the leading British deep-sea port since the days of the Norman Conquest. Portsmouth did not develop as a port until the 16th century but makes up for its shorter history by its romantic associations with such legendary ships as *HMS Victory,* the *Mary Rose,* and *HMS Warrior.* Portsmouth is also a popular seaside resort providing, together with its neighbour, Hayling Island, some seven miles of sandy beaches. Southsea Castle and massive Portchester Castle have interesting historical associations, and the ruins of Netley Abbey and the Bishop's Palace at Bishop's Waltham are both outstandingly picturesque.

Like most major ports, Southampton and Portsmouth have something of a cosmopolitan air about them, providing an intriguing contrast with the rural charms of the inland villages.

•

As you'd expect in a city with such a glorious maritime heritage, Southampton offers a huge choice of boat excursions, whether along the River Hamble, around the Solent, or over to the Isle of Wight. Blue Funnel Cruises operate from Ocean Village; Solent Cruises from Town Quay.

•

SOUTHAMPTON

From this historic port, Henry V set sail for Agincourt in 1415, the Pilgrim Fathers embarked on their perilous journey to the New World in 1620, and, on April 10th, 1912, the *Titanic* set off on its maiden voyage, steaming majestically into the Solent. More recently, in 2004, the *Queen Mary 2* set sail on her first voyage. The city's sea-faring heritage is vividly recalled at the excellent **Maritime Museum**, housed in the 14th century Wool House. The museum tells the story of the port from the age of sail to the heyday of the great ocean liners.

Tudor House, Southampton

As a major seaport, Southampton was a prime target for air raids during World War II and suffered grievously. But the city can still boast a surprising number of ancient buildings – no fewer than 60 scheduled Ancient Monuments and more than 450 listed buildings. Substantial stretches of the medieval **Town Walls** have miraculously survived, its ramparts interspersed with fortifications such as the oddly-named 15th century **Catchcold Tower** and **God's House Gate and Tower,** which now houses the city's archaeological museum. Perhaps the most impressive feature of the walls is **Bargate**, one of the finest medieval city gates in the country. From its construction around 1200 until the 1930s, Bargate remained the principal entrance to the city. Its narrow archway is so low that Southampton Corporation's trams had to be specially modified for them to pass through. Inside the arch stands a statue of George III, cross-dressing as a Roman Emperor. Bargate now stands in its own pedestrianised area; its upper floor once the former **Guildhall**.

Another remarkable survivor is the **Medieval Merchant's House** (English Heritage) in French Street which has been expertly restored and authentically furnished, now appearing just as it was when it was built around 1290. One of the most popular visitor attractions in Southampton is the **Tudor House Museum & Garden**, a lovely 15th century house with an award-winning Tudor Garden complete with fountain, bee skeps (baskets) and 16th century herbs and flowers.

Bargate, Southampton

Southampton's **City Art Gallery** in the Civic Centre is a treasure house of works ranging over six centuries, while the John Hansard Gallery in the University of Southampton and the Millais Gallery in Southampton Solent University specialise in contemporary art. Entry to all three galleries is free. The painter Sir John Millais was a native of Southampton, as was Isaac Watts, the hymnologist whose many enduring hymns include *O God, Our Help In Ages Past.* Other natives of Southampton include Admiral Earl Jellicoe, Benny Hill, Ken Russell, the MP John Stonehouse and the TV gardener Charlie Dimmock.

There's so much history to savour in the city, but Southampton has also proclaimed itself "a City for the New Millennium". Major developments include the flagship shopping area of WestQuay, the enhancement of the city's impressive central parks, the superbly appointed Leisure

City Walls, Southampton

16 SOUTHAMPTON CITY ART GALLERY

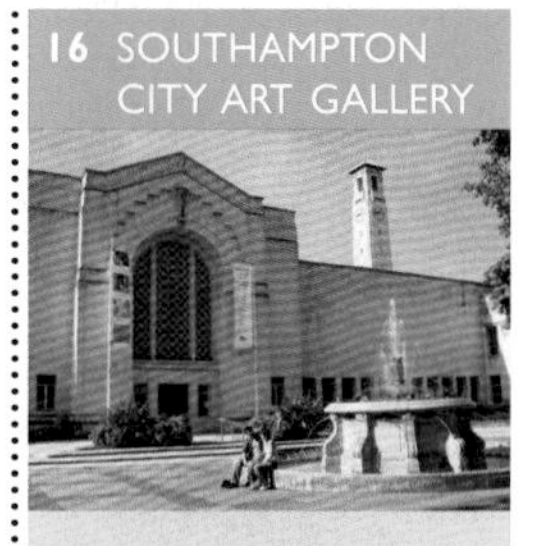

Southampton

An internationally renowed gallery, famous for its impressive collection and temporary exhibitions programme.

see page 140

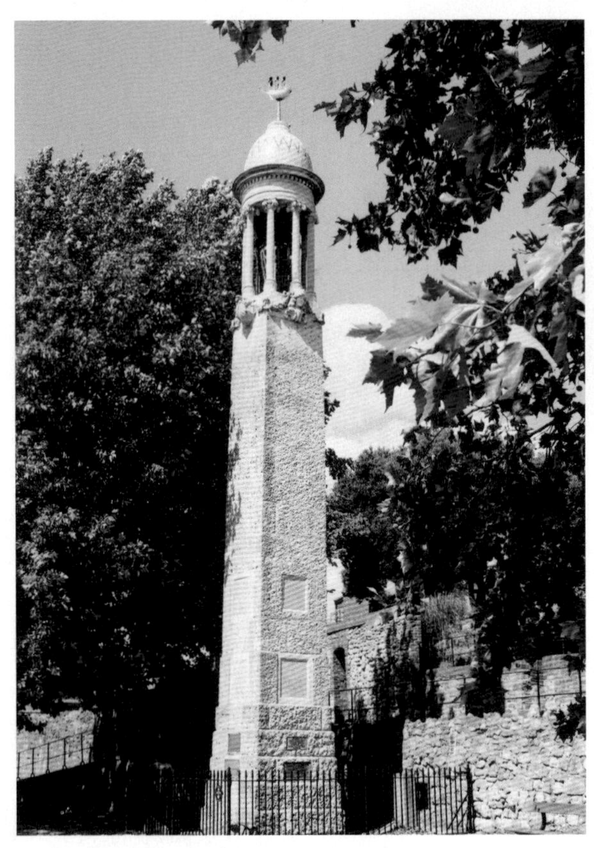

Mayflower Quay, Southampton

World; the state-of-the-art Swimming & Diving Complex which incorporates separate championship, diving and fun pools, and Ocean Village, an imaginatively conceived waterfront complex with its own 450-berth marina, undercover shopping, excellent restaurants and a multi-screen cinema.

The city also occupies an important place in aviation history. A short step from Ocean Village, **Solent Sky** presents the story of aviation in the Solent and incorporates the RJ Mitchell Memorial Museum. Mitchell lived and worked in Southampton in the 1930s and not only designed the Spitfire but also the S6 Seaplane which won the coveted Schneider Trophy in 1929. The centrepiece is the spectacular Sandringham Flying Boat which visitors can board and feel envious about the glamour and luxury of air travel in the past. Solent Sky is open from 10 to 4 Tuesday to Saturday, 12 to 4 Sunday; closed Monday except during school holidays.

AROUND SOUTHAMPTON

WEST END

4 miles NE of Southampton off the A27

An ideal destination for a family outing is **Itchen Valley Country Park** on the outskirts of Southampton. Its 440 acres of water meadows, ancient woodland, conifer plantations and grazing pasture lie either side of the meandering River Itchen, famous for its clear waters and excellent fishing. The Park is managed by Eastleigh Borough Council's Countryside Service to provide informal recreation, enhance and conserve wildlife habitats and as an educational resource. The best place to begin your visit is the High Wood Barn Visitor Centre, an attractive timber structure built in the style of a 17th century Hampshire Aisle Barn. From the Visitor Centre, waymarked trails help you to discover the different areas of the Park and an informative leaflet reveals the history and wildlife of a landscape shaped by hundreds of years of traditional farming and woodland management. Children are well-provided for at the park. In High Hill Field there's an adventure play area for the under-12s that includes an aerial runway, and behind the Visitor Centre a play area for the under-5s has giant woodland animals designed by local school-children and built by sculptor Andy Frost.

EASTLEIGH

5 miles NE of Southampton on the A335

Eastleigh is first mentioned in a charter of AD 932 but it wasn't until some 900 years later that it began to expand. That was when the Eastleigh Carriage and Engine Works were established in the town. At one time the works covered 60 acres and employed 3600 people. The town's railway connection is commemorated by Jill Tweed's sculpture, *The Railwayman*, which stands in the town centre.

Nearby, in a former Salvation Army building, is the **Eastleigh Museum** whose exhibits concentrate on the town's railway heritage. Visiting heritage, art, craft and photography exhibitions are also held here. The **Point Dance and Arts Centre** stages a full programme of theatre, dance, cinema and music events, while the **Beatrice Royal Contemporary Art and Craft Gallery** offers exhibitions of art, sculpture, ceramics, jewellery and textiles.

Just outside the town is the **Lakeside Country Park,** home to a variety of wild life and also a place for model boating, windsurfing and fishing. Here too is the Eastleigh Lakeside Railway, a miniature steam railway that provides trips around the park.

BISHOP'S WALTHAM

10 miles NE of Southampton on the B2177/B3035

Bishop's Waltham is a charming and historic small town. It was the country residence of the Bishops of Winchester for centuries and through the portals of their sumptuous **Palace** have passed at least 12 reigning monarchs. Amongst them were Richard the Lionheart returning from the Crusades, Henry V mustering his army before setting off for Agincourt, and Henry VIII entertaining Charles V of Spain (then the most powerful monarch in Europe) to a lavish banquet. The palace's days of glory came to a violent end during the Civil War when Cromwell's troops battered most of it to the ground. The last resident bishop was forced to flee, concealing himself beneath a load of manure.

Set within beautiful moated grounds the ruins remain impressive, especially the Great Hall with its 3-storey tower and soaring windows. Also here are the remains of the bakehouse, kitchen, chapel and lodgings for visitors. The Palace is now in the care of English Heritage and entrance is free.

The town itself offers visitors a good choice of traditional and

17 EASTLEIGH MUSEUM

Eastleigh

A re-creation of an engine drivers home and of part of a locomotive works helps to tell the story of what life was once like in the town.

see page 142

specialist shops, amongst them a renowned fishmonger, butcher, baker – even a candle-maker. And just north of the town you can visit one of the country's leading vineyards. Visitors to **Northbrook Springs Vineyard** are offered a tour of the vineyard which explains the complex, labour-intensive process of planting, growing, pruning and harvesting the vines, and a free tasting in the Vineyard Shop (open Tuesday to Sunday) of a selection of crisp, clear, flavourful wines.

South of Bishop's Waltham, at Waltham Chase, **Jhansi Farm Rare Breed Centre** is dedicated to the conservation of rare breed farm animals, some of them critically endangered. The Farm has a pets' corner housing a large variety of pure bred rabbits, guinea pigs, chipmunks and birds, a souvenir and pet shop, tea room, picnic and play area, nursery and water gardens, with events such as sheep shearing and hand spinning taking place throughout the season.

DROXFORD

13 miles NE of Southampton on the A32

Droxford is one of the larger and most attractive villages in the Meon Valley. It has some fine Georgian houses, an 18th century mill now converted into a private house, and a church dating from 1599 – one of very few built during the reign of Elizabeth I. From the churchyard, a path leading down to the River Meon would have been familiar to the 'Compleat Angler', Izaak Walton, who loved this river above all others. He was a frequent visitor to Droxford as his daughter was married to the rector and Izaak spent the last years of his life at the rectory.

Just across the river, the hamlet of Brockbridge once had its own railway station on the Meon Valley line. During World War II, Churchill, Eisenhower, de Gaulle and Jan Smuts all gathered here in a railway carriage to discuss the invasion of France.

BOTLEY

6 miles E of Southampton on the A334

Set beside the River Hamble, Botley is an attractive village of red brick houses which remains as pleasant now as when William Cobbett, the 19th century writer and political commentator, described it as "the most delightful village in the world….it has everything in a village I love and none of the things I hate". The latter included a workhouse, attorneys, justices of the peace – and barbers. The author of *Rural Rides* lived a very comfortable life in Botley between 1804 and 1817 and he is honoured by a memorial in the Market Square.

NETLEY

5 miles SE of Southampton off the A3025

A Victorian town on the shores of the Solent, Netley was brought into prominence when a vast military hospital was built here after the Crimean War. The foundation stone of **Netley Hospital** was laid by Queen Victoria in 1856 and the hospital remained in use until after

World War II. A disastrous fire in the 1960s caused most of the buildings to be demolished but the hospital's chapel, with its distinctive 100feet tower, did survive and now houses an exhibition about the hospital from the time of Florence Nightingale. The rest of the site has been developed as the **Royal Victoria Country Park** offering woodland and coastal walks, waymarked themed and nature trails, and trips around the park on a miniature steam railway.

Netley Abbey, Netley

Heritage of a different kind can be found at ruined **Netley Abbey** (English Heritage), a wonderfully serene spot surrounded by noble trees. "These are not the ruins of Netley" declared Horace Walpole in the mid-1700s, "but of Paradise". Jane Austen was equally entranced by the Abbey's romantic charm and she made many visits. Dating back to 1300, the extensive ruins provide a spectacular backdrop for open-air theatre performances during the summer.

BURSLEDON

6 miles SE of Southampton off the A3024

Anyone interested in England's industrial heritage should pay a visit to Bursledon. Ships have been built here since medieval times, the most famous being the *Elephant*, Nelson's flagship at the Battle of Copenhagen. The yard where it was built, now renamed the Elephant Boatyard, is still in business.

The village can boast another unique industrial site. When **Bursledon Brickworks** was established in 1897 the machinery installed was at the very forefront of brick-making technology. The works closed in 1974 but a charitable trust has now restored its gargantuan

Bursledon Windmill, Bursledon

•

Bursledon Windmill is the only working windmill in Hampshire. Built in 1813 at a cost of £800, its vanes ground to a halt during the great agricultural depression of the 1880s. Happily, all the machinery remained intact and after a lengthy restoration between 1976 and 1991, the sails are revolving once again whenever a good northerly or southerly wind is blowing. The mill produces stone-ground flour for sale and is open to visitors at weekends, or whenever the sails are turning!

•

To the south of Hamble is Hamble Common, an area of coastal heath providing a wide variety of habitats. On the shoreline stand the minimal ruins of a castle built in 1543 and at the eastern tip of the common is a Bofors anti-aircraft gun, installed in 1989 to replace one that had helped protect the docks and oil terminals further up Southampton Water during World War II.

machines, thus preserving the last surviving example of a steam-driven brickworks in the country. Special events are held here from time to time but the works are only open on a limited basis.

HAMBLE

7 miles SE of Southampton on the B3397

Famous throughout the world as a yachting centre, Hamble takes its name from the river, a mere 10 miles long, that flows past the village into Southampton Water. Some 3,000 vessels have berths in the Hamble Estuary so there's an incredible variety of boats thronging the river during the season, anything from vintage barges to the sleekest of modern craft. There are even a few fishing boats bringing in fresh fish to sell on the quay, which is also the starting point for the summer river bus offering trips along the river. On the western bank of the River Hamble, just upstream from the village, lies **Manor Farm Country Park**, an area of ancient woodland and farmland with the old traditional farmhouse at its heart. A typical Victorian farm has been reconstructed, with a wheelwright's shop and a Victorian schoolroom. Other attractions include vintage tractors and farm machinery, farm animals and riverside and woodland walks.

PARK GATE

8 miles SE of Southampton on the A27

Back in the days when strawberries still had real taste and texture, Park Gate was the main distribution centre for the produce of the extensive strawberry farms all around. During the season, scores of special trains were contracted to transport the succulent fruit to London, some 3,000 tons of it in 1913 alone. By the 1960s, housing had taken priority over fruit farms and today the M27 marks a very clear division between the built up areas to the south, and the unspoilt acres of countryside to the north.

OWER

5 miles NW of Southampton on the A3090

This hamlet on the edge of the New Forest is home to **Paultons Park**, 140 acres of landscaped parkland with more than 40 attractions that range from thrilling rides to bird gardens and museums.

PORTSMOUTH

The only island city in the UK, Portsmouth promotes itself as the 'Waterfront City'. Visitors can stroll for miles along the scenic waterfront that passes through Old Portsmouth and along Southsea's Victorian seafront. It's a great place for watching the great ships negotiating the Solent, ferries on their way to Hayling Island, Gosport or the Isle of Wight, and the scores of colourful pleasure craft.

Portsmouth is also often described as Flagship City. With good reason, since **Portsmouth Historic Dockyard** is home to the most famous flagship in British naval history, **HMS Victory.** From the outside it's a majestic, three-masted ship; inside it's creepily claustrophobic, except for the Admiral's and Captain's spacious, mahogany-panelled quarters. Visitors can pace the very same deck from which Nelson masterminded the decisive encounter with the French navy off Cape Trafalgar in 1805. Standing on this deck, ostentatiously arrayed in the gorgeous uniform of a British Admiral of the Fleet, Nelson presented a clear target to a sharp-sighted French sniper. The precise spot where Nelson fell and the place on the sheltered orlop (lowest) deck where he died are both marked by plaques.

HMS Warrior Engine Room at Historic Dockyard, Portsmouth

The death of Nelson was a tragedy softened by a halo of victory: the loss of the *Mary Rose,* some 260 years earlier was an unmitigated disaster. Henry VIII had ordered the ship, the second largest in his fleet, to be built. He was standing on Southsea Castle above Portsmouth in 1545, watching the *Mary Rose* manoeuvre, when it suddenly heeled over and sank. All but about 30 members of its 415-strong crew were lost. "And the king he screeched right out like any maid, 'Oh, my gentlemen! Oh, my gallant men!'" More than four centuries later, in 1982, the hulk of the *Mary Rose* was carefully raised from the seabed where it had lain for so long. The impressive remains are now housed in the timber-clad **Mary Rose Museum**. A recent

Historic Dockyard, Portsmouth

18 PORTSMOUTH HISTORIC DOCKYARD

Portsmouth

A superb day out for all the family. HMS Victory, HMS Warrior and the remains of the Mary Rose can all be seen as well as various interactive displays to test your skills.

see page 141

study claims that the sinking of the vessel was not due to the high wind, open gun ports and poor seamanship but to French gunfire. Having been holed and taking a quantity of water into her hull, she manoeuvred into a firing position, causing the water in the hold to move and capsize the vessel. The reasons given at the time are now held by some to have been invented to protect the reputation of the British Navy.

Another ship you can see at Portsmouth doesn't possess the same historical glamour as the *Victory* or the *Mary Rose,* but **HMS Warrior** merits a visit because when this mighty craft was commissioned in 1860, she was the Navy's first ironclad warship. A great advance in technology, but the distinctions between the officers' and crew accommodation show little difference from those obtaining in Nelson's day. Portsmouth's naval connection remains as strong as ever. In January 2009 a new kind of warship was greeted with a 15-gun salute, with hundreds of people, including the families of crew members. *HMS Daring* is the first of six Type 45 warships built to replace the ageing Type 42s.

Also within the dockyard area are the **Royal Naval Museum** which has a marvellous exhibition on the life and exploits of Nelson; and **The Dockyard Apprentice** where visitors can become a new apprentice for a day and learn the skills that helped construct the impressive Dreadnought battleships. Here too can be found **Action Stations**, a unique experience that brings the modern Royal Navy to life. Visitors can take command of one of the Navy's most advanced warships, 'fly' in a replica of a Merlin helicopter, and join the Royal Marines on exercise.

Opened in 2005 and dominating the Portsmouth skyline is the **Spinnaker Tower**, a striking building representing a billowing spinnaker sail. There are stunning sea views from the glass panoramic lift which stops at viewing platforms at 300feet, 315feet and 330feet high – the topmost one open to the elements. The tallest publicly-accessible structure in

Spinnaker Tower, Portsmouth

Britain, it reaches a final height of 550feet. It is set within Gunwharf Quays, a vibrant waterfront development with shops, bars and restaurants.

Like Southampton, Portsmouth suffered badly during World War II, losing most of its 17th and 18th century buildings. **St George's Church**, a handsome Georgian building of 1754 with large galleries, was damaged by a bomb but has been fully restored, and just to the north of the church, the barn-like **Beneficial Boy's School**, built in 1784, is another survivor. The oldest church building is **Portsmouth Cathedral** which dates back to 1188 although it was not consecrated as a cathedral until the 1920s. Naturally, the cathedral has strong connections with the Royal Navy: it contains the grave of a crew member of the *Mary Rose*; a fragment of the white ensign from *HMS Victory*; and some notable stained glass windows commemorating D-Day and the Normandy landings.

Portsmouth also offers visitors a wealth of varied museums, two of which deserve special mention: the **Royal Armouries**, housed in the huge Victorian Fort Nelson, claims to be 'Britain's Loudest Museum', with live firings every day; and the **Charles Dickens Birthplace Museum** at 393, Old Commercial Road, has been restored and furnished to show how the house looked when the great novelist was born here in 1812.

AROUND PORTSMOUTH

SOUTHSEA

1 mile S of Portsmouth on the A288

Now a suburb of Portsmouth, Southsea developed as a select residential area in the early 1800s. By the 1860s, it was well-established as a stylish seaside resort with elegant Victorian villas, tree-lined streets, green open spaces and colourful formal gardens.

One of the most interesting buildings in the town is **Southsea Castle** which was built in 1544 as one of Henry VIII's series of forts protecting the south coast from French attacks. It has been modified several times since then but the original keep is still intact and there are fine views across the Solent from the gun platforms. Inside, there's an exhibition on the military history of Portsmouth, displays of artillery and underground tunnels to explore.

Along the seafront are two more military museums: the **Royal Marines Museum** that tells the fascinating story of this elite group around the world, and the **D-Day Museum & Overlord Embroidery**, which commemorates the Allied invasion of Europe in 1944 and is most notable for the 83-metre-long Overlord Tapestry, a 20th century equivalent of the Bayeux Tapestry. Away from military matters, the **Natural History Museum** explores the diversity of wildlife in the area and includes a display showing what a natural history museum would

•

One major attraction in Southsea is the Blue Reef Aquarium where you can enjoy close encounters with sharks and rays, stroll through the spectacular underwater tunnel, watch otters at play in their riverside home and go eye-to-bulbous-eye with the amphibians in the Fascinating Frogs exhibition.

•

19 THE ROBIN HOOD

Havant

"Unexpected gem" of an 18th century town centre hostelry full of charm and character.

see page 142

have looked like in Victorian times. Between May and September, visitors can also enjoy walking through the Butterfly House filled with living insects and plants.

HAVANT

6 miles NE of Portsmouth on the B2149

Havant developed from a network of springs and a Roman crossroads to become a leading centre for the manufacture of leather goods, gloves and parchment. The **Havant Museum** has displays on the town and neighbouring places of interest as well as a special local studies collection of videos, photographs and maps. The museum also contains the nationally important Vokes Collection of Firearms. To the north of Havant lies **Stanton Country Park**, where the grounds include some interesting follies, an ornamental farm with animals, gardens, a tropical greenhouse, maze and puzzle garden, shop and tea room.

HORNDEAN

9 miles NE of Portsmouth off the A3

This busy large village has a long association with the brewing industry and, in particular, with **George Gale & Co**, a brewery that was founded in Horndean in 1847. Its award-winning HSB Prize Old Ale is brewed and bottled here and the company also produces a selection of traditional old country wines that range from birch & cowslip to damson & strawberry. Hampshire's only remaining independent family-owned brewery, the company offers guided tours by arrangement. Horndean is also home to the **Goss & Crested China Museum** which houses the world's largest collection of these popular Victorian and Edwardian souvenirs that have not been manufactured since the 1930s.

ROWLAND'S CASTLE

9 miles NE of Portsmouth off the B2149

This small village with its long green takes its name from a medieval castle whose ruins are largely obscured by a massive railway viaduct. To the southeast stands one of the area's most elegant stately homes, **Stansted Park**, a fine example of Caroline Revival architecture surrounded by 1700 acres of glorious park and woodland. Originally built in 1688, the house was virtually destroyed by a great fire in 1900 but was rebuilt in exactly the same style. The superbly grand state rooms contain some fine Dutch Old Master paintings and 18th century Brussels tapestries, and visitors are invited to enjoy a 'below stairs experience'. Outside, the grounds contain an exquisitely decorated chapel, a restored circular well head garden, an arboretum, falconry, Victorian glasshouses, woodland walks, children's play area and tea rooms.

WARBLINGTON

6 miles NE of Portsmouth off the A27

The **Church of St Thomas à Becket** here has a rather unusual timbered spire but the real curiosity is to be found in the graveyard – a pair of stone grave-watchers' huts.

These were erected at a time when body-snatching to provide corpses for medical schools was widespread. From these huts, men could guard the graves of recently interred corpses.

The cemetery is on the route of the long-distance Solent Way Footpath, one of many waymarked walks in the county.

EMSWORTH

6 miles NE of Portsmouth on the A27

This picturesque fishing village in the upper reaches of Chichester Harbour was once the principal port in the harbour. It's now best known for its annual **Emsworth Food Festival**, held each year in September, when the town's pubs, restaurants and cafés join forces to showcase locally produced speciality food.

HAYLING ISLAND

4 miles E of Portsmouth on the A3023

A traditional family resort for well over a century, Hayling Island manages to provide all the usual seaside facilities without losing its rural character, particularly in the northern part. Much of the foreshore is still open ground with wandering sand dunes stretching well back from the 4-mile-long shingle beach. Bathing is safe here and West Beachlands even boasts a European Blue Flag which is only awarded to beaches meeting 26 environmental criteria. One of Hayling's more unusual beach facilities is the line of old-fashioned beach huts, all of which are available to rent.

A good way to explore the island is to follow the **Hayling Billy Leisure Trail,** once the Hayling Billy railway line, which provides a level footpath around most of the 14 miles of shoreline.

Hayling is something of a Mecca for board sailors. Not only does it provide the best sailing in the UK for beginners and experts alike, it is also the place where board-sailing was invented. Many places claim that honour but Peter Chilvers has a High Court ruling to prove it. In 1982 a judge decided that Mr Chilvers had indeed invented the sailboard at Hayling in 1958. As a boy of ten, he used a sheet of plywood, a tent fly-sheet, a pole and some curtain rings to sail up an island creek. Fame recently came to a Hayling Island resident by way of an appearance on one of the Royal Mail's 2008 Christmas pantomime-themed stamps. Actress Wendy Adams-Evans represented the Wicked Queen from *Snow White* on the 81p stamp.

GOSPORT

2 miles W of Portsmouth on the A32

Gosport is home to another of Palmerston's forts – the circular **Fort Brockhurst** (English Heritage) which is in almost mint condition (currently closed to visitors). At the **Royal Navy Submarine Museum**, located at *HMS Dolphin*, visitors can experience a century of submarines. Stories of undersea adventures and the heroism of the Royal Navy's submarine services

•

The name 'Emsworth' will be familiar to devotees of PG Wodehouse who used it in several of his comic novels. He livedin Emsworth for some time in Record Road where a blue plaque marks his house. His stay in the village is recalled in the Emsworth Museum which also has exhibits reflecting its great fishing days, including a model of the Echo, the largest sailing fishing vessel to work out of any British port.

•

20 EXPLOSION! THE MUSEUM OF NAVAL FIREPOWER

Gosport

A hands on, interactive Museum telling the story of naval warfare, from the days of gunpowder to modern missiles.

see page 142

are recounted and there are also guided tours around **HMS Alliance**, a late World War II submarine.

The town's connections with the Royal Navy are further explored at **Explosion! The Museum of Naval Firepower** which is dedicated to the people who prepared armaments used by the Navy from the Battle of Trafalgar to the present day. As well as browsing through the unique collection of small arms, cannons, guns, mines and torpedoes, visitors can experience the pitch and roll of a moving gun-deck, help move barrels of gunpowder, and dodge mines on the seabed.

Away from the Navy's influence on the town, there is Gosport's splendid **Holy Trinity Church** which contains an organ that was played by George Frederick Handel when he was music master to the Duke of Chandos. The town bought the organ after the duke's death. Gosport also boasts one of the county's best local museums – **Gosport Museum & Gallery** – where the history of the area from prehistoric times is brought to life through a series of fascinating exhibits. And for those who enjoy a proper pint of ale, brewed in traditional fashion, the **Oakleaf Brewery** offers tours by arrangement.

PORTCHESTER

3 miles NW of Portsmouth on the A27

Standing at the head of Portsmouth Harbour, **Portchester Castle** is not only the grandest medieval castle in the county but also stands within the best-preserved site of a Roman fort in northern Europe. Sometime around AD 280, the Romans enclosed 8 acres of this strategic headland and used it as a base for their ships clearing the Channel of pirates. The original walls of the fort were 20feet high and 10feet thick, their depth much reduced later by local people pillaging the stone for their own buildings.

The medieval castle dates back to 1120 although the most substantial ruins are those of the royal palace built for Richard II between 1396 and 1399. Richard was murdered in 1399 and never saw his magnificent castle. Also within the walls of the Roman enclosure is **Portchester Church**, a superb Norman construction built between 1133 and 1150 as part of an Augustinian Priory. For some reason, the Priors moved inland to Southwick, and the church remained disused for more

Gosport Ferry, Gosport

than five and a half centuries until Queen Anne personally donated £400 for its restoration. Apart from the east end, the church is entirely Norman and, remarkably, its 12th century font of wondrously carved Caen stone has also survived the centuries.

FAREHAM

6 miles NW of Portsmouth on the A27

Fareham has expanded greatly since Thackeray described it as a "dear little Hampshire town". It still has considerable charm and the handsome houses on the High Street reflect its prosperous days as a ship-building centre. Many aspects of the town's history are featured in **Westbury Manor Museum** which occupies a large 17th century town house in the centre of Fareham. This old market town is also home to **The Royal Armouries at Fort Nelson** whose displays of artillery dating from the Middle Ages form one of the finest collections of its kind in the world. Among the 300 guns on show are a Roman catapult; a wrought-iron monster of 1450 that could fire a 60 kilogram granite ball almost a mile; Flemish guns captured at Waterloo; and parts of the notorious Iraqi 'Supergun'. Visitors can see some of the guns in action at daily firings and at special event days when the dramatic interpretations include accounts of the defence of Rorke's Drift, experiences under shellfire in the World War I trenches, and a Royalist account of the execution of Charles I.

TITCHFIELD

9 miles NW of Portsmouth on the A27

Just to the north of the village are the ruins of the 13th century **Titchfield Abbey**, its presence reflecting the former prominence of Titchfield as an important market town and a thriving port on the River Meon. The parish church contains a notable treasure in the form of the **Wriothesley Monument** which was carved by a Flemish sculptor in the late 1500s. This remarkable and massive work is a triple tomb chest depicting Thomas Wriothesley, 1st Earl of Southampton, along with his wife and son. It was the 1st earl who converted part of the now ruined abbey into a house and it was there that his grandson, the 3rd earl, entertained William Shakespeare.

WICKHAM

8 miles NW of Portsmouth on the A334

This village was the home of William of Wykeham (1324-1404), one of the most eminent men of his day. He served as Chancellor of England and Bishop of Winchester, and amongst many other benefactions was founder of both Winchester College and New College, Oxford.

To the northwest of the village is **Wickham Vineyard** which was established in the 1980s and has expanded over the years. The vineyard and modern winery are open to visitors who can take advantage of an audio tour, sample the wines and browse through the gift shop.

21 THE CROFTON

Fareham

A light and airy establishment offering top-quality food and drink and a warm welcome throughout the week.

see page 143

•

The mill by the bridge over the River Meon in Wickham will be of interest to American visitors since it contains beams from the American frigate,* Chesapeake, *which was captured in 1813 off Boston by the British frigate* Shannon. *The mill is now open as a craft retail centre.

•

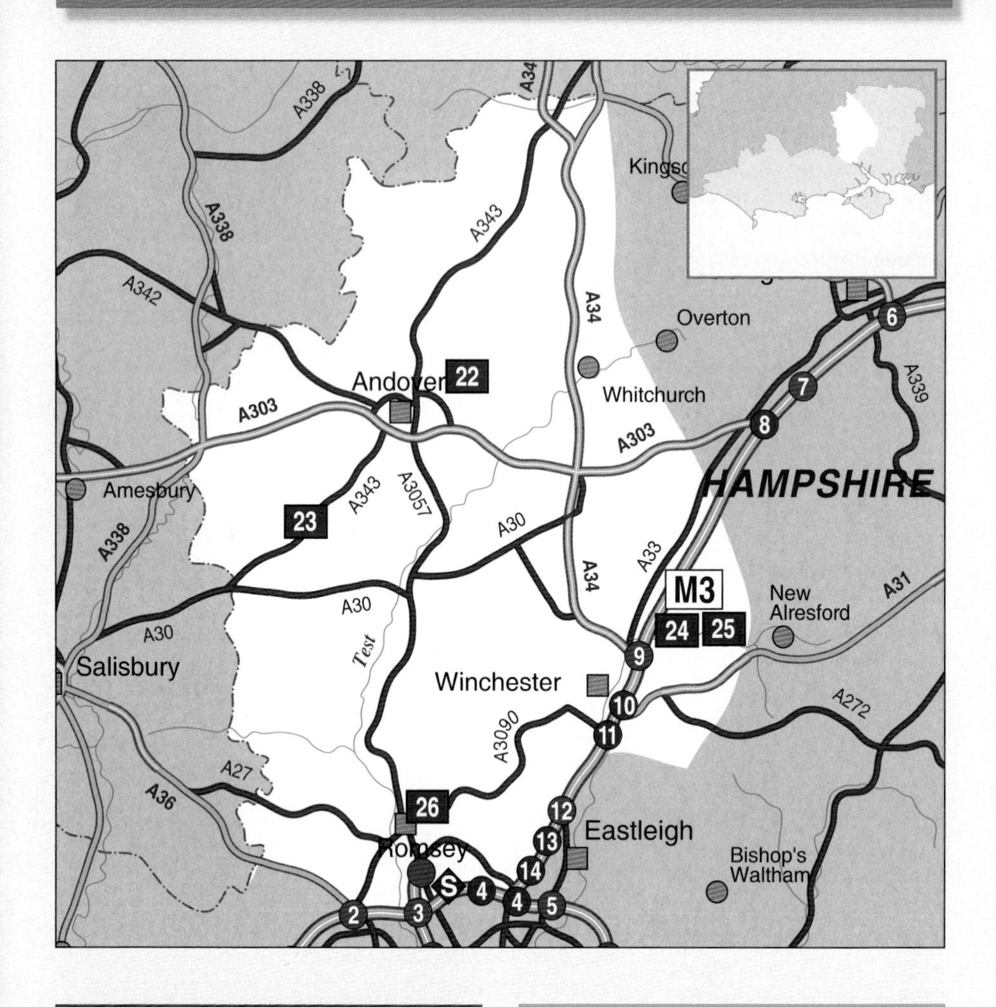

ACCOMMODATION

26 Ranvilles Farmhouse, Romsey — p 43, 146

FOOD & DRINK

24 The Chestnut Horse, Easton, nr Winchester — p 41, 144

PLACES OF INTEREST

22 Finkley Down Farm Park, Andover — p 34, 143

23 The Museum of Army Flying, Middle Wallop — p 37, 143

25 Avington Park, Winchester — p 41, 145

Northwest Hampshire

Some of Hampshire's grandest scenery lies in this part of the county as the North Downs roll westwards towards Salisbury Plain. There's just one sizeable town, Andover, and one major city, Winchester: the rest of the region is quite sparsely populated (for southern England) with scattered villages bearing evocative names such as Hurstbourne Tarrant and Nether Wallop. Winchester is of course in a class of its own with its dazzling cathedral, medieval buildings and King Arthur's legendary Round Table, but there are many other attractions in this area, ranging in time from the Iron Age Danebury Hill Fort, through the Victorian extravaganza of Highclere Castle, to Stanley Spencer's extraordinary murals in the Sandham Memorial Chapel at Burghclere. The 12th century Mottisfont Abbey is noted for its superb grounds, home to the National Collection of Old Fashioned Roses, while a further 11 National Collections and more than 40,000 exceptional plants can be found at the splendid Sir Harold Hillier Gardens & Arboretum in Ampfield. Also well worth visiting is Romsey with its glorious Norman abbey and stately Broadlands House, once the home of Prime Minister Lord Palmerston and later of Earl Mountbatten.

22 FINKLEY DOWN FARM PARK

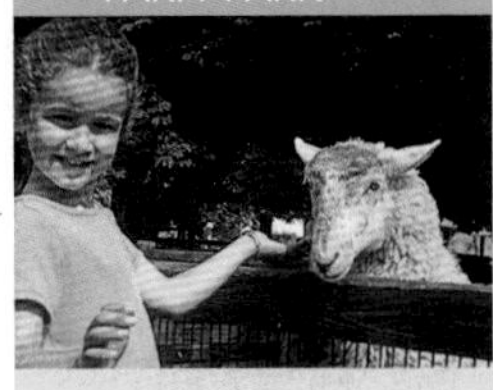

Andover

An enjoyable day out for the whole family, where the farmyard animals can be fed and petted. A large adventure playground will also keep the children entertained.

see page 143

A good way of getting to know Andover is to join one of the guided tours along the Andover Heritage Trail. Scheduled tours, lasting about 90 minutes, take place on Tuesday and Saturday afternoons but can also be arranged for groups at other times. More details on 01264 324068.

ANDOVER

Andover has expanded greatly since the 1960s when it was selected as a "spillover" town to relieve the pressure on London's crowded population. But the core of this ancient town, which was already important in Saxon times, retains much of interest. One outstanding landmark is **St Mary's Church**, completely rebuilt in the 1840s at the expense of a former headmaster of Winchester College. The interior is said to have been modelled on Salisbury Cathedral and if it doesn't quite match up to that sublime building, St Mary's is still well worth a visit.

Equally striking is the **Guildhall** of 1825, built in classical style, which stands alone in the Market Place where markets are still held every Tuesday and Saturday. Andover has also managed to retain half a dozen of the 16 coaching inns that serviced 18th century travellers at a time when the fastest stage coaches took a mere 9 hours to travel here from London. As many as 50 coaches a day stopped at these inns to change horses and allow the passengers to take refreshments.

For a fascinating insight into the town's long history, do pay a visit to the **Andover Museum** in Church Close. There are actually two museums here, both of them housed in buildings which began life as an elegant Georgian town house in 1750 and were later extended to serve as Andover's Grammar School from the 1840s to 1925. The Andover Museum traces the story of the town from Saxon times to the present day with a range of colourful exhibits which include a 19th century Period Room. There's also a fascinating display evoking Victorian Andover and a workhouse scandal of the time. The museum hosts an exciting programme of temporary exhibitions with subjects including art, craft, photography, history and much more. Former classrooms of the grammar school now house the **Museum of the Iron Age** which tells the story of Danebury, an Iron Age hillfort that lies 6 miles southwest of Andover.

Two miles east of Andover, **Finkley Down Farm Park** provides a satisfying day out for families with young children. Youngsters can feed and handle the animals, groom a pony, ride on a mini-tractor, and expend any excess energy in the well-equipped playground. Romany caravans and farming bygones are on display and other attractions include a tea room, gift shop and picnic area with a sandpit.

AROUND ANDOVER

FACCOMBE

9 miles N of Andover off the A343

This appealing little village, which is owned by the Faccombe Estate, is tucked away in the Hampshire countryside close to the Berkshire border, set on chalk Downs some 750feet above sea level, with the highest points of the North Downs, Pilot Hill and Inkpen

Beacon, both nearby. An extra attraction for walkers is the Test Way, a long-distance footpath which runs from Inkpen Beacon to the south coast following the track of the disused "Sprat & Winkle" railway.

About 5 miles west of Faccombe, just inside Berkshire, **Highclere Castle** is a wondrous example of Victorian neo-Gothic architecture at its most exuberant. If the central tower reminds you of another well-known building, that may be because the castle was designed by Sir Charles Barry, architect of the Houses of Parliament. Highclere stands on the site of a former palace of the Bishops of Winchester, overlooking an incomparably lovely park, one of 'Capability' Brown's greatest creations. The ornate architecture and furnishings of the castle interior delight many, others feel somewhat queasy at its unrelenting richness. Highclere is the family home of the 8th Earl and Countess of Carnavon. It was the present earl's great-grandfather who in 1922 was with Howard Carter at the opening of Tutankhamun's tomb. A small museum in the basement of the castle recalls that breath-taking moment. Another display reflects the family's interest in horse racing. For more than a century, Earls of Carnavon have owned, bred and raced horses, and the 7th earl was racing manager to the queen. In addition to the superb parkland, there's also a Walled Garden, planted entirely with white blooms, a gift shop, restaurant and tea rooms.

BURGHCLERE

11 miles NE of Andover off the A34

A couple of miles northeast of Highclere Castle, at Burghclere, the **Sandham Memorial Chapel** (National Trust) is, from the outside, a rather unappealing construction, erected in 1926 by Mr and Mrs JL Behrend in memory of a relation, Lieutenant Sandham, who died in World War I. Their building may be uninspired but the Behrends can't be faulted on their choice of artist to cover the inside walls with a series of 19 murals. Stanley Spencer had served during the war as a hospital orderly and 18 of his murals represent the day-to-day life of a British Tommy in wartime. The 19th, covering the east wall of the Chapel, depicts the Day of Resurrection with the fallen men and their horses rising up. The foreground is dominated by a pile of white wooden crosses the soldiers have cast aside. The whole series is enormously moving, undoubtedly one of the masterpieces of 20th century British art.

LONGPARISH

5 miles E of Andover on the B3048

Living up to its name, Longparish village straggles alongside the River Test for more than two miles. This stretch of the river is famously full of trout but no one has yet beaten the record catch of Colonel Peter Hawker who lived at Longparish House in the early 1800s.

In the 1990s, Middle Wallop, with its picturesque timber-framed thatched buildings became familiar to television viewers when it provided the main location for the 'Miss Marple' mysteries.

According to his diary for 1818, in that year this dedicated angler relieved the river of no less than one ton's weight of the succulent fish. A previous owner of the colonel's house had actually captured double that haul in one year, but the bounder had cheated by dragging the river.

Longparish Upper Mill, in a lovely location on the river, is a large flour mill with a working waterwheel. Visitors can see the restoration work in progress.

WHITCHURCH

6 miles E of Andover on the B3400

This small market town was once an important coach stop on the London to Exeter route. The coaching inns have gone but the town still boasts a unique attraction – the 18th century **Whitchurch Silk Mill,** the last such working mill in the south of England. Located on Frog Island in the River Test, the mill's waterwheel has been fully restored although today's power is provided by electricity. The mill now functions as a museum making silks for interiors and costume dramas such as the BBC's acclaimed production of *Pride and Prejudice*. Visitors can see the working waterwheel, watch the late-19th century looms weave the silk, have a go at weaving on a hand loom, view the textile and costume exhibition, and enjoy the riverside garden. There's also a tea room and gift shop. To the east of Whitchurch is **Bere Mill**, a weather-boarded construction where Frenchman Henri Portal set up a paper-making business in the early 18th century. By 1742 the mill had won the contract to supply banknote paper to the Bank of England and Portal moved his operation upstream to Laverstoke. The business continues from premises in Overton.

STOCKBRIDGE

6 miles S of Andover on the A3057/A30

The trout-rich River Test flows through, under and alongside Stockbridge's broad main street which reflects the street's earlier role as part of a drover's road. The town attracts many visitors for its famous antique shops, art galleries and charming tea rooms. Two exclusive clubs strictly control fishing on the River Test at this point but visitors may be lucky enough to catch glimpses of the fish from the bridge on the High Street.

Just to the south of Stockbridge are **Houghton Lodge Gardens**, the spacious gardens of an 18th century 'cottage orné' which have the tranquil beauty of the River Test as their border. Chalk cob walls shelter a kitchen garden with ancient espaliered fruit trees, glasshouses and herb garden, whilst in the Hydroponicum greenhouse plants are grown "without soil, toil or chemical pesticides".

MIDDLE WALLOP

7 miles SW of Andover on the A343

The village of Middle Wallop became famous during the Battle of Britain when the nearby airfield was the base for squadrons of Spitfires and Hurricanes. Many of the old buildings have been incorporated into the **Museum of Army Flying** which traces the development of Army Flying from the man-lifting balloons and kites of pre-World War I years, through various imaginative dioramas, to a helicopter flight simulator in which visitors can test their own skills of 'hand and eye' co-ordination. There's a collection of more than 35 helicopters and fixed wing aircraft and other attractions include a Museum Shop, licensed café & restaurant, and a grassed picnic area. The highlight of the museum's year is the Music in the Air event at the end of July. As the strains of a live orchestra ring out, the air is filled with breathtaking synchronised flying displays by aerial artistes such as the Red Devils.

Situated about a mile to the east of the village, **Danebury Vineyards** welcomes groups of visitors by arrangement for a guided tour of the 6 acres of vines and winery. Tastings and dinners can also be arranged. The vineyard was planted in 1988 on south facing slopes of free draining chalk, an excellent siting for the varieties of grape grown here. The British climate generally results in a late-ripening crop producing grapes which are most suitable for the white wines with which Danebury Vineyards has made its name. About three miles east of Middle Wallop, **Danebury Ring** is Hampshire's largest Iron Age hill fort. Occupied from about 550 BC until the arrival of the Romans, the site has been meticulously excavated and the finds are now displayed at the Museum of the Iron Age in Andover. Visitors can wander round the site and, with the help of explanatory boards, reconstruct the once-thriving community with its clearly defined roads, shops, homes and places of worship.

NETHER WALLOP

8 miles SW of Andover off the A343

The names of the three Wallops, (Over, Middle and Nether), have provided a good deal of amusement to visitors over the centuries, so it's slightly disappointing to discover that Wallop is just a corruption of the Old English word *waell-hop*, meaning a valley with a stream. At Nether Wallop, the prettiest of the three, the stream is picturesquely lined with willow trees, while the village itself is equally attractive with many thatched or timbered houses. The most notable building in Nether Wallop is **St Andrew's Church,** partly because of its Norman features and handsome West Tower of 1704, but also because of its striking medieval wall paintings which provide an interesting contrast with Stanley Spencer's at Burghclere. Some 500 years old, these lay hidden for generations under layers of plaster and were only rediscovered in the 1950s. The most impressive of them shows St George slaying the dragon. Outside St Andrew's stands

23 MUSEUM OF ARMY FLYING

Middle Wallop

The story of military aviation is told through a series of exciting displays, from the use of kites and gliders to todays combat helicopters.

see page 143

an item of great interest for collectors of churchyard oddities. It's a dark grey stone pyramid, 15feet high, with red stone flames rising from its tip. This daunting monument was erected at his own expense and in memory of himself by Francis Douce, 'Doctor of Physick', who died in 1760. Dr Douce also left an endowment to build a village school on condition that the parishioners would properly maintain the pyramid.

WEYHILL

3 miles W of Andover on the A342

In its day the October Weyhill Fair was an event of some importance. In Thomas Hardy's *Mayor of Casterbridge* it appears as the Weydon Priors Market where the future mayor sells his wife and child.

Just south of Weyhill, off the A303, the 22 acres of the **Hawk Conservancy Trust** is home to more than 150 birds of prey, including eagles, falcons, condors, kites and vultures. The highlights of a visit are the three flying displays every day, each with a different team of birds. Children can hold an owl, take a Raptor Safari Tractor ride, watch the runner duck racing, or just work off some energy in the adventure play area. For adults, there are bird viewing hides, a butterfly garden and a colourful wildflower meadow, or they can fly a hawk or just explore the beautiful woodland grounds. The grounds here are also home to Shire horses, Sika deer, Hampshire Down sheep and red squirrels that have been given their own aerial runway.

THRUXTON

5 miles W of Andover off the A303

This large village with many thatched cottages is well known for its **Motor Racing Circuit** which is built on a World War II airfield. Its annual calendar of events takes in many aspects of the sport including Formula Three, Touring Cars, British Super Bikes, Trucks and Karts.

PENTON MEWSEY

3 miles NW of Andover off the A342 or A343

For those who enjoy deciphering the cryptic place-names of English villages, Penton Mewsey offers a satisfying challenge. The answer goes like this: Penton was a 'tun' (enclosure or farm) paying a 'pen' (penny) as annual rent. That's the Saxon part. Later, in the early 1200s, Penton was owned by Robert de Meisy so his surname provided the second part of the village's name.

The town of Andover has now expanded to Penton Mewsey's parish boundaries but the village itself remains more rural than urban, and even has a field at its centre.

APPLESHAW

4 miles NW of Andover off the A342

The houses in the village of Appleshaw sit comfortably along both sides of its broad, single street. Many of them are thatched and a useful, century-old clock in the middle of the street, placed here to celebrate Queen Victoria's Jubilee, adds to the time-defying atmosphere. The former Vicarage, built in Georgian times, is as gracious as you would expect of that era, and the neo-Gothic architecture of the parish church, rebuilt in 1830, is in entire harmony with its earlier neighbours.

TANGLEY

5 miles NW of Andover off the A342 or A343

For the best views, approach Tangley from the east, along the country lane from Hurstbourne Tarrant. Its mostly Victorian church is notable for its rare font, one of only 38 in the whole country made of lead and the only one in Hampshire. Dating back to the early 1600s, it is decorated with Tudor roses, crowned thistles, and fleur-de-lys.

The old Roman road from Winchester to Cirencester, the **Icknield Way,** runs through the parish of Tangley. Most of this part of the county is designated an Area of Outstanding Natural Beauty and the scenery is enchanting.

WINCHESTER

One of the country's most historic and beautiful cities, Winchester was adopted by King Alfred as the capital of his kingdom of Wessex, a realm which then included most of southern England. There had been a settlement here since the Iron Age and in Roman times, as Venta Belgarum, it became an important military base. **The Brooks Experience**, located within the modern Brooks Shopping Centre, has displays based on excavated Roman remains with its star exhibit a reconstructed room from an early-4th century town-house.

When the Imperial Legions returned to Rome, the town declined until it was refounded by King Alfred in the late 800s. Alfred's street plan still provides the basic outline of the city centre and in 2003 his last known resting place was commemorated by the opening of Hyde Abbey Garden.

A Saxon cathedral had been built in the 7th century but the present magnificent **Cathedral**, easily the most imposing and

Winchester Cathedral, Winchester

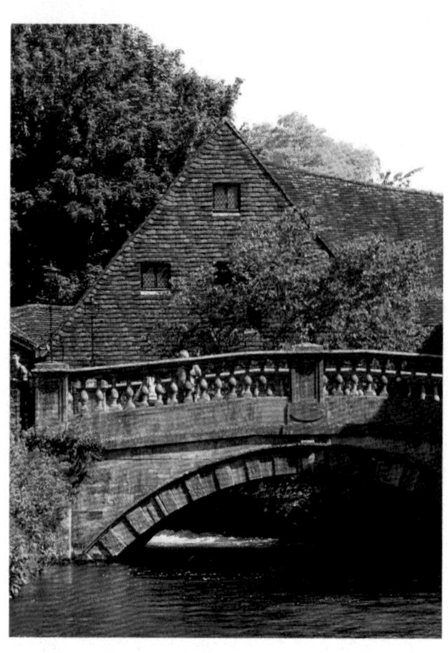

Winchester City Mill, Winchester

interesting building in Hampshire, dates back to 1079. It's impossible in a few words to do justice to this glorious building and its countless treasures such as the famous Winchester Bible, a 12th century illuminated manuscript that took more than 15 years to complete using pure gold and lapis lazuli from Afghanistan. Winchester Cathedral boasts the longest nave in Europe, a dazzling 14th century masterpiece in the Perpendicular style, a wealth of fine wooden carvings, and gems within a gem such as the richly decorated Bishop Waynflete's Chantry of 1486. Sumptuous medieval monuments, like the effigy of William of Wykeham, founder of Winchester College, provide a striking contrast to the simple black stone floorslabs which separately mark the graves of Izaak Walton and Jane Austen. One of the more unusual memorials is the statue of William Walker, a diver who spent six years, from 1906, working full-time under water as he laboriously removed the logs that had supported the cathedral for 800 years and replaced those rotting foundations with cement.

Within the beautiful Cathedral Close, popular with picnickers, are two other buildings of outstanding interest. No. 8, College Street, a rather austere Georgian house with a first-floor bay window, is **Jane Austen's House** in which she spent the last six weeks of her life in 1817. The house is private but a slate plaque above the front door records her residence here. Two years after Jane Austen was buried in the Cathedral, the poet John Keats stayed in Winchester and wrote his timeless *Ode to Autumn – 'seasons of mist and mellow fruitfulness'.* Right next door stands **Winchester College,** the oldest school in England, founded in 1382 by Bishop William of Wykeham to provide education for seventy 'poor and needy scholars'. Substantial parts of the 14th century buildings still stand, including the beautiful Chapel. The Chapel is always open to visitors and there are guided tours around the other parts of the college from April to September. If you can time your visit during the school holidays, more of the college is available to view.

Another literary connection is with Anthony Trollope who attended Winchester College briefly and later transformed the city into the 'Barchester' of his novels. A true incident at a Winchester almshouse provided the basis for his novel, *The Warden.*

The city's other attractions are so numerous one can only mention a few of the most important. **The Great Hall**, off the High Street, is the only surviving part of the medieval castle rebuilt by Henry III between 1222 and 1236. Nikolaus Pevsner considered it "the finest medieval hall in England after Westminster Hall". On one wall hangs the great multi-coloured Round Table traditionally associated with King Arthur but actually made in Tudor times – the painted figure at the top closely resembles Henry VIII. Located within the castle grounds are no fewer than six military museums, including the Gurkha Museum, the King's Royal Hussars Museum whose displays include an exhibit on the famous Charge of the Light Brigade, and the Royal Green Jackets Museum which contains a superb diorama of the Battle of Waterloo.

Other buildings of interest include the early-14th century **Pilgrim Hall**, part of the Pilgrim School, and originally used as lodgings for pilgrims to the shrine of St Swithun; the **Westgate Museum**, occupying one of the city's medieval gateways which also served as a debtors' prison for 150 years; and **Wolvesey Castle** (English Heritage), the residence of the Bishops of Winchester since AD 963. The present palace is a gracious, classical building erected in the 1680s, flanked by the imposing ruins of its 14th century predecessor which was one of the grandest buildings in medieval England. It was here, in 1554, that Queen Mary first met Philip of Spain and where the wedding banquet was held the next day. Also well worth a visit is the 15th century **Hospital of St Cross,** England's oldest almshouse once described by Simon Jenkins as "a Norman cathedral in miniature". Founded in 1132 by Henri du Blois, grandson of William the Conqueror, it was extended in 1446 by Cardinal Beaufort, son of John of Gaunt. It is still home to 25 Brothers and maintains its long tradition of hospitality by dispensing the traditional Wayfarer's Dole to any traveller who requests it. To the east of the city lies a very modern attraction, **INTECH**, which explores the technologies that shape our lives.

AROUND WINCHESTER

ITCHEN ABBAS

4 miles NE of Winchester on the B3047

One of the finest stately homes in England, **Avington Park** dates back to the 11th century but the grand State Rooms were added in 1670 and include a Great Saloon with a magnificent gold plasterwork ceiling, painted wall panels depicting the four seasons, along with many remarkable paintings. Avington Park is open on Sunday and Bank Holiday afternoons during the summer, and is available for private functions at other times.

TWYFORD

3 miles S of Winchester, on the B3335

Hampshire churchyards are celebrated for their ancient yew trees, but the one at Twyford is truly exceptional. A visitor in 1819

24 THE CHESTNUT HORSE

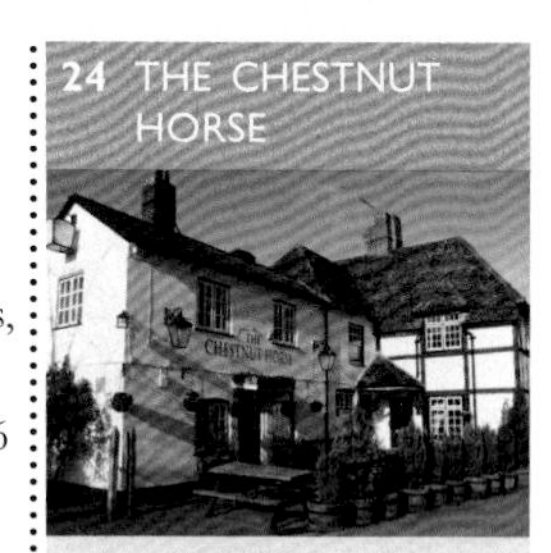

Easton

Delightful traditional 16th century hostelry serving outstanding cuisine and award-winning ales.

see page 144

25 AVINGTON PARK

Itchen Abbas, Winchester

One of the finest stately homes in England, it is open for visits on Sundays and Bank Holidays and is also available for private functions.

see page 145

Twyford Waterworks Museum, housed in the town waterworks which opened in 1898, explains the evolution of water supply during the 20th century.

described the clipped tree as resembling "the top of a considerable green hillock, elevated on a stump". The grand old yew is still in apparently good health and provides a dark green foil to the trim Victorian church of striped brick and flint which was designed by Alfred Waterhouse, architect of the Natural History Museum in London.

Three well-known historical figures have strong associations with the village. Benjamin Franklin wrote much of his autobiography while staying at Twyford House; Alexander Pope attended school here until he was expelled for writing a lampoon on the Master; and it was at the old Brambridge House that Mrs Fitzherbert was secretly married to the Prince Regent, later George IV, in 1785.

Montifont Abbey & Gardens, Romsey

COLDEN COMMON

5 miles S of Winchester on the B3354

Just to the east of Colden Common, **Marwell Zoological Park** is home to more than 200 species of animals, from meercats and red pandas to snow leopards and rhinos. Set in a 100-acre park, Marwell boasts the largest collection of hoofed animals in the UK, nine species of cat and many endangered species ranging from Amur Tigers – the largest in the world – to Leafcutter ants. Adventure playgrounds, a restaurant, gift shops and special events all combine to make the park a grand day out for all the family.

AMPFIELD

8 miles SW of Winchester on the A3090

Ampfield was once a busy pottery centre and bricks made from local clay were used to build the Church of St Mark in the 1830s. One of the vicars here was the father of the Revd W Awdry, creator of Thomas the Tank Engine. But the main attraction at Ampfield is the **Sir Harold Hillier Gardens & Arboretum**, one of the most important modern plant collections in the world. Sir Harold began his unique collection in 1953 and the 180-acre site is now home to the greatest assembly of hardy trees and shrubs in the world. The 42,000 plants from temperate regions all around the world include 11 National Plant Collections, more than 250 Champion Trees and the largest Winter Garden in Europe. Amenities within the grounds include a stylish licensed restaurant, gift shop and interpretation area explaining the role and history of the gardens.

Broadlands, Romsey

ROMSEY

11 miles SW of Winchester on the A27/A3090

"Music in stone", and "the second finest Norman building in England" are just two responses to **Romsey Abbey**, a majestic building containing some of the best 12th and 13th century architecture to have survived. Built between 1120 and 1230, the Abbey is remarkably complete. Unlike so many monastic buildings which were destroyed or fell into ruin after the Dissolution, the abbey was fortunate in being bought by the town in 1544 for £100 – the bill of sale, signed and sealed by Henry VIII, is displayed in the south choir aisle. Subsequent generations of townspeople have carefully maintained their bargain purchase. The abbey's most spectacular feature is the soaring nave which rises more than 70feet and extends for more than 76feet. Amongst the abbey's many treasures is the 16th century **Romsey Rood** which shows Christ on the cross with the hand of God descending from the clouds.

Just across from the Abbey, in Church Court, stands the town's oldest dwelling, **King John's House**, built around 1240 for a merchant. It has served as a royal residence but not, curiously, for King John who died some 14 years before it was built. He may though have had a hunting lodge on the site. The house is now a museum and centre for cultural activities; the garden has been renovated and replanted with pre-18th century plants.

The **Moody Museum** occupies the Victorian home of the Moody family who were cutlers in Romsey from the 18th century up until the 1970s. Visitors are greeted by (models of) William Moody and his sister Mary in a reconstruction of the family parlour and the exhibits include fixtures and fittings from the family's gun shop. Railway enthusiasts will want to seek out a curious exhibit located behind the infants' school in Winchester Road. **Romsey Signal Box** is a preserved vintage signal box in working order, complete with signals, track and

26 RANVILLES FARMHOUSE

Romsey ★★★★★

Nestled within five acres of attractive gardens Ranvilles is a perfect place to relax and enjoy life and you can even bring your pet.

see page 146

Close to the village of East Wellow, is Headlands Farm Fishery where there are two lakes available for fishing for carp, tench, perch, roach, pike and trout. Other facilities on site include rod hire, flies for sale and hot drinks.

other artefacts.

Romsey's most famous son is undoubtedly the flamboyant politician Lord Palmerston, three times Prime Minister during the 1850s and 1860s. Palmerston lived at Broadlands, just south of the town, and is commemorated by a bronze statue in the town's small triangular Market Place.

Broadlands is a gracious Palladian mansion that was built by Lord Palmerston's father in the mid-1700s. The architect was Henry Holland; the landscape was modelled by the ubiquitous 'Capability' Brown. The important collections of furniture, porcelain and sculpture were acquired by the 2nd Viscount Palmerston. The house passed to the Mountbatten family and it was Lord Louis Mountbatten who first opened Broadlands to the public shortly before he was killed in 1979. The present owner, Lord Romsey, has established the Mountbatten Exhibition in tribute to his grandfather's remarkable career as naval commander, diplomat, and last Viceroy of India. An audio-visual film provides an overall picture of the Earl's life and exhibits include his dazzling uniforms, the numerous decorations he was awarded, and an astonishing collection of the trophies, mementoes and gifts he received in his many rôles.

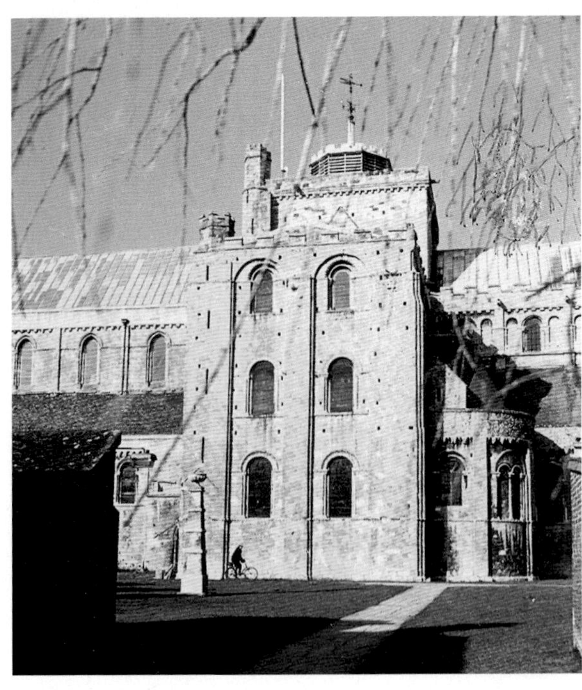

Romsey Abbey, Romsey

EAST WELLOW

14 miles SW of Winchester off the A27

The **Church of St Margaret** is the burial place of Florence Nightingale, who lies beneath the family monument, her final resting place bearing the simple inscription: *FN 1820-1910*. The church itself has several interesting features, including 13th century wall paintings and Jacobean panelling.

MOTTISFONT

10 miles W of Winchester off the A3057

Mottisfont's little Church of St Andrew boasts a wealth of 15th century stained glass, including a superb Crucifixion, and should not be overlooked on a visit to **Mottisfont Abbey** (National Trust). Built as an Augustinian priory in the 12th century, the abbey was converted into a country mansion after the Dissolution and was further modified in the 1700s. Some parts of the original priory have survived, amongst them the monks' cellarium – an undercroft with vast pillars – but the main attraction inside is the drawing room decorated with a Gothic trompe l'oeil fantasy by Rex Whistler. He was also commissioned to design the furniture but World War II intervened and he was killed in action. The superb grounds contain the National Collection of old-fashioned roses, established in 1972, a lovely pollarded lime walk designed by Sir Geoffrey Jellicoe, and some superb trees, including what is thought to be the largest plane tree in England.

CRAWLEY

5 miles NW of Winchester off the B3049

Crawley is a possibly unique example of an early-20th century model village. The estate was bought in 1900 by the Philippi family who then enthusiastically set about adding to the village's store of genuine traditional cottages a number of faithful fakes built in the same style. (They also provided their tenants with a state-of-the-art bath house and a roller skating rink). Sensitive to tradition and history, they did nothing to blemish the partly Norman church, leaving its unusual interior intact. Instead of stone pillars, **St Mary's Church** has mighty wooden columns supporting its roof, still effective more than 500 years after they were first hoisted into place.

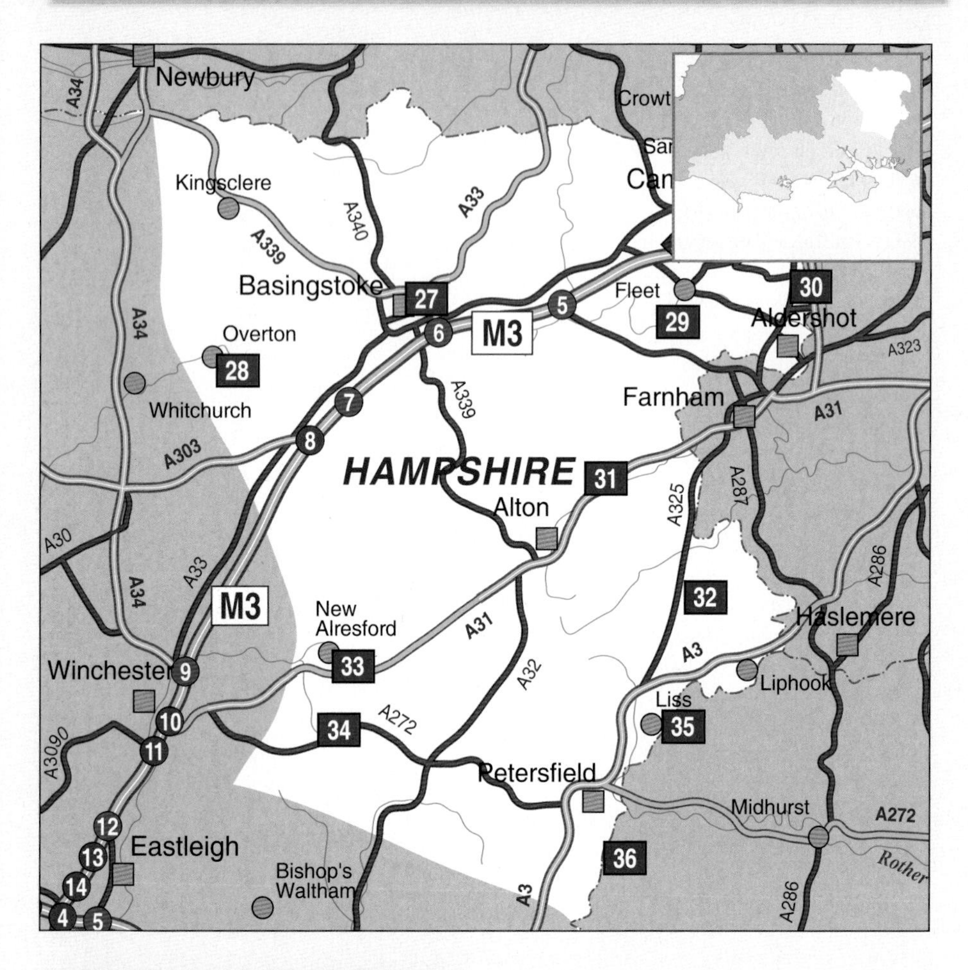

ACCOMMODATION

30	Park Lodge, Farnborough	p 53, 147
33	Haygarth Bed & Breakfast, Alresford	p 57, 149
35	The Flying Bull Inn, Rake, nr Liss	p 59, 150

FOOD & DRINK

28	Honey Pot Tea Rooms & Restaurant, Overton, nr Basingstoke	p 52, 147
29	The Wyvern, Church Crookham, nr Fleet	p 53, 146
31	The Hen & Chicken, Upper Froyle, nr Alton	p 54, 148
32	The Crown Inn, Arford, nr Headley	p 56, 148
35	The Flying Bull Inn, Rake, nr Liss	p 59, 150
36	The White Hart Inn, South Harting	p 60, 150

PLACES OF INTEREST

27	Milestones, Basingstoke	p 48, 146
34	Hinton Ampner Gardens, Bramdean, nr Alresford	p 57, 149

Northeast Hampshire

Northeast Hampshire lies within easy commuting distance of London, so it's not surprising that this corner of the county is quite heavily populated, dotted with prosperous, sprawling towns such as Farnborough, Farnham and Basingstoke. What *is* surprising is that, once you turn off the busy main roads, you can find yourself driving along narrow country lanes.

This area forms part of the North Downs. Honouring the perverse tradition of English place-names, the downs are actually uplands, softly-rolling, wooded hills in whose folds lie scores of picturesque villages. Even though, as the crow flies, central London is little more than 30 miles away, for many of the north-eastern Hampshire villages, even today, the metropolis might just as well be 300 miles distant.

There are few grand houses in the area, although The Vyne near Basingstoke and the Duke of Wellington's home, Stratfield Saye House, are both very imposing. Two smaller dwellings, however, attract hundreds of thousands of visitors to this corner of the county: Jane Austen's House at Chawton, near Alton, and a few miles to the south in the village of Selborne, The Wakes, home of the celebrated naturalist, Gilbert White. Lovers of steam railways can combine a visit to these two houses with a ride on the Watercress Line which runs between Alton and Alresford.

We begin this tour of north-eastern Hampshire at Basingstoke, a vibrant, modern town whose name goes back to Saxon times. It was then that a farmer with a name something like Base, along with his extended family, or 'ing', established a 'stok', (stock or farm-house) beside the River Lodden.

27 MILESTONES

Basingstoke

A fascinating insight into the industrial and everyday life of the area, with re-creations of Victorian shops and businesses.

 *see page 146*

BASINGSTOKE

Basingstoke's tourist information people never tire of telling visitors that their busy, prosperous town with its soaring multi-storey buildings boasts no fewer than 25 parks and open spaces. A useful leaflet available from the Tourist Information Centre gives details of them all, ranging from the 16-hectare **War Memorial Park**, an 18th century park complete with bandstand, aviary and sports facilities, to **Southview Cemetery**, a site with a fascinating history. Some 800 years ago, during the reign of King John, England languished under an interdict pronounced by the Pope. Throughout the six years from 1208 to 1214, any baby christened, or dead person buried, lacked the official blessing of Mother Church. At Basingstoke during those years, the deceased were interred in a graveyard known as the Liten and when the interdict was finally lifted, the ground was consecrated and a chapel built, the **Chapel of the Holy Ghost.** Today, it's a striking ruin surrounded by a well-managed site which provides a peaceful refuge from the bustling town.

As befits such a thriving place, Basingstoke offers visitors a wide choice of attractions: theatre, cinema, a vast Leisure Park and, opened in 2002, **Festival Square** whose 1 million square feet of shopping and leisure contains some 165 shops, 26 bars, restaurants and cafés, and a 10-screen cinema.

Housed in the old Town Hall of 1832, is the excellent **Willis Museum** (free) which charts the town's history with lively displays featuring characters such as "Fred", a Roman skeleton, and "Pickaxe", a 19th century farm worker "forced to scrape a living from the streets of Basingstoke as a scavenger". The museum is named after George Willis, a local clockmaker and former mayor of Basingstoke who established the collection in 1931. Naturally, locally made grandfather clocks feature prominently in the displays.

Chapel of the Holy Ghost, Basingstoke

A more recent attraction is **Milestones,** a living history museum of the 19th and early-20th centuries. The vast hi-tech structure houses a network of streets complete with reconstructed shops, a working pub, factories, cobbled streets and staff in period costume. You can call into the gramophone shop to listen to the 'latest' hits on 78s, or drop into

Abrahams the Confectioners for a 2oz bag of boiled sweets. Other highlights include the Tasker and Thorneycroft collections of agricultural and commercial vehicles, and the fascinating AA collection. The complex also contains a café and gift shop and at the nearby **Viables Craft Centre** visitors can watch craftspeople at work

Basing House, Basingstoke

AROUND BASINGSTOKE

SHERBORNE ST JOHN

2 miles N of Basingstoke off the A340

A mile or so north of the village, **The Vyne** (National Trust) is a tremendously impressive mansion that was built in the early 1500s for Lord Sandys, Lord Chamberlain to Henry VIII. Set within a thousand acres of beautiful gardens and parkland, the house enjoys an idyllic setting with lawns sweeping down to a shimmering lake. A classical portico was added to the house in 1654, the first of its kind in England. The Vyne's treasures include a fascinating Tudor chapel with Renaissance glass, a Palladian staircase, some remarkable statuary and a wealth of old linenfold oak panelling and fine furniture.

SILCHESTER

7 miles N of Basingstoke off the A340

Excavation of the town which the Romans called **Calleva Atrebatum** took place at the turn of the 19th/20th centuries and revealed some remarkable treasures, most of which are now on display at Reading Museum. The dig also revealed the most complete plan of any Roman town in the country but, rather oddly, the site was 're-buried' and now only the 1.5 mile city wall is visible – the best-preserved Roman town wall in Britain. Also impressive is the recently restored 1st century amphitheatre which lay just beyond the town walls.

Tucked in next to part of the Roman wall is the pretty **Church of St Mary** which dates from the 1100s. It boasts a superb 16th century screen with a frieze of angels and some unusual bench-ends of 1909 executed in Art Nouveau style.

PAMBER HEATH

7 miles N of Basingstoke off the A340

There are three 'Pambers' set in the countryside along the A340. At Pamber End stand the picturesque ruins of a once-magnificent 12th/

•

Basing House was once one of the grandest residences in the realm. Built during the reign of Henry VIII, it rivalled even the king's extravagant mansions. Less than a hundred years later, during the Civil War, Cromwell's troops besieged the house for an incredible three years. When Basing House was finally captured the victorious New Army put it to the torch, but some mightily impressive ruins still stand, along with a magnificent 16th century Grange Barn.

•

A mile or so west of Hartley Wintney stands West Green House. Owned by the National Trust, the house is surrounded by lovely gardens featuring a dazzling variety of trees, plants and shrubs.

13th century **Priory Church**, idyllically sited in sylvan surroundings. Set apart from the village, they invite repose and meditation. Pamber Green, as you might expect, is a leafy enclave; but for anyone in search of a good country pub, the Pamber to make for is Pamber Heath. Lots of pubs have a few pots scattered around, but the collection at The Pelican in Pamber Heath is something else. There are hundreds of them hanging from the ceiling beams, in every shape and colour you can imagine, some pewter and some ceramic.

STRATFIELD SAYE

7 miles NE of Basingstoke off the A33

About 4 miles west of Eversley, **Stratfield Saye House** was just one of many rewards a grateful nation showered on the Duke of Wellington after his decisive defeat of Napoleon at Waterloo. The duke himself doesn't seem to have been reciprocally grateful: only lack of funds frustrated his plans to demolish the gracious 17th century house and replace it with an even more impressive mansion which he intended to call Waterloo Palace. Quite modest in scale, Stratfield Saye fascinates visitors with its collection of the duke's own furniture and personal items such as his spectacles, handkerchiefs and carpet slippers. A complete room is devoted to his favourite charger, Copenhagen, who carried him on the day of the battle of Waterloo and is buried in the grounds here. More questionable exhibits are the priceless books in the library, many of them looted from Napoleon's own bibliotheque. A good number of the fine Spanish and Portuguese paintings on display share an equally dubious provenance, "relieved" during the duke's campaign in those countries as "spoils of war". That was accepted military practice at the time and, these quibbles apart, Stratfield Saye House is certainly one of the county's "must-see" attractions.

To the west of the estate is the **Wellington Country Park** where there are fine walks and numerous attractions.

HARTLEY WINTNEY

8 miles NE of Basingstoke on the A30

Riding through Hartley Wintney in 1821, William Cobbett, the author of *Rural Rides* and a conservationist long before anyone had thought of such a creature, was delighted to see young oaks being planted on the large village green. They were the gift of Hartley Wintney's lady of the manor, Lady Mildmay, and were originally intended to provide timber for shipbuilding. Fortunately, by the time they matured they were no longer needed for that purpose and today the **Mildmay Oaks** provide the village centre with a uniquely sylvan setting of majestic oak trees.

While you are in Hartley Wintney a visit to the old **Church of St Mary**, on Church Lane off the A323, is well worth while. Parts of the building date back to medieval times, but the fascination of this church lies in the fact that, after being completely renovated in 1834, it has remained almost totally unaltered ever since. High-sided box pews line the main aisle, there are elegant galleries for choir and congregation spanning the nave and both transepts, and colourful funeral hatchments add to St Mary's time-warp atmosphere.

EVERSLEY

11 miles NE of Basingstoke on the A327

Charles Kingsley, author of such immensely popular Victorian novels as *The Water Babies* and *Westward Ho!* was Rector of Eversley for 33 years from 1842 until his death in 1875 and is buried in the churchyard here. Some large half-timbered labourers' cottages were built as a memorial to him and the gates of the village school, erected in 1951 for the Festival of Britain, include a figure of a boy chimney sweep, the main character in *The Water Babies*. Kingsley was an attractive personality with a burning passion for social justice, but modern readers don't seem to share the Victorian enthusiasm for his works. It's a sad fate for a prolific man of letters, although perhaps not quite so dispiriting as that met by one of Kingsley's predecessors as preacher at Eversley. *He* was hanged as a highwayman.

ODIHAM

7 miles E of Basingstoke on the A327

Odiham Castle, Odiham

Odiham Castle, located by the canal near North Warnborough to the west of the town, must have a very good claim to being one of the least picturesque ruins in the country. It looks like something rescued from a giant dentist's tray, with gaping window holes and jagged, crumbling towers. Back in 1215, though, Odiham Castle was a state-of-the-art royal residence. Great pomp and circumstance attended King John's stay at the castle, then just seven years old, the night before he set off to an important meeting. The following day, in a meadow beside the River Thames called Runnymede, John reluctantly ascribed his name to a bill of rights. That document, known as Magna Carta, proved to be the embryo of democracy in western Europe.

Odiham itself is one of the most attractive villages in the county, with a handsome High Street and a 15th century church, **All Saints Parish Church**, the largest in Hampshire, in which collectors of curiosities will be pleased to find a rather rare item, a hudd. A portable wooden frame covered with cloth, the hudd provided Odiham's rector with graveside shelter when he was

28 THE HONEY POT TEAROOMS & RESTAURANT

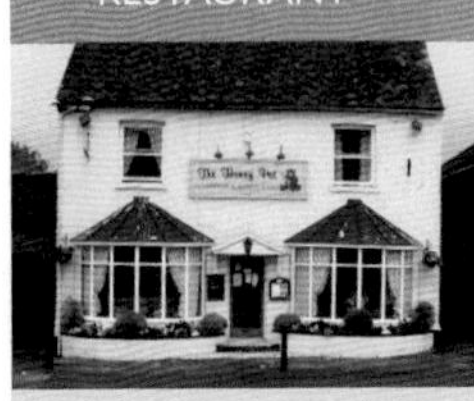

Overton

Licensed establishment offering extensive choice of appetising home-cooked food.

see page 147

conducting burials in inclement weather. In a corner of the graveyard stands the **Pest House**, built around 1625 as an isolation ward for patients with infectious diseases. From 1780 until 1950, it served as an almshouse and is now open to visitors on most weekends.

STEVENTON

6 miles SW of Basingstoke, off the B3400

At Steventon Rectory on December 16th 1775, Cassandra Austen presented her husband, George, with their seventh child, Jane. George was the rector of Steventon and Jane was to spend the first 25 years of her short life in the village. There is now very little evidence of her time here. The rectory was later demolished but there are memorials to the Austen family in the church where George Austen served for 44 years. It was at Steventon that Jane wrote *Pride and Prejudice*, *Sense and Sensibility* and *Northanger Abbey*. When the Revd George retired in 1800, the family moved to Bath. After her father's death, five years later, Jane and her mother took the house in Chawton that is now the Jane Austen Museum.

OVERTON

8 miles W of Basingstoke on the B3400

A large village near the source of the River Test, Overton has a broad main street lined with handsome houses. During the stage coach era, it was an important staging post on the London to Winchester route and the annual sheep fair was one of the largest in the county selling at its peak up to 150,000 lambs and sheep. The fair flourished for centuries, only coming to an end in the early 1930s.

To the north of Overton is **Watership Down**, made famous by Richard Adams' book of the same name. The down spreads across a high ridge from which there are superb downland views. The down is now a nature reserve providing sanctuary for a variety of birds and mammals, including, of course, rabbits. The down lies on the long-distance footpath, the Wayfarer's Walk, which runs from Inkpen Beacon, just across the border in Berkshire, to Emsworth on the Hampshire coast.

KINGSCLERE

8 miles NW of Basingstoke on the A339

Collectors of curiosities might like to make a short excursion to the peaceful village of Kingsclere where the weather-vane on top of the parish church has baffled many visitors. With its six outstretched legs and squat body, the figure on the vane has been compared to a skate-boarding terrapin. Local historians, however, assert that it actually represents a bed bug and was placed here by the command of King John. The king had been hunting in the area when a thick fog descended and he was forced to spend the night at the Crown Hotel in Kingsclere. Apparently, he slept badly, his slumber continually disturbed by the attentions of a bed bug. The next morning, he ordered that the townspeople should forever be reminded of his restless night in Kingsclere by erecting this curious memorial to his tormentor.

ALDERSHOT

Back in 1854, Aldershot was a village of some 800 inhabitants. Then the Army decided to build a major camp here and the population has grown steadily ever since to its present tally of around 60,000. The story of how Aldershot became the home of the British Army is vividly recounted at the **Aldershot Military Museum** which stands in the middle of the camp and is a must for anyone with an interest in military history. Housed in the last two surviving Victorian barrack blocks, its tiny appearance from the outside belies the wealth of fascinating displays contained inside. For example, there's a detailed cutaway model of a cavalry barracks showing how the soldiers' rooms were placed above the stables, an economic form of central heating described as "warm, but aromatic".

It was soldiers at Aldershot who became the first military aviators in Britain, using Farnborough Common for their flying and building their aircraft sheds where the Royal Aircraft Establishment stands today. **The Parachute Regiment and Airborne Forces Museum** has many interesting exhibits illustrating the part these pioneers played during the early days of the 20th century and during two World Wars. There are two further military museums to be found here: the **Army Medical Services Museum,** telling the story of medical services from 1660 to the present day, and the **Army Physical Training Corps Museum** where the Corps history is recounted with the help of numerous exhibits, pictorial records – and some Victorian gymnastic equipment.

In the town's Manor Park, the **Heroes Shrine** commemorates the dead of World War I, while a nearby walled and sunken garden, shaded by deodar trees, honours the fallen of World War II. Another celebrated military figure, the Duke of Wellington, is represented by an imposing bronze statue crowning Round Hill, just outside the town. The statue originally stood atop the Triumphal Arch at Hyde Park Corner in London but was moved to Aldershot in 1885.

AROUND ALDERSHOT

FARNBOROUGH

3 miles N of Aldershot on the A331

The town is best known for the **Farnborough Air Show** which is held every other year. The town's unique aviation heritage is explored at the **Farnborough Air Sciences Museum** which holds an extensive collection of exhibits, records and artefacts. The museum is open every Saturday and Sunday.

Less well-known is **St Michael's Abbey,** now a

29 THE WYVERN

Church Crookham

Wyvern is a warm and friendly pub, located at the heart of Church Crookham. One for all the family.

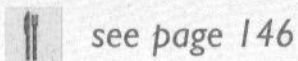

see page 146

30 PARK LODGE

Farnborough

An 1860's building, with a contemporary twist. Experience a warm welcome and the best sausages in town.

see page 147

31 THE HEN AND CHICKEN

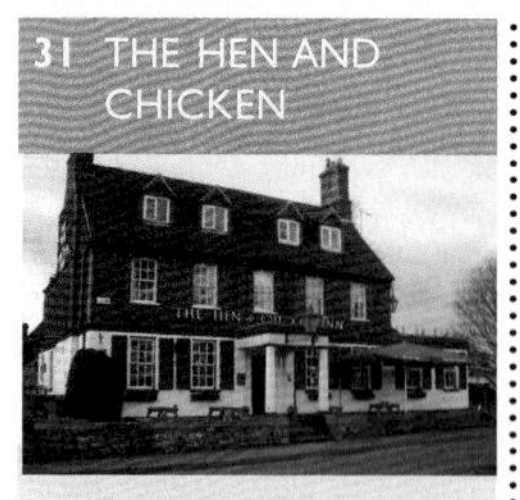

Upper Froyle, nr Alton

An historic building with tremendous character, serving wonderfully prepared food.

see page 148

Benedictine foundation but with a curious history. After the fall of Napoleon III, his wife the Empress Eugenie came to live at a large house called Farnborough Hill where she was later joined by her husband and her son, the Prince Imperial. Napoleon died at Chislehurst after an operation to remove bladder stones; her son was killed in the Zulu War. The heartbroken Empress commissioned the building of an ornate mausoleum for their tombs as part of a monastery in the flamboyant French style. The first monks arrived in 1895 from Solesmes Abbey, France, and they still continue their regime of liturgy, study and manual work. The abbey is open to the public and has a small farm and apiary that supplies not only the monks but also the abbey shop. Guided tours are available on Saturday and Bank Holiday afternoons.

ALTON

Surrounded by some of Hampshire's loveliest countryside, Alton is an appealing market town with a history stretching back far beyond Roman times (the name actually means old town). The town's market, held on Tuesdays, is more than a thousand years old and at the time of the *Domesday Book* was the most valuable the survey recorded anywhere in the country. Alton boasts a large number of old coaching inns, and the impressive, partly-Norman **St Lawrence's Church** which was the setting for a dramatic episode during the Civil War. In 1643, a large force of Roundheads drove some eighty Royalists into the church where 60 of them were killed. The Royalist commander, Colonel Boles, made a last stand from the splendid Jacobean pulpit, firing repeatedly at his attackers before succumbing to their bullets. The church door and several of the Norman pillars are still pock-marked with holes from bullets fired off during this close-combat conflict. More cheerful are the comical carvings on these pillars of animals and birds, amongst them a wolf gnawing a bone and two donkeys kicking their heels in the air.

Nearby is the old cemetery and the well-tended **Grave of Fanny Adams.** The expression "Sweet Fanny Adams" arose from the revolting murder in 1867 of an 8-year-old girl in the town who was hacked into pieces by her assassin. With macabre humour, sailors used the phrase "Sweet Fanny Adams" to describe the recently-issued

Market Square, Alton

tinned mutton for which they had a certain mistrust. Over the years, the saying became accepted as a contemptuous description for anything considered valueless. A poor memorial for an innocent girl.

There's a different sort of monument in Amery Street, a narrow lane leading off the market place. On a small brick house is a plaque commemorating the Elizabethan poet Edmund Spenser who came to Alton around 1590 to enjoy its "sweet delicate air".

Well worth a visit while you are in Alton is the **Allen Gallery** in Church Street (free), home to an outstanding collection of English, Continental and Far Eastern pottery, porcelain and tiles. Housed in a group of attractive 16th and 18th century buildings the gallery's other attractions include the unique Elizabethan Tichborne Spoons, delightful watercolours and oil paintings by local artist William Herbert Allen, a walled garden and a comfortable coffee lounge. Across the road, the **Curtis Museum** (free) concentrates on exploring 100 million years of local history with displays devoted to the "shocking tale of Sweet Fanny Adams", other local celebrities such as Jane Austen and Lord Baden-Powell, and a colourful Gallery of Childhood with exhibits thoughtfully displayed in miniature cases at an ideal height for children.

AROUND ALTON

CHAWTON

2 miles S of Alton off the A31

From the outside, the home in which Jane Austen spent the last eight years of her life, **Chawton House**, and where she wrote three of her most popular novels (*Mansfield Park, Emma* and *Persuasion*), is a rather austere-looking 17th century building. Once you step inside, however, the mementoes on show are fascinating. In the parlour is the small round table where she wrote; in her bedroom the patchwork quilt she made with her mother and sister still lies on the bed; whilst in the old bake house is her donkey cart. Another room is dedicated to her brothers, Frank and Charles, who both had distinguished careers in the Royal Navy. Outside, there's a pretty garden stocked with many

On the western edge of the town of Alton is The Butts, a pleasant open area of grassland that was once used for archery practice and is now the setting for various events such as the annual Victorian Cricket Match.

Allen Gallery, Alton

32 THE CROWN INN

Headley

A 16th Century house, which is set in a picturesque setting, serving a beautiful menu and is quintessentially English.

see page 148

From Selborne village centre there are several walks, one of which leads to the 'Zig-Zag' path constructed by Gilbert and his brother in 1753. It winds its way up to the 'Hanger' (a wood on a steep hillside) that overlooks the village. The land at the summit is part of an area of meadow, woodland and common which is owned by the National Trust – the spot provides panoramic views across the South Downs.

old varieties of flowers and herbs. Chawton village itself is a delightful spot with old cottages and houses leading up to the village green outside Jane's house.

SELBORNE

4 miles SE of Alton on the B3006

Like the nearby village of Chawton, Selborne also produced a great literary figure. **The Wakes** was the home of Gilbert White, a humble curate of the parish from 1784 until his death in 1793. He spent his spare hours meticulously recording observations on the weather, wild-life and geology of the area. Astonishingly, a percipient publisher to whom Gilbert submitted his notes recognised the appeal of his humdrum, day-to-day accounts of life in what was then a remote corner of England. *The Natural History and Antiquities of Selborne* was first published in 1788, has never been out of print, and still provides what is perhaps the most entertaining and direct access to late-18th century life, seen through the eyes of an intelligent, sceptical mind.

Visitors to The Wakes can see the original manuscript of his book along with other personal belongings, and stroll around the peaceful garden with its unusual old plant varieties.

The house also contains the **Oates Museum** which celebrates the Francis Oates, the Victorian explorer, and his nephew Captain Lawrence 'Titus' Oates who was with Captain Scott on his doomed expedition to the South Pole. Titus' last words – "I am just going outside. I may be some time" – are known around the world, as is Scott's diary entry describing Oates' selfless deed as "the act of a very gallant gentleman". The Wakes and the Oates Museum are open daily, and there's an excellent book and gift shop, and a tea-room specialising in 18th century fare.

Gilbert White is buried in the graveyard of the pretty **Church of St Mary**, his final resting place marked by a stone bearing the austere inscription *GW 26th June 1793*. A fine stained glass window depicts St Francis preaching to the birds described in Gilbert's book. Outside in the churchyard, is the stump of a yew tree which was some 1400 years old when it succumbed to the great storm of January 1990.

Selborne Pottery was established by Robert Goldsmith in 1985. Each piece of pottery made here is hand-thrown and turned, and the distinctive pots are not only functional but also decorative.

NEW ALRESFORD

10 miles SW of Alton off the A31

Pronounced *Allsford*, 'New' Alresford was created around 1200 by a Bishop of Winchester, Geoffrey de Lucy, as part of his grand plan to build a waterway from Winchester to Southampton. Where the river Arle flows into the Itchen, he constructed a huge reservoir covering 200 acres, its waters controlled to keep the Itchen navigable at all seasons. The Bishop's reservoir is now reduced to some 60 acres but it's still home to countless wildfowl and many otters. Known today as **Old Alresford Pond**, it's one of the most charming features of this dignified Georgian town. Alresford can also boast one of the county's most beautiful streets, historic Broad Street, lined with elegant, colour-washed Georgian houses interspersed with specialist shops and inviting hostelries.

Alresford's most famous son was Admiral Lord Rodney, a contemporary of Lord Nelson, who built the grand Manor House (private) near the parish church, but the town can also boast two famous daughters. One was Mary Sumner, wife of the Rector of Alresford, who founded the Mother's Union here in 1876. The other was Mary Russell Mitford, author of the fascinating collection of sketches of 18th century life, *Our Village,* published in five volumes between 1824-1832. Mary's prolific literary output was partly spurred on by the need to repay the debts of her spendthrift father. Dr Mitford managed to dissipate his own inherited fortune of many thousands of pounds; his wife's lavish dowry which almost doubled that income disappeared equally quickly, and when Mary at the age of ten won the huge sum of £20,000 in a lottery, the good doctor squandered that as well. Mary's classic book tells the story.

One of Alresford's attractions that should not be missed is the **Watercress Line**, Hampshire's only preserved steam railway and so named because it was once used to transport watercress from the beds around Alresford to London and beyond. The line runs through 10 miles of beautiful countryside to Alton where it links up with main line services to London. Vintage steam locomotives make the 35-minute journey up to eight times a day, and there are regular dining trains as well as frequent special events throughout the year. Footplate rides and train-driving lessons are available.

HINTON AMPNER

11 miles SW of Alton on the A272

The River Itchen, renowned for its trout and watercress beds, rises to the west of the village to begin its 25-mile journey to the sea at Southampton; the **Itchen Way** footpath follows the river throughout its course. To the south of the village are **Hinton Ampner Gardens** (National Trust). They were created by Ralph Dutton, 8th and last Lord Sherborne, who inherited the house in 1936 and then planned a superb garden that combines formal and informal planting. The design produces some delightful walks with some unexpected vistas. The house itself, which contains a stunning collection of furniture and paintings, is open on Tuesday and Wednesday afternoons in the summer, and on weekend afternoons in August.

TICHBORNE

12 miles SW of Alton off the A31

Two intriguing stories are

33 HAYGARTH BED & BREAKFAST

Alresford

3-star comfortable en suite accommodation in pretty Georgian town.

see page 149

34 HINTON AMPNER GARDENS

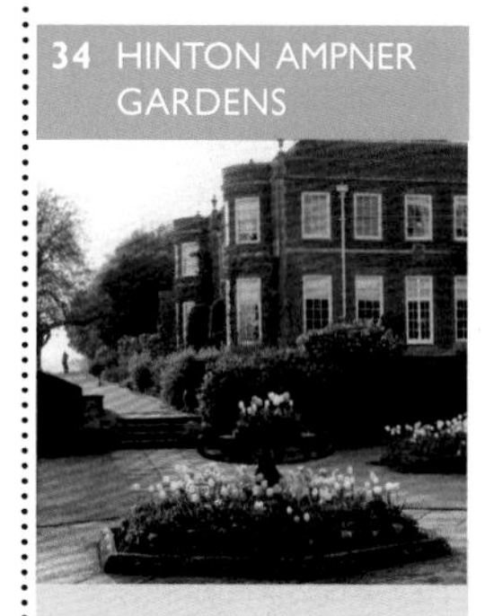

Bramdean, nr Alresford

Delightful house and gardens, remodelled by the late Lord Sherborne. The tranquil garden includes walks, lily pond and superb topiary.

see page 149

Petersfield Heath is an extensive recreational area with a pond for fishing and boating in the summer months. In October, the heath is the setting for the annual Taro Fair. Also within the heath is an important group of Bronze Age barrows. There are more than 20 of them scattered between the bracken and pine trees, making this the largest Bronze Age Burial ground in the south of England.

associated with this lovely village of thatched and half-timbered cottages. The legend of the **Tichborne Dole** dates from the reign of Henry I. At that time the owner of Tichborne Park was the dastardly Sir Roger Tichborne. As his crippled wife, Mabella, lay dying her last wish was to provide food for the poor. Sir Roger agreed – but only from an area she could crawl around. The brave woman managed to encircle an area of more than 20 acres of arable land, carrying a flaming torch as she did so. Ever since then the Park's owners have provided bags of flour every year to the villages of Tichborne and Cheriton. The field is still known as 'The Crawls'.

Equally notorious is the episode of the **Tichborne Claimant**. In 1871 a certain Arthur Orton, son of a Wapping butcher, returned from Wagga Wagga, Australia, claiming to be the heir to the estate. Although he bore no resemblance to the rightful heir who had disappeared while sailing round the world, Arthur was 'recognised' by the widow as her son and supported in his claim. She, apparently, detested her late husband's family. Arthur's claim was rejected in a trial that lasted 100 days and he was put on trial for perjury. After a further 188 days he was found guilty and sentenced to 14 years in prison.

PETERSFIELD

An appealing market town, Petersfield is dominated by the bulk of **Butser Hill**, 900feet high and the highest point of the South Downs offering grand panoramic views over the town and even, on a clear day, to the spire of Salisbury Cathedral, some 40 miles distant. In the 1660s, Samuel Pepys noted his stay in Petersfield, at a hotel in which Charles II had slept before him. Another king is commemorated in the town square where William III sits on horseback, incongruously dressed in Roman costume. Unusually, the statue is made of lead.

Most of the elegant buildings around the square are Georgian, but the **Church of St Peter** is much older, dating back to Norman times and with a fine north aisle to prove it. Just off the Square, the **Flora Twort Gallery** was once the home and studio of the accomplished artist of that name who moved to Petersfield at the end of World War I. Her delightful paintings and drawings capture life in the town over some 40 years – "reminders of some of the things we have lost" as she put it shortly before her death at the age of 91 in 1985. The ground floor of the gallery is now a restaurant serving morning coffee, lunches and afternoon teas. From the gallery, a short walk along Sheep Street, (which has some striking timber-framed 16th century houses and Georgian cottages), brings you to **The Spain**, a pleasant green surrounded by some of the town's oldest houses. It apparently acquired its rather unusual name because dealers in

Spanish wool used to hold markets there.

Other attractions include the Dragon Gallery, providing a showcase for contemporary artists; the Petersfield Museum, housed in the Victorian Courthouse; and the Teddy Bear Museum, the first in the country to be dedicated to these cuddly comforters. Another unusual attraction is the **Physic Garden** behind 16 High Street. Set in an ancient walled plot, the garden has been planted in a style that would have been familiar to the distinguished 17th century botanist John Goodayer, a native of Petersfield.

Petersfield is a fine area for walking and there are several of vaying length, including town trails, Hangers Way and the Serpent Trail.

AROUND PETERSFIELD

STEEP

1 mile N of Petersfield off the A3

Appropriately, the village is reached by way of a steep hill. Steep is famous as the home of the writer and nature poet Edward Thomas who moved here with his family in 1907. It was while living at 2 Yew Tree Cottages that he wrote most of his poems. In 1909 he and his wife Helen moved to the Red House (private) where his daughter Myfanwy was born in 1913. Many years later, in 1985, she unveiled a plaque on the house. Her former home featured in two of her father's poems, *The New House* and *Wind and Mist*. Thomas was killed in action in World War I. His death is commemorated by two engraved lancet windows installed in 1978 in All Saints Church, and by a memorial stone on Shoulder of Mutton Hill above the village. It was in Steep in 1898 that the educational pioneer John Badley established Bedales, the first boarding school for both sexes in the country. His 'preposterous experiment' proved highly successful. The school has its own art gallery and a theatre, both of which stage lively programmes of events and exhibitions open to the public.

LIPHOOK

12 miles NE of Petersfield off the A3

Just south of Liphook, the **Hollycombe Steam Collection** boasts the largest gathering of working steam machines in Britain. Visitors can enjoy original 'white knuckle' rides in the Edwardian Steam Fairground which contains Mr Field's Steam Circus – the world's oldest working mechanical ride – or ride behind a steam locomotive as it travels high on the hill, providing marvellous views over the Sussex Weald. Elsewhere, steam is used to power an astonishing variety of machines, amongst them a sawmill, steam road engines and farm machinery. In strong contrast to all this activity are the peaceful woodland gardens, Grade 2* listed, which date back to the early 1800s. For opening times of this volunteer-run attraction call 01428 724900.

35 THE FLYING BULL INN

Rake

Friendly pub in delightful village offering home-cooked food, real ales and very comfortable en suite accommodation.

see page 150

•

To the west of Liphook, Bohunt Manor Gardens are owned by the Worldwide Fund for Nature which has made the grounds a refuge for a collection of ornamental waterfowl. There's a pleasant lakeside walk, herbaceous borders and many unusual trees and shrubs.

•

36 THE WHITE HART INN

South Harting

This stunningly decorated property is both a restaurant and a pub. A truly great place worth visiting.

see page 150

UPPARK

4 miles SE of Petersfield on the B2146

Just over the county border in West Sussex, **Uppark** (National Trust), is a handsome Wren-style mansion built around 1690 and most notable for its interior which contains a wealth of paintings, textiles, ceramics and a famous doll's house. Uppark was completely redecorated and refurnished in the 1750s by the Fetherstonhaugh family and their work has remained almost entirely unchanged – not only the furniture but even some of the fabrics and wallpapers remain in excellent condition. Outside there's a pretty Regency garden that has been restored to the original Repton design and commands stunning views away to the sea. Uppark has an intriguing connection with the author HG Wells. When Wells was a young boy, Sir Harry Fetherstonhaugh was the lord of Uppark. He married late in life to his dairymaid. They had no children and after Sir Harry's death she lived on at Uppark. Wells's mother was employed as her housekeeper and the boy's recollections of life at the big house are fondly recorded in his autobiography.

BURITON

2 miles S of Petersfield off the A3

An ancient church surrounded by trees and overlooking a large tree-lined duck pond is flanked by an appealing early-18th century manor house (private) built by the father of Edward Gibbon, the celebrated historian. The younger Gibbon wrote much of his magnum opus *Decline and Fall of the Roman Empire* in his study here. Gibbon was critical of the house's position, "at the end of the village and the bottom of the hill", but was highly appreciative of the view over the Downs: "the long hanging woods in sight of the house could not perhaps have been improved by art or expense".

To the south of Buriton is the Queen Elizabeth Country Park, the largest of Hampshire's public open spaces, and home to a very extensive variety of wildlife, notably flowers and butterflies.

CHALTON

5 miles S of Petersfield off the A3

Situated on a slope of chalk down, Chalton is home to **Butser Ancient Farm,** a reconstruction of an Iron Age farm that has received worldwide acclaim for its research methodology and results. There's a magnificent great roundhouse, prehistoric and Roman crops are grown, ancient breeds of cattle roam the hillside, and metal is worked according to ancient techniques. The latest project here is the construction of a replica Roman villa, complete with hypocaust, using the same methods as the Romans did. A wonderful living laboratory, the farm is open on the last weekend of each month from March to September when there are themed events.

HAMBLEDON

8 miles SW of Petersfield, off the B2150

A village of Georgian houses and

well-known for its vineyard, Hambledon is most famous for its cricketing connections. It was at the Hambledon Cricket Club that the rules of the game were first formulated in 1774. The club's finest hour came in 1777 when the team, led by the landlord of the Bat and Ball Inn, beat an All England team by an innings and 168 runs! A granite monument stands on **Broadhalfpenny Down** where the early games were played.

EAST MEON

5 miles W of Petersfield off the A32 or A272

Tucked away in the lovely valley of the River Meon and surrounded by high downs, East Meon has been described as "the most unspoilt of Hampshire villages and the nicest". As if that weren't enough, the village also boasts one of the finest and most venerable churches in the county. The central tower of **All Saints Church** has walls 4feet thick dating back to the 12th century, and is a stunning example of Norman architecture at its best. Inside, the church's greatest treasure is its remarkable 12th century Tournai font of black marble, exquisitely carved with scenes depicting the fall of Adam and Eve. Only seven of these wonderful fonts are known to exist in England, (four of them in Hampshire) and East Meon's is generally regarded as the most magnificent of them all.

Court House, East Meon

Just across the road from the church is the 15th century **Courthouse** which also has walls 4feet thick. It's a lovely medieval manor house where for generations the Bishops of Winchester, as Lords of the Manor, held their courts. The venerable old building would have been a familiar sight to the 'compleat angler' Izaac Walton who spent many happy hours fishing in the River Meon nearby.

WEST MEON

8 miles W of Petersfield on the A32

A sizeable village set beside the River Meon, West Meon has a graveyard that provided the final resting place for two very different characters. In 1832, Thomas Lord, founder of the famous cricket ground in London, was buried here; in 1963, the ashes of the notorious spy Guy Burgess were sprinkled on the grave of his mother in a suitably clandestine night-time ceremony.

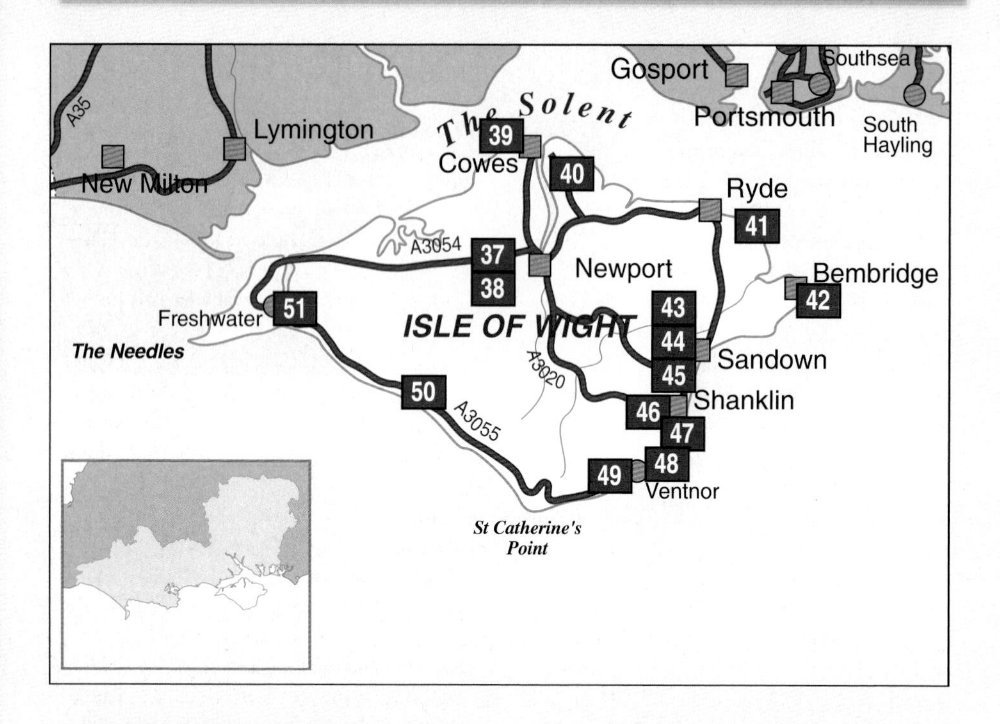

ACCOMMODATION

39	Rawlings Restaurant Hotel, Cowes	p 67, 152
42	Wight Coast & Country Cottages, Bembridge	p 72, 153
43	Hazelwood Apartments, Sandown	p 74, 154
44	Alendel Hotel, Sandown	p 75, 155
45	Mount Brocas Guest House, Sandown	p 75, 155
46	St Georges House Hotel, Shanklin	p 76, 156
48	Winterbourne Country House, Bonchurch, nr Ventnor	p 77, 158
51	The Royal Standard, Freshwater	p 81, 161

FOOD & DRINK

37	The Eight Bells Inn, Carisbrooke, nr Newport	p 64, 151
39	Rawlings Restaurant Hotel, Cowes	p 67, 152
44	Alendel Hotel, Sandown	p 75, 155
46	St Georges House Hotel, Shanklin	p 76, 156
47	Saffrons, Shanklin	p 76, 157
49	El Toro Contento Tapas Bar, Ventnor	p 78, 159
51	The Royal Standard, Freshwater	p 81, 161

PLACES OF INTEREST

38	Carisbrooke Castle, Carisbrooke, nr Newport	p 65, 152
40	Barton Manor, Whippingham, nr East Cowes	p 69, 152
41	Seaview Wildlfe Encounter, Seaview	p 71, 154
50	Dinosaur Farm Museum, Brighstone	p 80, 160

The Isle of Wight

The Isle of Wight has adopted a motto which declares: "All this beauty is of God". It echoes the poet John Keats "A thing of beauty is a joy for ever", the first line of his poem *Endymion* which he wrote while staying on the island in the hope that its crisp country air would improve his health.

Other distinguished visitors have described Wight as "The Garden Isle", and "England's Madeira" and about half of its 147 square miles have been designated Areas of Outstanding Natural Beauty. But it was quite late in the day before the island became popular as a resort. This was partly because for centuries, right up until the 1600s, the island was a first port of call for pestiferous French raiders who made the islanders' lives a misery with their constant incursions. These attacks ceased following the Napoleonic wars but the turning point came in the 1840s when Queen Victoria and Prince Albert bought an estate near East Cowes. They demolished the existing house and Albert designed and built an Italianate mansion he named Osborne House. A few years later, the Poet Laureate, Alfred, Lord Tennyson, bought Farringford on the eastern side of the island. Socially, the Isle of Wight had arrived. Tourists flock here in their thousands, and at peak times there are some 350 ferry crossings every day.

Most of the island's 125,000 residents live in the northeast quadrant of the island, with its main resort towns of Sandown and Shanklin strung along the east coast. The rest of the island is wonderfully peaceful with a quiet, unassertive charm all of its own. There are many miles of footpaths, bridleways and cycle paths, making it easy to explore – and more than 60 miles of coastline.

37 THE EIGHT BELLS

Newport

This is a delightful property with beautiful surroundings. Definitely one for families with children of all ages and the food is lovely. The beef is recommended.

see page 151

NEWPORT

Set around the River Medina, Newport has a history going back to Roman times. In Cypress Road, excavations in 1926 uncovered the well-preserved remains of a **Roman Villa**, a 3rd century farmhouse in which one side of the building was given over entirely to baths. Visitors can follow the bather's progress through changing room, cold room, warm and hot rooms with underfloor heating systems, and integral cold and hot plunge baths. A Roman style garden has been re-created in the grounds and provides an interesting insight into the wealth of new plants the Romans introduced into Britain.

Newport received its first charter back in 1190 but the growth of the small town received a severe setback in 1377 when it was completely burnt to the ground by the French. Recovery was slow and it wasn't until the 17th century that Newport really prospered again. Indirectly, the new prosperity was also due to the French since the island was heavily garrisoned during the Anglo-French wars of that period. Supplying the troops with provisions and goods brought great wealth to the town.

Some striking buildings have survived, amongst them **God's Providence House**, built in 1701 and now a tea room; John Nash's elegant **Guildhall** of 1816 which is now occupied by the Museum of Island History; a charming Tudor **Old Grammar School,** and the parish **Church of St Thomas** whose foundation stone was laid in 1854 by Queen Victoria's consort, Prince Albert. The church contains the tomb of the tragic Princess Elizabeth, daughter of Charles I, who died of a fever at the age of 14 while a prisoner at nearby Carisbrooke Castle.

There's also an 18th century brewer's warehouse near the harbour which now houses the **Quay Arts Centre**, incorporating a theatre, two galleries, a craft shop, café and bar; another old warehouse is home to the **Classic Boat Museum**. Among the highlights here are a 1910 river launch and *Lady Penelope*, a fabulous speedboat once owned by the 1950s socialite Lady Docker. Other exhibits include beautifully restored sailing and power boats, along with engines, equipment and memorabilia.

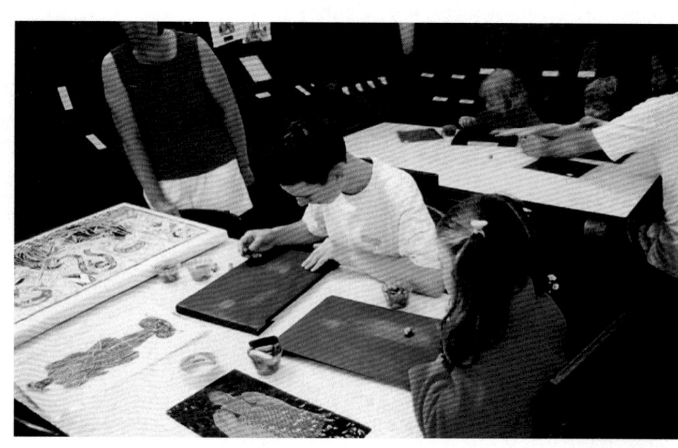

Brass Rubbing Centre, Newport

Next door to the Boat Museum is the **Isle of Wight Bus Museum** which displays an impressive array of island buses and coaches in a former grain store warehouse. Established in 1997, a collection of vintage buses and coaches display the Island's road transport heritage. Among the exhibits are a former Ryde tramcar dating from 1889, a 1927 Daimler and a Bristol Lodekka that completed a successful trip to Nepal. There are also several vehicles under reconstruction and a wealth of photographs and memorabilia.

To the northwest of Newport, **Parkhurst Forest** offers miles of woodland walks, while over to the northeast, at Wootton, **Butterfly World and Fountain World** is home to hundreds of exotic butterflies flying free inside a beautifully landscaped indoor garden with ponds, streams, fountains and waterfalls. Other attractions include an Italian water garden, a Japanese water garden with Koi Carp, a restaurant, garden centre and shop.

CARISBROOKE

1 mile SW of Newport, on the B3323/B3401

Another quote from John Keats: "I do not think I shall ever see a ruin to surpass **Carisbrooke Castle**". The castle is set dramatically on a sweeping ridge and it's quite a steep climb up from the picturesque village to the massive gatehouse. This was built in 1598 but the oldest parts of the castle date back to Norman times, most notably the mighty keep which, apart from Windsor Castle, is the most perfect specimen of Norman architecture in Britain. Archaeologists believe that the castle stands on the site a Roman fort built some thousand years earlier.

During the season costumed guides, or 'storytellers' as English Heritage prefers to call them, conduct visitors around the noble ruins. The most poignant of their stories concern Charles I and his youngest daughter, Elizabeth. Charles was imprisoned here in the months before his trial and the guides will point out the mullioned window through which he unsuccessfully attempted to escape. After the King's execution, Cromwell's Council of State ordered that his daughter Elizabeth, "for her own safety", should also be incarcerated at Carisbrooke. The 14-year-old implored them not to send her to her father's former prison, but they were adamant. Elizabeth was a sickly child and less than a week after her arrival at the castle she "was stricken by fever and passed away, a broken-hearted child of fourteen". The story touched the heart of Queen Victoria who set up a monument in St Thomas' Church in Newport where the Princess was buried. The effigy, in pure white Carrara marble, bears an inscription stating that it had been erected "as a token of respect for her virtues, and of sympathy for her misfortunes by Victoria R 1856". The royal connection with the Island goes back much further:

•

Church Litten Park in Newport, on the site of an old churchyard whose Tudor gateway still remains, is a peaceful spot and interesting for its memorial to Valentine Gray, a 9-year-old chimney sweep whose death in 1822 as a result of ill-usage by his master caused a national outcry.

•

38 CARISBROOKE CASTLE

Carisbrooke

Dating from Saxon times, Carsibrooke Castle was once prison to Charles I

see page 152

In Carisbrooke village, St Mary's Church contains the elaborate canopied tomb of Lady Wadham, an aunt of Jane Seymour. The Perpendicular tower is covered with carvings, including a clearly discernible group of singers.

in the 11th century Odo, half-brother to William the Conqueror, sought sanctuary here after being accused of committing a treasonable act; he was soon caught and arrested by William himself.

More cheerful aspects of a visit to the castle include the Donkey Centre. Donkeys walking a treadmill were once used to turn the huge 16th century wheel in the Wellhouse to draw water from a well 161feet deep. A light at the bottom of the well gives some idea of its depth. Before donkeys were trained to raise the water, the task was performed by prisoners and nowadays visitors are invited to have a go at walking the treadmill themselves. Also within the Castle grounds are a Coach House Exhibition and Victorian Island Exhibition, the Isle of Wight Museum and a tea room.

ARRETON

3 miles SE of Newport on the A3056

From Downend, it's less than a mile to **Arreton Manor** which claims, with some justification, to be "the most beautiful and intriguing house on the Isle of Wight". There was a house on this site long before Alfred the Great mentioned Arreton in his will of AD 885 and the manor was owned by successive monarchs from Henry VIII to Charles I. The present house was built during the reigns of Elizabeth and James I and it's a superb example of the architecture of that period, with mellow stone walls and Jacobean panelling complemented by furniture from the same era. Perhaps the most appealing aspect of Arreton is that indefinable atmosphere of a house that has been lived in for centuries. Other attractions here include an Elizabethan-style garden with a miniature maze and water terraces, rose garden, armour collection, gift shop, tea-rooms and picnic area.

In Arreton village, there's a 12th century church and, right next door, the **Island Brass Rubbing Centre** where visitors can learn this simple skill. On the main road between Sandown and Newport, **Arreton Barns** describes itself as a traditional working craft village and

Arreton Manor, Arreton

offers a wide selection of crafts including ceramics, glassware and canework. There's a craft shop, lavender and lace shop, a medieval carp pond, pub and tea rooms. It is also the home of the **Shipwreck Centre & Maritime Museum**, which between 1978 and 2006 had been located in Bembridge. The larger premises within an established tourist attraction allow for expanded displays and a separate Lifeboat Museum. A mile or so southwest of Arreton Manor stands another grand old house, **Haseley Manor & Children's Farm**. The superbly restored house contains tableaux explaining the different eras of its existence, a working pottery, a play area for small children, a tea room and a gift shop. Outside, the attractions include magnificent herb, flower and water gardens, a children's farm and adventure playground and a picnic area.

COWES

Cowes' origins as the most famous yachting resort in the world go back to the early 1800s. It was then a rather shabby port whose main business was shipbuilding. In 1811, the Duke of Gloucester came to stay and as part of the rather limited entertainment on offer watched sailing matches between local fishermen. The duke's patronage led to amateur gentlemen running their own race and founding a club. The Prince Regent joined in 1817 and on his accession as George IV it was first re-christened the Royal Yacht Club, and then the Royal Yacht Squadron with its headquarters in one of Henry VIII's castles. Nowadays, **Cowes Week** has become the premier yachting event of the year and also a fixture in the aristocratic social calendar.

Shipbuilding was for centuries the main industry of East Cowes, spanning ships for the Royal Navy, lifeboats, flying boats and seaplanes. Many of the seaplanes took part in the Schneider Trophy races, which brought great excitement to the Solent in the inter-war years. Sir Donald Campbell's *Bluebird* was built here, and the hovercraft had its origins in what is now the home of Westland Aerospace. Westland's factory doors were painted with a giant Union Jack to mark the Queen's Jubilee in 1977 – a piece of patriotic paintwork that has been retained by popular demand. Two museums in Cowes have a nautical theme. The **Sir Max Aitken Museum** in an old sailmaker's loft in West Cowes High Street houses Sir Max's remarkable collection of nautical paintings, instruments and artefacts, while the **Cowes Maritime Museum** charts the island's maritime history and has a collection of racing yachts that includes the Uffa Fox pair *Avenger* and *Coweslip*. (Uffa Fox, perhaps the best known yachtsman of his day, is buried in the Church of St Mildred at Whippingham.)

On the Parade, near the Royal Yacht Squadron, the **Isle of Wight Model Railways Exhibition** has

39 RAWLINGS RESTAURANT HOTEL

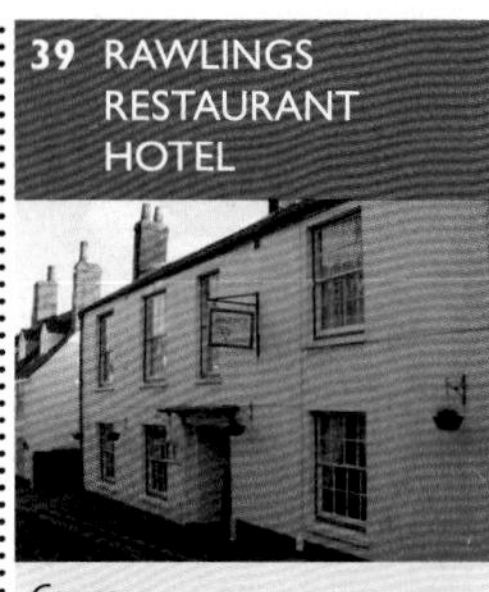

Cowes

This excellent hotel provides everything a yachtsman and their family could want!

see page 152

Osborne House and its grounds featured prominently in the film Mrs Brown (2001) starring Judi Dench and Billy Connolly which explored the controversial relationship between the queen and her Scottish ghillie, John Brown.

for almost 20 years been one of the most admired attractions of its kind in the country. Across the River Medina, linked by a chain ferry, East Cowes is most famous for **Osborne House** (English Heritage), a clean-cut, Italianate mansion designed and built by Prince Albert in 1846. Queen Victoria loved "dear beautiful Osborne" and so did her young children. They had their very own house in its grounds, a full-size Swiss Cottage, where they played at house-keeping, cooking meals for their parents, and tending its vegetable gardens using scaled-down gardening tools. In the main house itself, visitors can wander through both the State and private apartments which are crammed with paintings, furniture, ornaments, statuary and the random bric-à-brac that provided such an essential element in the décor of any upper-class Victorian home. Osborne House possessed a special place in the queen's affections. It had been built by the husband she adored with an almost adolescent infatuation: together they had spent many happy family days here. After Albert's premature death from typhoid in 1861, she often returned to Osborne. Her staff had instructions to lay out the Prince's clothes in his dressing-room each night, and the queen herself retired to bed with his nightshirt clasped in her arms. In 1901 she returned to Osborne for the last time, dying here in her 83rd year, her death co-incidentally signalling the beginning of the slow decline of the British Empire over which she had presided as Queen-Empress.

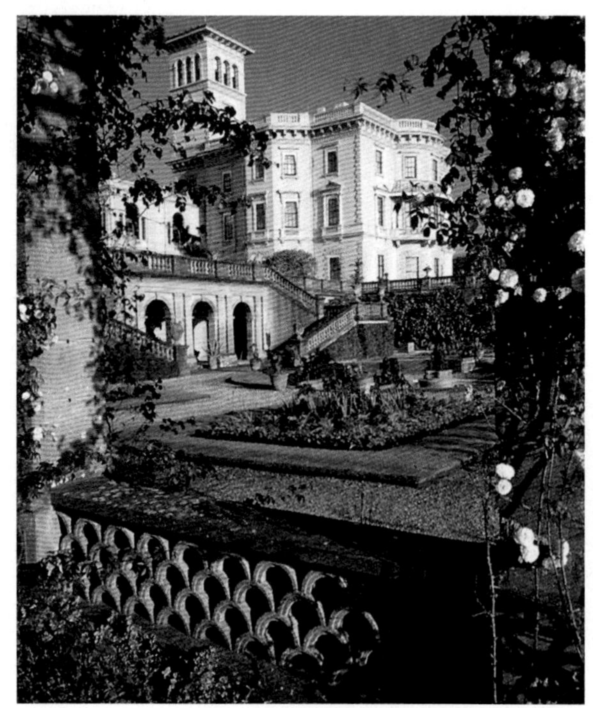

Osborne House, Cowes

WHIPPINGHAM

2 miles SE of Cowes on the A3021

Queen Victoria also acquired **Barton Manor** at nearby Whippingham, a peaceful retreat whose grounds are occasionally open to the public. Prince Albert had a hand in the design of the gardens and of the ornate **Church of St Mildred**, where the contractor and co-designer was AJ Humbert, who was also responsible for Sandringham House in Norfolk. The royal family regularly worshipped at St Mildred's, which is predictably full of royal memorials, including a monument to Victoria's son-in-law Prince Henry of Battenberg, who succumbed to malaria in Africa at the age of 38. Alfred Gilbert's wonderful art nouveau screen in the chancel arcade is a unique work of art, and other notable pieces are a bronze angel and font, both of them designed by Princess Louise, a daughter of the queen; a memorial to Albert, and a chair used by the queen.

Barton Manor, Whippingham

WOOTTON CREEK

6 miles SE of Cowes off the A3054

Wootton is notable for its ancient bridge and mill-pond, and as the western terminus of the Isle of Wight Steam Railway, with an old wooden booking office and signal box moved from elsewhere on the island. It is also the home of **Butterfly World & Fountain World**. This complex comprises a sub-tropical indoor garden with hundreds of exotic butterflies flying free; a colourful Italian garden with computer-controlled fountains; a Japanese garden with Oriental buildings and a koi carp lake; and a five-acre garden centre.

FISHBOURNE

2 miles W of Ryde on the A3054

Fishbourne is the port where the car ferry from Portsmouth docks. Nearby **Quarr Abbey** is a handsome redbrick Benedictine monastery built around 1910 near

40 BARTON MANOR

Whippingham

Once owned by Queen Victoria and Prince Albert, Barton was mentioned in the Domesday Book. The estate is open on special days in aid of charity.

 *see page 152*

Quarr Old Abbey, Fishbourne

the ruins of a 12th century Cistercian Abbey. The old abbey, founded by a certain Baldwin de Redvers, enjoyed 400 years of prestige and influence, owning much of the land and many of the grand houses, before its destruction in 1536.

The stone for the original Quarr Abbey at Fishbourne came from the quarries at nearby Binstead, where a major family draw is **Brickfields Horse Country**, a centre that is home to more than 100 animals, from magnificent shire horses to miniature ponies, farm animals and pets. Open daily throughout the year, the numerous attractions include racing pigs (the Lester Piglet Derby!), wagon rides, a parade of Cowboys and Indians, a blacksmith's forge and museums focusing on carriages, tractors and many aspects of farm life. The shire horses are the particular pride and joy of the centre's owner Phil Legge, whose 'Montgomery' and 'Prince' won him top honours in an All-England ploughing match.

Isle of Wight Steam Railway, Havenstreet

HAVENSTREET

3 miles SW of Ryde off the A3054

Royal patronage and the growth of the island as a holiday destination went hand in hand with the development of a comprehensive railway system. Between 1862 and 1900 the whole Island was criss-crossed by railways, which in 1923 became part of the Southern Railway and alter came under the aegis of British Railways. As car ownership increased, the railways declined, and by the 1960 only the Ryde Pier- Shanklin route remained, currently operated by trains that previously ran on the Northern Line of the London Underground. 1971 saw the re-opening of a preserved line from Wootton to Haverstreet, extended in the 1990s to Smallbrook Junction, linking with the Ryde-Shanklin line. Havenstreet is the Headquarters and nerve centre of the **Isle of Wight Steam Railway** which has a small workshop and museum, gift shop and refreshment room here. The locomotives working the line date back as far as 1876 and include a tiny A1 class engine acquired from the London, Brighton & South Coast Railway in 1913, and a W14, named *Calbourne*, which was built in 1891 and came to the island in 1925. The carriages and goods wagons are of a similar vintage and have been lovingly restored. Trips through some scenic countryside take place daily from late-May to mid-September, and on other selected days in March, April and October.

RYDE

Ryde is the largest town on the island and its attractions include a huge expanse of sandy Blue Flag beach and a half-mile long pier, one of the first to be built in Britain. Passenger ferries from Portsmouth dock here, the hovercraft service settles nearby, and the car ferry from the mainland disgorges its cargo a couple of miles to the west. The town is essentially Victorian, a popular resort in those days for affluent middle-class families. Then, as now, visitors enjoyed strolling along the elegant Esplanade with its sea views across Spithead Sound to Portsmouth.

Reminders of the town's Georgian and Victorian heyday are still there in abundance, among them a fine arcade in Union Street opened in 1837, the year of Queen Victoria's accession. The town has some important churches: **All Saints**, designed by Sir George Gilbert Scott, the Roman Catholic **St Mary's** with a Pugin chapel, and **St Thomas**, which is now a heritage centre featuring an exhibition of memorabilia associated with the transportation of convicts to Australia – many of the convicts left these shores in ships moored off Ryde.

In the middle of Appley Park stands **Appley Tower**, built as a station for troops guarding Spithead and now open to the public as a centre for fossils, crystals, natural gems, oracles and rune readings. Another public space is **Puckpool Park**, a leisure area behind the sea wall between Ryde and Seaview. It surrounds what was once a battery, built in the 19th century; its last gun was removed in 1927. At the Westridge Centre, just off the A3055 road to Brading, **Waltzing Waters** offers an indoor water, light and music spectacular performed several times daily in a comfortable modern theatre.

SEAVIEW

2 miles E of Ryde on the B3330/B3340

To the east of Ryde, the aptly named resort of Seaview has a good, gently sloping beach with clean firm sand, ideal for making sandcastles. There are little rock pools where small children can play in safety while trying to catch the abundant crabs and shrimps. Lines of clinker-built wooden dinghies bob about on the waves, and out to sea rise two of "Palmerston's Follies" – forts constructed in the 1850s as a warning signal to the French to keep away.

A short distance west of Seaview, on the B3330, is one of the Island's chief visitor attractions, the **Seaview Wildlife Encounter**. Previously known as Flamingo Park, the site has been at the forefront of bird and wildlife conservation for more than 35 years, and the new name reflects the new aims and increased diversity of resident wildlife. Among the most favourite inmates are the wallabies, the meerkats and the seriously endangered Humboldt penguins, and the Tropical House has proved an instant success. The

•

To the southwest of Ryde lies Rosemary Vineyard which grows 11 different varieties of vine to produce a selection of estate bottled wines, fruit juices and liqueurs. Visitors can learn about the wine-making process, sample the wines and enjoy refreshments in the café that overlooks the estate.

•

41 SEAVIEW WILDLIFE ENCOUNTER

Seaview

As one of the Island's leading attractions this nature haven specialises in hands-on feeding which encourages everyone to participate.

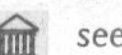
see page 154

Old Church, St Helens

42 WIGHT COAST & COUNTRY COTTAGES

Bembridge

This company offers a magnificent range of self-catering cottages all over the Isle of Wight.

see page 153

centre is open from 10am to 5pm (last entrance 4pm) from April to the end of September and from 10am to 4pm (last entrance 3pm) during October.

ST HELENS

3 miles SE of Ryde on the B3330

Famed for its picturesque harbour and magnificent village green, St Helens straggles down the hillside above the mouth of the River Yar, a quiet spot beloved by yachtsmen. It must be the only English village to be named after a Roman Emperor's wife – the Helen who was the wife of Constantine and in whose honour a church was erected here in AD 704. Another "royal" figure, the Queen of Chantilly was actually born in the village, and if the name is unfamiliar to you, seek out **Sophie Dawes' Cottage** which bears a wall plaque stating that "Sophie Dawes, Madame de Fouchères, Daughter of Richard Dawes, Fisherman and Smuggler, known as the Queen of Chantilly, was born here in 1792". As a young girl, Sophie left St Helens to seek her fortune in London where she worked (non-professionally) in a Piccadilly brothel for a while before ensnaring the exiled Duc de Bourbon and becoming his mistress. The duke paid for her education and when he was able to return to France, took her with him, marrying her off to a compliant Baron. Eventually, she married her duke, now Prince de Condé and having made sure that his will was in order, contrived his murder. Although she was tried for the crime, political considerations led to the case being quietly dropped. Sophie returned to England with her ill-gotten gains but in her last years she seems to have been stricken with remorse and gave lavishly to charity.

BEMBRIDGE

4 miles SE of Ryde on the B3350

The most easterly point of the island, this popular sailing centre was itself an island until the reclamation of the huge inland harbour of Brading Haven in the

1880s. The story of that major work was told from 1978 to 2006 at the **Shipwreck Centre & Maritime Museum**, which is now located at Arreton Barns (qv). A fascinating exhibition of life in Bembridge, past and present, is portrayed in photographs and artefacts at the **Bembridge Heritage Centre** in Church Road. Also well worth a visit is the **Bembridge Windmill** (National Trust). Dating from around 1700, it is the only windmill to have survived on the island and much of its wooden machinery is still intact. There are spectacular views from the top floor.

There are some excellent walks starting from the village, especially the coastal path from Bembridge to Sandown. On top of **Bembridge Down** (National Trust) stands an early-Victorian fort, a reminder that this downland was used by the military as a vantage point for the defence of Sandown Bay and Spithead from invasion.

Windmill, Bembridge

BRADING

4 miles S of Ryde on the A3055

For what is little more than a large village, Brading is remarkably well-stocked with visitor attractions. Amongst them are a diminutive **Town Hall** with whipping post and stocks outside, and a fine 12th century church housing some striking tombs of the Oglander family. The most ancient of the village's sights is the **Brading Roman Villa** which in the 3rd century was the centre of a rich and prosperous farming estate. Discovered in 1880, the villa covers some 300 square feet and has fine mosaic floors with a representation of that master-musician, Orpheus, charming wild animals with his lyre.

The oldest surviving house on the island, opposite the late-Gothic parish church, is now the half-timbered home of **The Brading Experience**, formerly the Isle of Wight Waxworks, an all-weather family attraction displaying scenes and characters from island history. Naturally, there's a Chamber of Horrors, as well as a World of

Town Hall, Brading

Nature Exhibition, The World of Wheels, some delightful gardens, and a shop. Close by, **The Lilliput Antique Doll & Toy Museum**, established in Brading in 1974, exhibits more than 2,000 dolls and toys, ranging across the centuries from around 2000 BC to 1945. The collection also includes dolls' houses, tinplate toys, trains, rocking horses, and some very rare German and French bisque dolls.

On the edge of the village stands **Morton Manor**, a lovely old house dating back to 1249, largely rebuilt in 1680, and now set amidst one of the finest gardens in England. The landscaped grounds feature rose and Elizabethan sunken gardens, ponds and cascades, and many mature specimen trees including 90 varieties of Japanese maple and the largest London Plane you're ever likely to see. Other attractions include the Stable Shop, licensed tearooms, a safe children's play area with a traditional Elizabethan Turf Maze, and even a vineyard. In fact, Brading has two vineyards. The other is the well-known **Adgestone Vineyard**, planted in 1968 and the oldest on the island. Entry is free, as is the wine tasting, there are pony trap rides around the vineyard during the season, a gift shop and café.

A mile or so northwest of the village of Brading, **Nunwell House & Gardens** should definitely not be missed. The picturesque house has been a family home since 1522 and is of great historic and architectural interest. It was here that Sir John Oglander, an ancestor of the present owner, was host to Charles I on his last night of freedom and modern day visitors can still see the Parlour Chamber in which they met. The house is beautifully furnished, there are exhibits recalling the family's military connections, and Nunwell is surrounded by 5 acres of tranquil gardens enjoying views across the Solent.

Some of the grandest views on the island can be enjoyed from **Brading Down**, just west of the village on the minor road that leads to Downend.

43 HAZELWOOD APARTMENTS

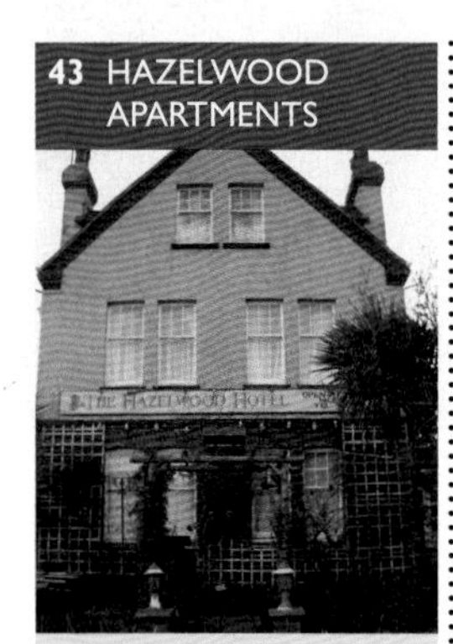

Sandown

Two great self catering apartments in the centre of the lively seaside town of Sandown.

see page 154

SANDOWN

"A village by a sandy shore" was how a guide-book described Sandown in the 1870s. Since then, its superb position on sweeping Sandown Bay has transformed that village into the island's premier resort. Now a lively town, Sandown offers its visitors every kind of seaside attraction, including a Blue Flag beach. There are miles of flat, safe sands where a Kidzone safety scheme operates during the season; a traditional pier complete with theatre; colourful gardens; a Sunday market; abundant sporting facilities, and even pleasure flights from the nearby airfield.

On the edge of town, the **Isle of Wight Zoo** specialises in breeding severely endangered exotic species and is home to the UK's largest variety of Royal Bengal, Siberian and Chinese tigers. The zoo is also a World Health Organisation centre for venomous snakes, their venom extracted for use in antidotes for snake bites. You may well see TV "Snake Man" Jack Corney handling these lethal reptiles and children who are photographed with a small harmless snake are presented with a handling certificate to prove it! There are all-weather snake and parrot shows, a kiddies' play area and Pets' Corner, a seafront pub and café, the Zoofari Gift Shop, and a snack bar. A Road-Runner Train operates frequent services between the zoo and the town centre.

On Culver Parade, the **Dinosaur Isle** is especially popular with children who love its life-sized monsters – the Isle of Wight is renowned for the number and quality of the dinosaur remains and other fossils that have been discovered here. The museum, "120 million years in the making", has excellent displays on all aspects of the island's geology. As part of its educational programme, museum staff will advise you on the best places to look for fossils and, when you return with your discoveries, will identify them for you. The centre is open every day from 10am.

ALVERSTONE

2 miles NW of Sandown off the A3055

A couple of miles west of Haseley Manor, the secluded and picturesque village of Alverstone sits beside the tiny River Yar. It has everything you expect of an English village – except for a pub. The deeds of the estate's owner, Lord Alverstone, specifically forbid the sale of intoxicating liquor within the village.

NEWCHURCH

2 miles W of Sandown on the A3056

Amazon World Zoo Park is a popular family attraction that tells the story of the rain forest with the help of a large number of exotic animals and birds – conservation is the name of the game here. There are many diverse habitats here, all specially created so that the exotic animals, birds and reptiles can live in as near natural landscapes as possible.

One of the highlights in Newchurch is the annual **Garlic Festival,** held on a weekend in August and attracting some 25,000 visitors. You can sample the aromatic root at the Garlic Farm where it is used in such products as garlic ice cream, Tansylvanian pickles and 'Vampire Relishes'.

SHANKLIN

2 miles SW of Sandown on the A3055

Like Sandown, Shanklin was just a small village a century or so ago. The old village has survived intact, a charming little complex of thatched houses standing at the

44 ALENDEL HOTEL

Sandown

This is a really friendly, family run hotel, who ensure your holiday is comfortable as well as cheerful.

see page 155

45 MOUNT BROCAS GUEST HOUSE

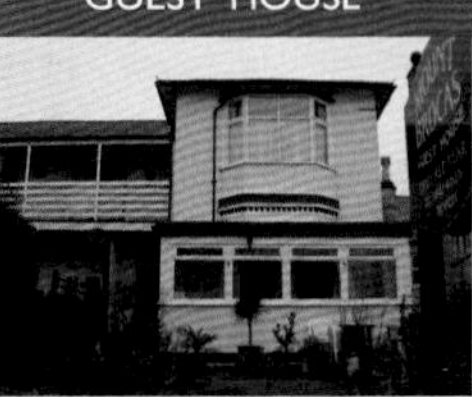

Sandown

Tastefully decorated rooms are available in the seaside resort of Sandown in the Isle of Wight. This property is a tranquil and enjoyable one.

see page 155

•

Throughout the season, the Sandown Bay area hosts a wide range of special events – from the Regatta in August to Sunday markets, from the Isle of Wight Power Boat Festival in May to the National Strong Man finals in September.

•

head of the **Shanklin Chine.** The famous Chine is a spectacular ravine some 300feet deep, 180feet wide, noted for its waterfalls and rare flora. There's a Nature Trail to follow or you can join a guided tour. The **Heritage Centre** contains an interesting exhibit on PLUTO (the Pipeline Under The Ocean) secretively constructed during World War II to transport fuel from the island to the continent during the D-Day landings. There's also a memorial to the soldiers of 40 Commando who trained in this area for the disastrous assault on Dieppe in 1942.

The old village stands on a 150feet-high cliff from which the ground slopes gently down to the safe, sheltered Blue Flag beach, with its long, seafront esplanade. With its scenic setting, many public gardens, and healthy climate, Shanklin has appealed to many celebrities. Charles Darwin was particularly fond of the town, the American poet Longfellow fell in love with it, and John Keats was a familiar figure in Sandown throughout the summer of 1818.

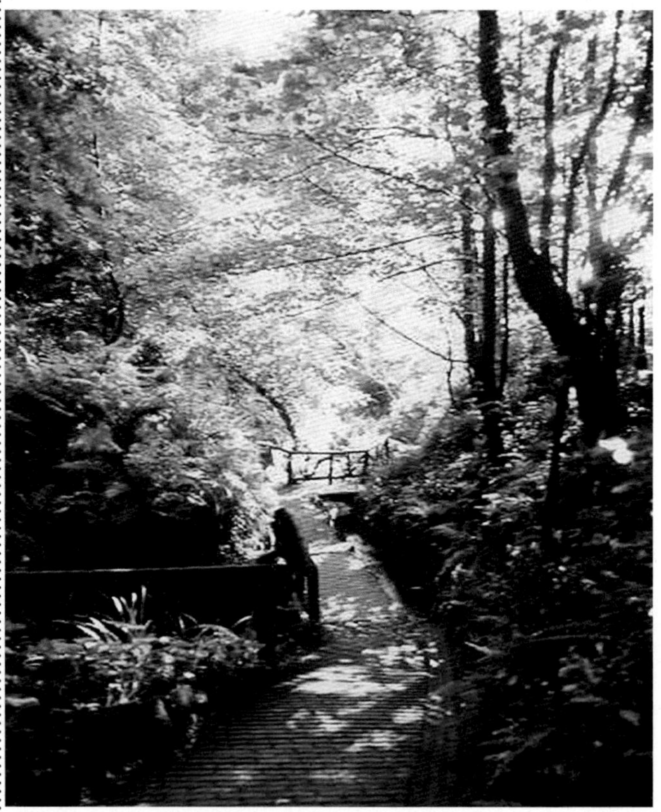

Shanklin Chine Woodland Bridge, Shanklin

46 ST GEORGES HOUSE HOTEL

Shanklin

Set in a tourist location of Shanklin, this hotel is extremely inviting and is perfect for a break away of crisp sea air.

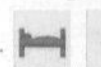

see page 156

47 SAFFRONS

Shanklin

Visit Saffrons for a delicious meal that will have you telling everyone. A family run establishment that has tremendous hospitality.

see page 157

The grassy open space known as **Keats Green** commemorates his stay here during which he wrote some of his best-known poems.

GODSHILL

4 miles W of Shanklin on the A3020

A short drive inland from Shanklin leads to the charming village of Godshill, which with its stone-built thatched cottages and its medieval **Church of All Saints** is one of the most popular stops on the tourist trail. The double-naved church, whose 15th century pinnacled tower dominates the village, contains some notable treasures, including a 15th century wall painting of Christ crucified on a triple-branched lily, a painting of Daniel in the Lions' Den and many monuments to the Worsleys and the Leighs, two of the leading island families.

Godshill has much to entertain visitors, including the magical **Model Village** with its 1:10 scale stone houses, trains and boats, even a football match taking place on the green, and the **Natural History Centre** with its famed shell collection, minerals and aquarium. The miniature village was built with the help of model-makers from Elstree film studio and after two years' preparation was opened to the public in 1952. The models are made of coloured cement and the detail is quite incredible. Real straw was prepared in the traditional way for thatching; the church on the hill took 600 hours of work before being assembled in its position; each house has its own tiny garden with miniature trees and shrubs. The airfield is in the style of small landing strips of the 1920s and 1930s, and the little railway is modelled on the older Island systems. Things get even smaller in the model garden of the model Old Vicarage, where there is another (1:100 scale) model village with yet another Old Vicarage, and within its garden another (1:1000 scale) model village – a model of a model of a model!

BONCHURCH

2 miles S of Shanklin on the A3055

The poet Algernon Swinburne spent some of his childhood in Bonchurch, and is buried in the churchyard of St Boniface. Charles Dickens wrote part of *David Copperfield* while staying in this quiet village. His first impressions of the place were very favourable – "I think it is the prettiest place I ever saw". He seemed likely to make it his permanent home, but he soon grew to dislike the weather and the place and returned to his familiar Broadstairs.

VENTNOR

Along the south-eastern corner of the island stretches a 6-mile length of ragged cliffs known as **Undercliffe**. Clinging to the slopes at its eastern end, Ventnor has been described as "an alpinist's town" and as "a steeply raked auditorium with the sea as the stage". Promoted as a spa town in the 1830s, its distinguished visitors

48 WINTERBOURNE COUNTRY HOUSE

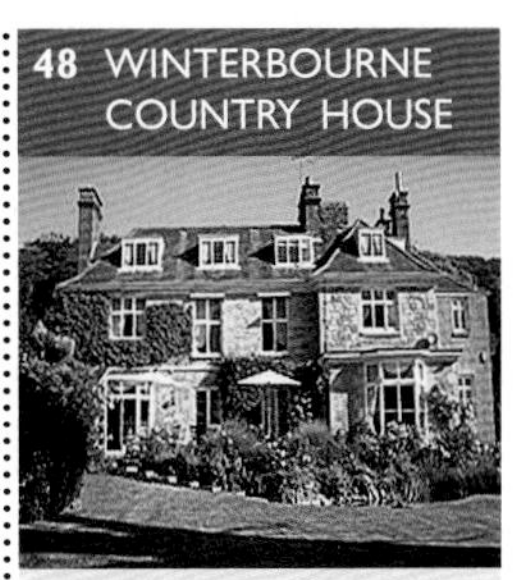

Bonchurch

"The prettiest place I ever saw in my life, at home or abroad" Charles Dickens, 1849.

see page 158

49 EL TORO CONTENTO TAPAS BAR

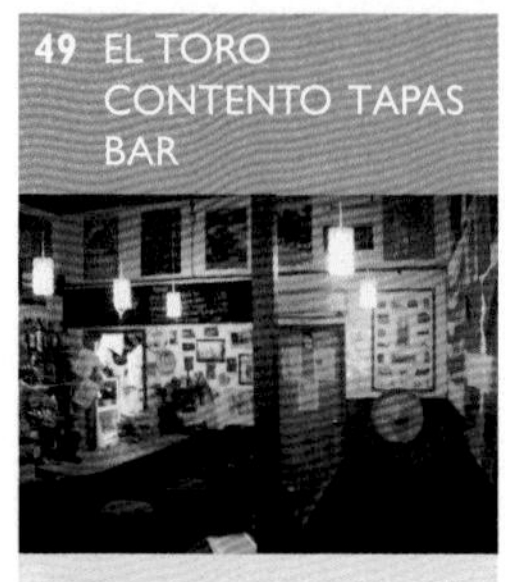

Ventnor

This is an absolutely tremendous Tapas bar. A real piece of Spain, in the middle of the Isle of Wight. The Paella served at El Toro Contento is out of this world.

see page 159

have included a young Winston Churchill and an elderly Karl Marx, and the town retains much of its Victorian charm.

Ventnor Heritage Museum houses a fascinating collection of old prints, photographs and working models relating to the town's history, while **Ventnor Botanical Gardens** shelters some 10,000 plants in 22 acres of grounds, amongst them many rare and exotic trees, shrubs, alpines, perennials, succulents and conifers. In the gardens' Visitor Centre the exhibits include an interactive display called The Green Planet – the Incredible Life of Plants. Many unusual varieties of plants are on sale in the shop here. There's a picnic area and children's playground, and during August the Gardens host open-air performances of Shakespearean plays. Also snuggling in the garden grounds is the **Smuggling Museum**, whose 300 exhibits illustrate 700 years of smuggling lore.

Back in town, the **Coastal Visitor Centre** provides a fascinating and educational insight into the island's coastal and marine environment, with special features on animal and plant life, coastal defences and living with landslides a problem very familiar to the island as well as to many parts of England's south coast.

Above the town, **St Boniface Down** (National Trust), at 785feet the highest point on the island, provides some dizzying views across coast and countryside.

WROXALL

2 miles N of Ventnor on the B3327

Owls, falcons, vultures and donkeys all call Wroxall their home! The **Owl & Falconry Centre**, in what used to be the laundry and brewhouse of Appuldurcombe House, stages daily flying displays with birds of prey from around the world and holds courses in the centuries-old art of falconry.

Appuldurcombe House itself was once the grandest mansion on the whole island with gardens laid out by 'Capability' Brown, but the house was badly bombed in 1943 and has never been lived in since. The building has been partly restored and visitors can stroll in the 11 acres of ornamental grounds landscaped by 'Capability' Brown which provide an enchanting setting for picnics.

Heaven for 200 donkeys and many other animals is the **Isle of Wight Donkey Sanctuary** at Lower Winstone Farm. The rescue centre is a registered charity relying entirely on donations, and visitors have several ways of helping,

Appledurcombe House, Wroxhall

including the Adopt-a-Donkey scheme.

ST LAWRENCE

2 miles W of Ventnor on the A3055

Nestling in the heart of the Undercliff, the ancient village of St Lawrence has a 13th century church that once laid claim to being the smallest in Britain. It was extended in 1842 but remains diminutive, measuring just 20 feet by 12 feet. Lord Jellicoe, hero of the Battle of Jutland, lived for some years in St Lawrence and often swam in Orchard's Bay, a small cove where Turner sketched.

Close to the village is the **Rare Breeds Waterfowl Park** set in 30 acres by the coast. The park includes one of the largest collections in Britain of rare farm animals, plus animals and birds from all over the world. The meerkats who arrived in 1999 have been so successful at breeding that their quarters have had to be extended. Other arrivals for the millennium were the first litter of Kune Kune pigs from New Zealand. The park is also home to over 100 species of waterfowl and poultry, there's a guinea pig 'village' and chipmunk mansion, special children's areas, a unique temperate waterfall house, lakeside cafeteria and gift shop.

The coast road continues to **St Catherine's Point**, the most southerly and the wildest part of the island, in an area of Special Scientific Interest. Steps lead down to St Catherine's lighthouse (guided tours by arrangement) and a path leads up to the summit of St Catherine's Hill, where the remains of a much older lighthouse, known as the Pepperpot, can be seen. Close by is the Hoy Monument erected in honour of a visit by Tsar Nicholas

A little further west, **Blackgang Chine** has been developed from an early Victorian scenic park into a modern fantasy park with dozens of attractions for children. Also inside the park are two heritage exhibitions centred on a water-powered sawmill and a quayside, with displays ranging from cooper's and wheelwright's workshops to a shipwreck collection, a huge whale skeleton and a 19th century beach scene complete with a bathing machine. The coastline here is somewhat fragile, and a large slice of cliff has been lost to storms and gales in recent years.

SHORWELL

5 miles SW of Newport on the B3323

Pronounced 'Shorell' by Caulkheads, as Isle of Wight natives are known, this village of thatched stone cottages has no fewer than three venerable manor houses within its boundaries. West Court, Wolverton, and North Court were built respectively during the reigns of Henry VIII, Elizabeth I, and James I. They possess all the charm you would expect from that glorious age of English architecture but sadly none of them is open to the public. However, you can visit **St Peter's Church** to gaze on its mesmerisingly beautiful 15th

•

Just west of St Lawrence, old farm buildings have been converted into Isle of Wight Studio Glass, where skills old and new produce hand-made glass of the highest quality. There's an extensive showroom and shop.

•

•

The small village of Shorwell boasts Yafford Mill, an 18th century water mill in full working order. It's surrounded by ponds and streams where you'll find Sophie, the resident seal, and within the grounds there are paddocks which are home to rare cattle, sheep and pigs, a collection of antique farm machinery, a steam engine and narrow-gauge railway. There are also waymarked nature walks, a playground, picnic area, gift shop, tea gardens and a licensed bar.

•

50 DINOSAUR FARM MUSEUM

nr Brighstone

Traditional village inn serving quality home-made food and real ales.

see page 160

century wall-painting and admire its 500-year-old stone pulpit covered by an elaborate wooden canopy of 1620. The church also has a real oddity in a painting on wood of the Last Supper, brought from Iceland in 1898.

BRIGHSTONE

7 miles SW of Newport on the B3399

One of the prettiest villages on the island, Brighstone was once notorious as the home of smugglers and wreckers. Today, the National Trust runs a shop (selling legitimate goods) in a picturesque row of thatched cottages, and there's a little museum depicting village life down the years.

The island has long been known for its fossil finds, especially relating to dinosaurs. It was on a clifftop near the village that the bones of a completely new species of predatory dinosaur were recently unearthed. The 15ft carnivore, which lived in the cretaceous period about 120 million to 150 million years ago, has been named *cotyrannus lengi* after Gavin Leng, a local collector who found the first bone.

On Military Road (A3055) near Brighstone, the **Dinosaur Farm Museum** came into being following the unearthing in 1992 of the skeleton of a brachiosaurus, at that time the island's largest and most spectacular dinosaur discovery. A mile or so west of Brighstone is the National Trust's **Mottistone Manor Garden**, a charming hillside garden alongside a privately owned Elizabethan manor house. The garden is particularly known for its herbaceous borders, terraces planted with fruit trees, and a restored organic kitchen garden. On Mottistone Common, where New Forest ponies graze, are the remains of a Neolithic long barrow known as the Longstone.

CALBOURNE

5 miles W of Newport on the B3401

The most enchanting part of this picturesque village of thatched cottages is Barrington Row, usually known as Winkle Street. This row of charming old dwellings stands opposite the village stream (the Caul Burn) and an ancient sheepwash. The village's All Saints' Church dates from the 13th century and its treasures include a handsome 16th century brass of William Montacute, son of the Earl of Salisbury. The grandest building in the area is Swainston Manor, now a luxury hotel. It stands on the site of earlier buildings owned by the bishops of Winchester. The 12th century Bishop's Chapel can still be seen next to the hotel.

To the west of the village is **Calbourne Mill & Museum**, a 17th century water mill in working order with milling taking place every day at 3pm except on Saturdays. Sharing the site is a Museum of Rural Life, and visitors can also enjoy the spacious grounds or go punting on the millpond.

FRESHWATER

11 miles SW of Newport on the A3055

Freshwater and the surrounding

area are inextricably linked with the memory of Alfred, Lord Tennyson. In 1850, he succeeded Wordsworth as Poet Laureate, married Emily Sellwood, and shortly afterwards moved to **Farringford,** just outside Freshwater. The house, set in 33 acres of parkland, is now a hotel where visitors can relax in the luxuriously appointed drawing room with its delightful terrace and views across the downs. Tennyson was an indefatigable walker and however foul the weather would pace along nearby High Down dramatically arrayed in a billowing cloak and a black, broad-brimmed sombrero. As Tennyson grew older, he became increasingly impatient with sightseers flocking to Farringford hoping to catch sight of the now-legendary figure. He moved to his other home at Blackdown in Sussex where he died in 1892. After his death, the area he loved so much was re-named **Tennyson Down** and a cross erected high on the cliffs in his memory.

There are more remembrances of the great poet in the **Church of All Saints** in Freshwater town where Lady Tennyson is buried in the churchyard and a touching memorial inside commemorates their son Lionel, "an affectionate boy", who died at the age of 32 while returning from India.

About a mile south of the town, **Freshwater Bay** was once an inaccessible inlet, much favoured by smugglers. Today, the bay is the start point of the 15-mile Tennyson Trail, which ends at Carisbrooke and its scenic beauty attracts thousands of visitors every year. They also make pilgrimage in their thousands to **Dimbola Lodge,** one of the most important shrines in the history of early photography. It was the home of Julia Margaret Cameron (1815-1879) who bought the house in 1860 to be close to her friend Tennyson. Three years later, she was given a camera and immediately devoted herself with her usual energy to mastering the technical and artistic aspects of what was then called the "Black Art". (Because handling the chemicals involved usually left the photographer's hands deeply stained). The coal-house at Dimbola Lodge was turned into a dark room and within a year, Julia had been elected a member of the Photographic Society of London. She photographed most of the leading lights of the artistic community of the time including Thackeray, Darwin, GF Watts and

51 THE ROYAL STANDARD

Freshwater

This smart hotel provides a great mix of original Victorian features with a quality contemporary décor.

see page 161

Dimbola Lodge, Freshwater

The Needles Park at Alum Bay has good views and offers a wide range of family entertainments, a breathtaking chairlift from the clifftop to the beach, boat trips to the lighthouse, a glass-making studio and many other attractions.

his wife the actress Ellen Terry, who all at some time lived locally. Perhaps the most famous of her images is the classic portrait of Tennyson himself, a craggy, bearded figure with a visionary gaze. Dimbola Lodge was acquired by the Julia Margaret Cameron Trust in 1993 and it has been converted into a museum and galleries devoted to her photography. There's also a gift shop, antiquarian bookshop, and vegetarian restaurant.

From the bay itself, there are regular cruises around the island's most spectacular natural feature, the dreaded **Needles**. The boat trip takes you through the swirling waters around the lighthouse, and past the line of jagged slabs of gleaming chalk towering some 200feet high. The sea has gouged deep caves out of the cliffs. Two of them are known as Lord Holmes' Parlour and Kitchen, named after a 17th century governor of the island who once entertained his guests in the 'Parlour' and kept his wines cool in the 'Kitchen'.

The Needles are undoubtedly at their most impressive when viewed from the sea, but they are still a grand sight from the land. There are some particularly striking vistas from the **Needles Old Battery** (National Trust), a Victorian coastal fort standing 250feet above the sea. Visitors pass through a 200ft long tunnel and emerge onto a platform with panoramic views.

In the car park at **Alum Bay** is a monument to Marconi, who sent messages to a tug in Alum Bay and set up the first wireless station here in 1897. The first paid Marconigram was sent in the following year by Lord Kelvin.

YARMOUTH

9 miles W of Newport on the A3054

A regular ferry links this picturesque little port to Lymington on the mainland. Yarmouth was once the principal port on the island which was why Henry VIII ordered the building of **Yarmouth Castle** (English Heritage) in 1547. It was garrisoned until 1885 but is now disused, though much remains. The town also boasts a quaint old **Town Hall**, a working pier, and a 13th century church rather unhappily restored in 1831. It's worth going inside to see the incongruous statue on the tomb of Sir Robert Holmes, Governor of the Island in the mid-17th century. During one of the countless conflicts with the

Yarmouth Castle, Yarmouth

French, Sir Robert had captured a ship on board which was a French sculptor with an unfinished statue of Louis XIV. The sculptor had been on his way to Versailles to model the king's head from life. Sir Robert decided that the elaborate statue of the king (in full French armour) would do nicely for his own tomb. The sculptor was ordered to replace the royal head with Sir Robert's. No doubt deliberately, the artist made a poor fist of the job and the head is decidedly inferior to the rest of the statue. A mile west of yarmouth, Fort Victoria Country Park is one of the major leisure complexes on the Island and uses the area around one of Palmerston's forts. Attractions for all ages include unspoilt sandy beaches, woodland walks, a huge model railway, a state-of-the-art Planetarium and Astronomy centre, an aquarium, speedboat trips and eating outlets.

NEWTOWN

5 miles W of Newport off the A3054

Founded in the 13th century by a Bishop of Winchester, Newtown once had a large, busy harbour, but silting led to its decline as a maritime centre and the harbour is now a nature reserve. At its height, the town was the most important on the island and regularly sent two MPs to Westminster; among them were John Churchill, later the 1st Duke of Marlborough, and Prime Minister George Canning. The town's most notable building is the **Old Town Hall**, erected in 1699 and now owned by the National Trust. A small, unassuming building of brick and stone, it contains many interesting documents and memorabilia. The records include the exploits of Ferguson's Gang, an anonymous group of benefactors who gave donations to save selected properties. It is not recorded why this building was chosen, but in 1934 one of the gang went into the National Trust offices and discreetly dropped £500 on the secretary's desk to save the town hall.

At Porchfield, 2 miles east of Newtown, fun in the country for the whole family is promised at **Colemans Animal Farm**, where visitors are encouraged to stroke and feed the animals. Children will also love the huge wooden play area, the sandpit, the straw maze and the mini-farm with pedal tractors.

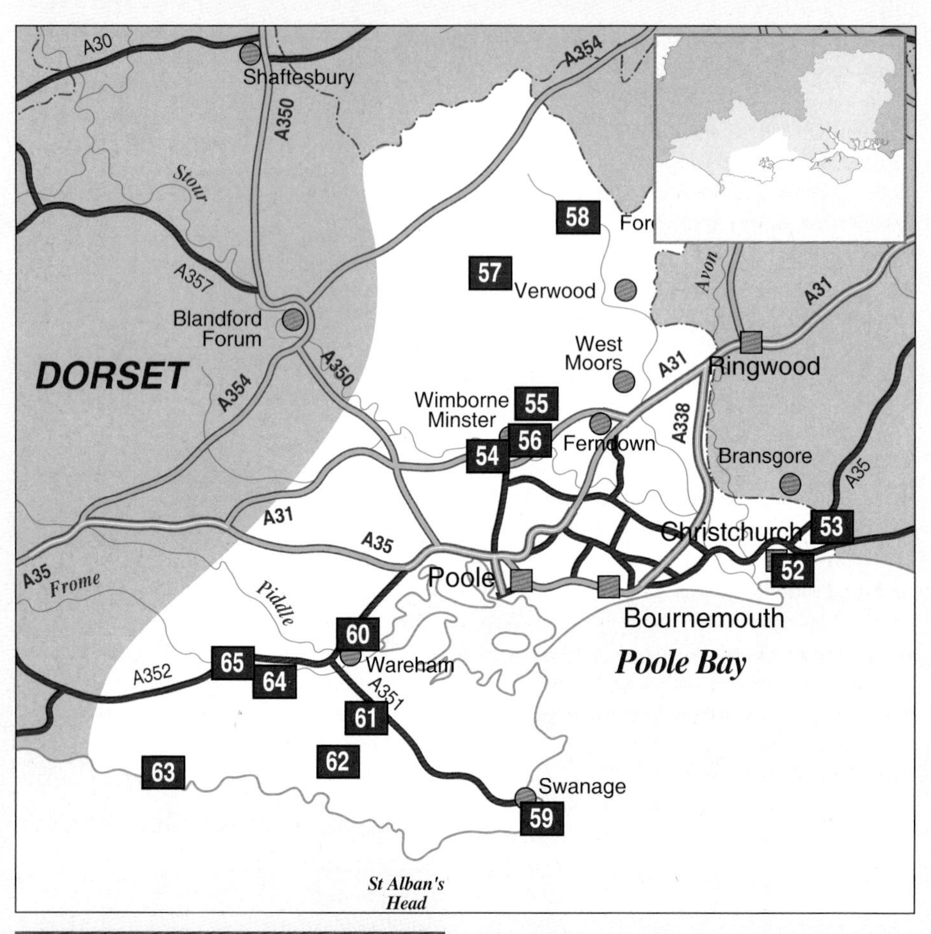

ACCOMMODATION

60	The Red Lion Hotel, Wareham	p 96, 167
62	Kimmeridge Farmhouse, Kimmeridge, nr Wareham	p 97, 169
62	Bradle Farmhouse, Bradle, nr Wareham	p 97, 169
63	The Cromwell House Hotel, Lulworth Cove	p 97, 168
64	Luckford Lake, West Holme, nr Wareham	p 98, 168
65	Luckford Wood House, East Stoke, nr Wareham	p 98, 170

FOOD & DRINK

53	The Amberwood, Walkford, nr Christchurch	p 89, 162
54	Angels Cafe, Wimborne	p 91, 164
55	The Stocks Inn, Furzehill, nr Wimborne	p 91, 163
56	Horns Inn, Wimborne	p 91, 165
57	Drovers Inn, Gussage All Saints, nr Wimborne	p 92, 164
58	Fleur-de-Lys, Cranborne	p 93, 166
59	Brook Tea Rooms, Swanage	p 93, 166
60	The Red Lion Hotel, Wareham	p 96, 167
62	Clavell's Café, Kimmeridge, nr Wareham	p 97, 169
63	The Cromwell House Hotel, Lulworth Cove	p 97, 168

PLACES OF INTEREST

52	The Museum of Electricity, Christchurch	p 88, 162
61	Barbrook Blue Pool, Furzebrook, nr Wareham	p 97, 168

East Dorset

Within a comparatively small area, East Dorset provides an extraordinary variety of attractions. It contains the county's two largest towns, Bournemouth and Poole, (virtually one, nowadays), where, along with all the other attractions, you can enjoy one of the best beaches in Britain during the day and a first class symphony concert in the evening.

Across Poole Harbour, the Isle of Purbeck is famous for the marble which has been quarried here since Roman times. The Isle of Purbeck's 'capital', the engaging seaside resort of Swanage, is linked by the steam-hauled Swanage Railway to the magnificent ruins of Corfe Castle. Set on a high hill above the charming village of the same name, this is one of the grandest sights in southwest England and should not be missed. Two other historic houses in the area also deserve special mention: Kingston Lacy which boasts an incomparable collection of 17th century Old Masters, and Cloud's Hill, the comfortless cottage where the enigmatic World War I hero T.E. Lawrence spent his last years. And no visitor to East Dorset should leave without paying a visit to glorious Wimborne Minster, a triumph of medieval architecture. To the west of Swanage are two of the most spectacular natural features in the county: the enchanting Lulworth Cove and the soaring limestone arch carved by the sea known as Durdle Door. Inland, a string of villages along the River Piddle, (delicately modified in Victorian times to 'Puddle') culminates in historic Tolpuddle, honoured in trades' union history as the home of the Tolpuddle Martyrs.

BOURNEMOUTH

In 1998, *Harpers & Queen* magazine predicted that Bournemouth was on its way to becoming the "coolest city on the planet" and another dubbed the town "Britain's Baywatch", a reference to the comely young lifeguards who patrol the seven miles of golden beaches. The British Tourist Authority's guide reckons that Bournemouth has "more nightclubs than Soho" as well as a huge range of hotels, shops, bars, restaurants and entertainment venues. The town also supports two symphony orchestras. In July 2005, in the hope of attracting more of Britain's 250,000 surfers to the town, Bournemouth council announced the construction of a 1600feet-long artificial reef capable of producing breakers up to 16ft-high. Beach users will also benefit as the reef will create a peaceful lagoon.

Russell Cotes Art Gallery & Museum, Bournemouth

Already, some 5.5 million visitors each year are attracted to this cosmopolitan town which has been voted the greenest and cleanest resort in the UK – there are more than 2000 acres of Victorian parks and gardens, and the town centre streets are washed and scrubbed every morning.

Two hundred years ago, the tiny village of Bourne was a mere satellite of the bustling port of Poole, a few miles to the west. The empty coastline was ideal for smugglers and Revenue men were regularly posted here to patrol the area. One of them, Louis Tregonwell, was enchanted by Bourne's glorious setting at the head of three deep valleys, or chines. He and his wife bought land here, built themselves a house and planted the valleys with the pines that give the present-day town its distinctive appearance. Throughout Victorian times, Bournemouth, as it became known, grew steadily and the prosperous new residents beautified their adopted town with wide boulevards, grand parks, and public buildings, creating a Garden City by the Sea.

They also built a splendid **Pier** (1855), the work of the peerless Eugenius Birch, the most famous of the pier designers. Born in 1818,

Birch was an artist and mechanic who worked on bridges and railways in the UK and India before turning skills to the classic English pier. **St Peter's Church** is much visited for its superb carved alabaster by Thomas Earp, and the tomb in which Mary Shelley, the author of *Frankenstein*, is buried along with the heart of her poet-husband, Percy Bysshe Shelley. Bournemouth's museums include the clifftop **Russell-Cotes Art Gallery & Museum**, based on the collection of the globe-trotting Sir Merton Russell-Cotes; and the **Bournemouth Aviation Museum** at Bournemouth International Airport, home to a collection of vintage jet aircraft – including the last flying Sea Fury fighter – which are flown on a regular basis. Opposite the airport, in seven acres of landscaped grounds, **Adventure Wonderland** offers a full day's fun with attractions ranging from an animal cuddle corner to Mensa Maze, theatre shows, sporting facilities and dozens of rides.

Back in town, the **Oceanarium**, located alongside the Pier, explores the wonders of the natural world beneath the surface of seas, lakes and rivers. Displays include life under the Amazon, the Caribbean and the lagoons of Hawaii. A popular feature here is Turtle Beach, home to rescued green turtles. A few steps from the Oceanarium, the **IMAX Cinema** shows 3D films on a screen the size of 5 double-decker buses on top of each other.

And if you're looking for a novel experience, and a really spectacular aerial view of the town and coastline, **Bournemouth Eye,** in the Lower Gardens near the pier, offers day or night ascents in a tethered balloon which rises up to 500feet.

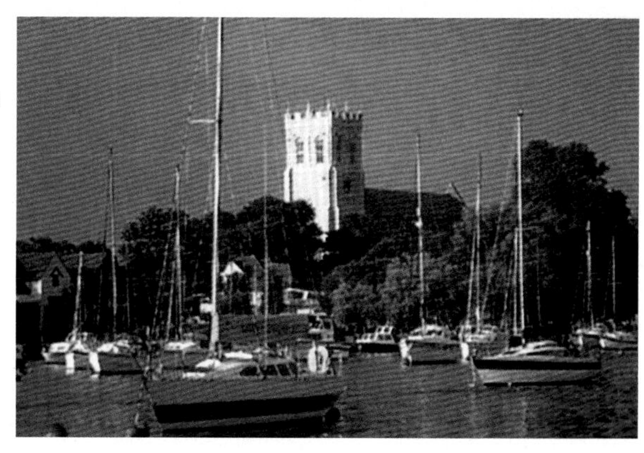

Coastal Christchurch, Christchurch

AROUND BOURNEMOUTH

CHRISTCHURCH

5 miles E of Bournemouth on the A35

An excellent way of exploring Christchurch is to follow the **Blue Plaques Millennium Trail** which commemorates sites around the town from Neolithic times to the 20th century. A booklet detailing this trip through time is available from the tourist information centre in the High Street.

Pride of place on the trail goes to **Christchurch Priory**, a magnificent building begun in 1094 and reputedly the longest parish church in England, extending for 311feet. It has an impressive Norman nave, some superb

•

On Christchurch Town Quay, at the meeting of the rivers Stour and Avon, is Place Mill, which dates back to Anglo-Saxon times and was mentioned in the Domesday Book. The mill has been restored and although it is unable to grind corn, you can still see the wheel turning when tidal conditions are right. The body of the mill is now an art gallery with changing exhibitions by local artists, interesting displays of artefacts, and a gift shop.

•

52 THE MUSEUM OF ELECTRICITY

Christchurch

Museum of Electricity is a must for all ages. Everything here is electric, from an old Bournemouth tram to a pair of boot warmers!

 *see page 162*

medieval carving, and a vast 14th century stone reredos with a Tree of Jesse. Other treasures include the magnificent Salisbury Chantry, some fine misericords and, in the beautiful Lady Chapel, a pendant vault believed to be the earliest of its kind in the country. From the Lady Chapel, a stairway of 75 steps leads to St Michael's Loft, originally a school for novice monks and later a grammar school for boys. It now houses **St Michael's Loft Museum** which tells something of the long history of the priory. Another stairway – a spiral one of 176 steps – winds its way up the tower of the church; from the top there are extensive views out over the town and harbour. Call 01202 485804 for opening times of the museum.

Just north of the priory are the remains of **Christchurch Castle**, built in the late 11th century and slighted (rendered militarily useless) after the Civil War. The site here contains the Constable's Hall which boasts the oldest Norman chimney in Britain, constructed around 1150.

Other nearby attractions include the **Red House Museum & Gardens** which is housed in a former Georgian workhouse and provides some interesting local history as well as a peaceful enclave in the heart of the town; and the **Museum of Electricity**, which occupies a stately Edwardian power station and has something for everyone – from dozens of early domestic appliances to a pair of boot warmers. Open Monday to Thursday 12 to 4.30 Easter to end September, also on Fridays during school holidays.

To the south of Christchurch are the ancient ditches known as **Double Dykes**, an area that offers great walking along with superb views. The dykes cut across the heathland of Hengistbury Head which forms the southern side of the town's large natural harbour. The headland is now a nature reserve, one of the few uninhabited parts of this otherwise built-up stretch of coastline. Not far from Double Dykes, Britain's first air show took place in 1910. It was attended by some of the greatest names in early aviation, including Wilbur Wright, Blériot and the Hon Charles Rolls, who was killed when his Wright Flyer crashed at this event.

MUDEFORD

7 miles E of Bournemouth off the A337

Standing at the entrance to Christchurch Harbour, Mudeford has a picturesque quay with piles of lobster pots, a fresh fish stall, fishermens' cottages and an old inn. It is still the centre of the local fishing industry and the quay provides a great vantage point for watching yachts and windsurfers as they come up "The Run" into the harbour. The beach here is clean and sandy with a lifeguard service during the summer months when beach huts, deck chairs and canoes can all be hired, and ferry services cross the harbour to Mudeford Sandbank. Day cruises to the Needles and Yarmouth on the Isle of Wight are also available.

HIGHCLIFFE

9 miles E of Bournemouth on the A337

The most easterly community in Dorset, Highcliffe has a fine beach and views of the eastern tip of the Isle of Wight. The bustling village centre hosts a Friday market but the major attraction here is **Highcliffe Castle** (English Heritage), an imposing mansion of gleaming white stone originally built between 1831 and 1835. It was damaged by fire in the 1960s but the exterior was restored in the 1990s although most of the interior remains unrepaired. Guided tours are available every Tuesday afternoon during the summer; the grounds, visitor centre, galleries and gift shop are open all year round.

POOLE

4 miles W of Bournemouth, on the A35/A350

Once the largest settlement in Dorset, Poole is now a pleasant, bustling port. Its huge natural harbour, actually a drowned river valley, has a shoreline of some 50 miles and is the most extensive anchorage in Europe with a history going back well beyond Roman times. A 33feet long Logboat, hollowed from a giant oak tree and dating back to around 295 BC, has been found off Brownsea Island, the largest of several islands dotting the harbour. Poole's extensive sandy beaches boast more Blue Flag awards than any other UK strand, and every Thursday evening in August there's a beach party with sports, calypso bands, barbecues and a spectacular firework finale.

The Quay is a great place to relax with a drink and watch people "just messing about in boats" or participating in one of the many watersports available. Nearby is the **Waterfront Museum**, which celebrates 2000 years of maritime heritage, and the internationally famed **Poole Pottery** which has been producing high-quality pottery for more than 125 years. Its visitor centre stands on the site of the old factory. Here, visitors can watch a video summarising two millennia of ceramic production and see the age-old processes under way, and children can have a go themselves at this tricky craft. The Pottery Shop offers factory-direct prices and special savings on seconds, there are superb displays of the Pottery's distinctively designed creations, and a brasserie and bar overlooking the harbour.

Poole is well-provided with public parks offering a wide range of activities, and the town also

53 THE AMBERWOOD

Walkford

Traditional village inn serving excellent food, wine and real ales; regular live entertainment.

see page 162

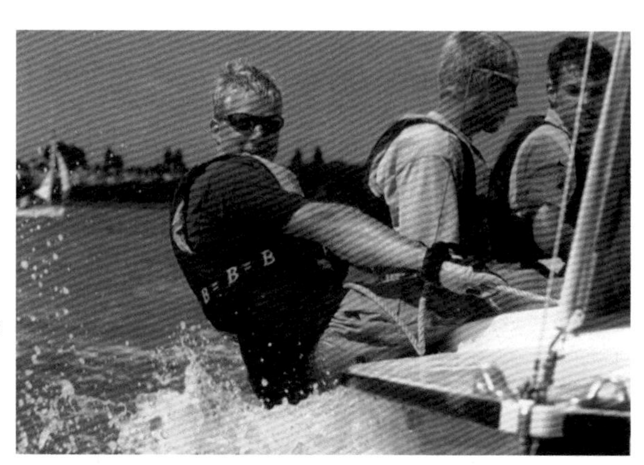

Rockley Point Sailing Centre, Poole

•

In the High Street of Wimborne Minster, the Priest's House is a lovely Elizabethan house set amidst beautiful gardens. It houses the Museum of East Dorset Life which re-creates 400 years of history in a series of rooms where the decoration and furnishings follow the changing fashions between Jacobean and Victorian times. There's also an archaeology gallery with hands-on activities, a Gallery of Childhood, delightful walled garden and summer tea room.

•

boasts one of the county's great gardens, **Compton Acres,** which was created in the 1920s by Thomas William Simpson who spent the equivalent of £10 million in today's money. Amongst its varied themed areas, which include a lovely Italian Garden, the Japanese Garden enjoys an especially fine reputation. Japanese architects and workmen were brought over to England to create what is reputed to be the only completely genuine Japanese Garden in Europe, an idyllic setting in which only the most troubled spirit could not find solace. Magnificent sculptures enhance the grounds which also contain restaurants, a delicatessen, model railway exhibition and shops. From the Colonnade viewpoint there are grand views over Poole Harbour to the Purbeck hills beyond.

From Poole Quay there are regular cruises along the coast and ferries to **Brownsea Island** (National Trust), where there are quiet beaches with safe bathing. Visitors can wander through 500 acres of heath and woodland which provide one of the few remaining refuges for Britain's native red squirrel. In 1907, General Robert Baden-Powell carried out an experiment on the island to test his idea of teaching boys from all social classes the scouting skills he had refined during the Boer Wars. Just 20 boys attended that first camp: in its heyday during the 1930s, the world-wide Scouting Movement numbered some 16 million members in more than 120 countries. In 1898, in the Haven Hotel at Sandbanks, at the entrance to Poole Harbour, Marconi established one of the world's first radio stations, which received signals sent from a transmitter on the Needles.

CORFE MULLEN

7 miles NW of Bournemouth off the A31

With a population of more than 10,000 Corfe Mullen has a good claim to be the largest village in the country. Much of it is modern housing for commuters to Poole and Bournemouth but the old village beside the River Stour has retained its charm. The ancient mill, mentioned in the *Domesday Book*, has had its wheel rebuilt and is turning once again, albeit inside a glass case at the centre of a tearoom. There's a medieval church whose first rector, Walter the Clerk, was installed in 1162; a delightful 300-year-old manor house (private); and a traditional pub with a flagstone floor in one of the bars.

WIMBORNE MINSTER

7 miles NW of Bournemouth on the A349/A31

Happily, the A31 now by-passes this beguiling old market town set amongst meadows beside the rivers Stour and Allen. The glory of the town is **Wimborne Minster** which, in 2005, celebrated 1300 years of ministry. It's a distinctive building of multi-coloured stone boasting some of the finest Norman architecture in the county and is also notable for its 14th century astronomical clock, and the

'Quarterjack', a life-sized figure of a grenadier from the Napoleonic wars, which strikes the quarter hours on his bells. Inside, the unique Chained Library, founded in 1686, contains more than 240 books, amongst them a 14th century manuscript on vellum.

In King Street you can see Wimborne as it was in the early 1950s – but at one tenth the size. **Wimborne Model Town** presents a meticulous miniature version of the town, complete with an Old English fair and a working small-scale model railway. Also in the heart of the town, **Verwood Heathland Heritage Centre** has permanent displays of the local Verwood pottery industry. The centre occupies a former pottery drying shed and visitors may get the opportunity to throw a pot or two themselves.

On the outskirts of Wimborne, **Honeybrook Country Park** has a family yard with lots of pure breed animals, dray and pony rides, an adventure playground, a period farmhouse, a natural maze, river and countryside walks, tea room and picnic areas. The park also hosts events such as country sports days, tug-of-war competitions, beer tasting and barn dances.

A mile or so northwest of Wimborne, **Kingston Lacy** (National Trust) is an imposing 17th century mansion which has been the home of the Bankes family for more than 300 years and exerts an irresistible attraction for anyone who loves the paintings of such Old Masters as Brueghel, Titian, Rubens and Van Dyck. Apart from those owned by the queen, the pictures on display here are generally acknowledged by experts as forming the finest private collection in the country. Kingston Lacy's fabulous gilded-leather Spanish Room and elegant Grand Saloon, both with lavishly decorated ceilings, and a fascinating exhibit of Egyptian artefacts dating back to 3000 BC, all add to the interest of a visit. Outside, you can wander through 250 acres of wooded parkland which contains a genuine Egyptian obelisk of c.150 BC and is also home to a herd of splendid Red Devon cattle. A new addition in 2005 was the Edwardian Japanese Tea Garden which follows traditional Japanese design with features such as a waiting pavilion, a dry stream raked with gravel, and a thatched tea house. Also within the grounds of the Kingston Lacy estate are **Badbury Rings,** an Iron Age hill fort reputedly the site of a great campaign by King Arthur.

A couple of miles to the east of Wimborne, **Stapehill Abbey** was built in the early 1800s as a Cistercian nunnery providing a peaceful place for retreat and contemplation. Visitors can enjoy the serenity of the restored Nuns' Chapel, stroll around the cloisters and enjoy the glorious award-winning gardens. Inside, there are reconstructions of a Victorian parlour, kitchen and washroom, and an outstanding Countryside Museum recording rural life in the area. Stapehill is also home to a group of working craftspeople -

54 ANGELS CAFÉ

Wimborne

A pleasant riverside café with freshly prepared meals for every taste.

see page 164

55 THE STOCKS INN

Wimborne

This pub is a historic gem, offering the best food that Dorset has to offer.

see page 163

56 HORNS INN

Wimborne

Welcoming traditional hostelry with family-friendly atmosphere in semi-rural location.

see page 165

57 DROVERS INN

Gussage All Saints

This 17th Century traditional Dorset Cob building offers stunning views of the surrounding countryside as you enjoy the seasonal cooking.

see page 164

special events are held throughout the year, and the site also contains a licensed coffee shop and picnic areas.

Just to the east of Stapehill are **Knoll Gardens & Nursery** whose gardens were planted some 30 years ago and are famous for the mature trees and shrubs that provide a wealth of colour throughout the seasons. The gardens specialise in grasses and perennials but in all there are more than 6000 plant species, including many fine trees. Tumbling waterfalls and ponds in an informal English setting add to the appeal.

HORTON

12 miles NW of Bournemouth off the B3078

Just outside the village stands Horton Tower (private), a 6-storey triangular folly built in the mid-1700s by Humphrey Sturt, the lord of the manor, as an observatory from which he could watch the movement of deer. The tower appeared in the film *Far From the Madding Crowd.*

WIMBORNE ST GILES

15 miles NW of Bournemouth off the B3081

A pretty village set beside the River Allen, Wimborne St Giles is notable for its **Church of St Giles**. It was rebuilt after a fire by the distinguished architect Sir Ninian Comper who also contributed the fine stained glass. Also worth seeing are the marvellous monuments, notably to Sir Anthony Ashley and to the 7th Earl of Shaftesbury (who is even more memorably honoured by the statue of Eros in Piccadilly Circus).

VERWOOD

12 miles N of Bournemouth on the B3081

Just north of Verwood village, **The Dorset Heavy Horse Farm Park** offers a real hands-on experience with these mighty beasts. You can drive a horse and wagon, or a vintage tractor, enjoy a tractor & trailer ride or have a go at logging or ploughing with the heavy horses. Suitable for all ages and weather conditions, the centre also has a display of gypsy caravans, animal feeding and handling, pedal tractors and go carts, a straw slide barn and a resident menagerie of donkeys, llamas, kune kune pigs, miniature ponies and pigmy goats. There's also a café, picnic area and gift shop. Call 01202 824040 for opening times.

Stocks, Wimborne St Giles

CRANBORNE

15 miles N of Bournemouth on the B3078

A picturesque village in a glorious setting, Cranborne sits on the banks of the River Crane with a fine church and manor house creating a charming picture of a traditional English village. The large and imposing **Church of St Mary** is notable for its Norman doorway, 13th century nave, and exquisite 14th century wall-paintings. **Cranborne Manor** was built in Tudor and Jacobean times for the Cecil family, now Marquesses of Salisbury, who still live there. The house is not open to the public but visitors can explore the gardens on Wednesdays during the season, and the Cranborne Manor Garden Centre, which specialises in old fashioned roses, is open all year. The present manor house stands on the site of a royal hunting lodge built by King John for his hunting forays in **Cranborne Chase.** Much of the huge forest has disappeared but detached areas of woodland have survived and provide some splendid walks.

To the south of the village lies **Edmonsham Hall,** a superb Tudor manor house with Georgian additions that has been owned by the same family since the 1500s. Guided tours of the house are conducted by the owner; the grounds contain a walled organic garden, a 6-acre garden with unusual trees and spring bulbs, and a stable block that is a fine example of Victorian architecture.

SWANAGE

Picturesquely set beside a broad, gently curving bay with fine, clear sands and beautiful surrounding countryside, Swanage is understandably popular as a family holiday resort. A winner of Southern England in Bloom, the town takes great pride in the spectacular floral displays in its parks and gardens, and its other awards include the prestigious European Blue Flag for its unpolluted waters, and the Tidy Britain Group's "Seaside Award". Swanage offers its visitors all the facilities necessary for a traditional seaside holiday, including boat-trips, (with sightings of bottle-nosed dolphins if you're lucky), water-sports, sea angling and an attractive, old-fashioned pier and bandstand. The **Mowlem Theatre** provides a seasonal programme of films, shows and plays, and on Sunday afternoons the Recreation Ground resounds to the strains of a brass band. On the clifftops, **Durlston Country Park** covers some 260 acres of delightful countryside; on the front, the **Beach Gardens** offer tennis, bowls and putting, or you can just rent a beach hut or bungalow and relax. One attraction not to be missed is a ride on the **Swanage Railway** along which magnificent steam locomotives of the old Southern Railway transport passengers some 6 miles through lovely Dorset countryside to Norden, just north of Corfe Castle.

In the town itself, the **Town Hall** is worth seeing for its ornate façade, the work of Christopher Wren. Wren didn't build it for Swanage, however. It was originally part of Mercers Hall in Cheapside,

58 FLEUR-DE-LYS

Cranborne

The **Fleur-de-Lys** is a handsome 16th century Grade II listed building. The customers can look forward to some of the best food in the region.

see page 166

59 BROOK TEA ROOMS

Swanage

A friendly atmosphere, magnificent views and freshly cooked locally sourced food.

see page 166

A couple of miles north of Swanage, Studland Bay offers a lovely 3-mile stretch of sandy beach, part of it clearly designated as an exclusive resort for nudists only.

London. When the Mercers Hall was being demolished, a Swanage man named George Burt scavenged the fine frontage and rebuilt it here. He also brought the graceful little **Clock Tower** which stands near the pier but once used to adorn the Surrey end of London Bridge; a gateway from Hyde Park for his own house; and cast-iron columns and railings from Billingsgate Market. No wonder older residents of the town refer to Swanage as "Little London".

There is, however, one monument that is purely Swanage – the **King Alfred Column** on the seafront. This commemorates the king's victory here over a Danish fleet in AD 877. The column is topped by cannonballs that would have been of great assistance to Alfred had they been invented at the time.

Collectors of curiosities will want to make their way to Tilly Whim Hill, just south of Swanage, which is also well-known for its murky **Caves.** High above the Caves stands the **Great Globe,** a huge round stone, some 10 feet in diameter and weighing 40 tons, its surface sculpted with all the countries of the world. At its base, stone slabs are inscribed with quotations from the Old Testament psalms, Shakespeare and other poets. They include moral injunctions such as "Let prudence direct you, temperance chasten you, fortitude support you", and the information that, "if a globe representing the sun were constructed on the same scale, it would measure some 1,090 feet across".

AROUND SWANAGE

LANGTON MATRAVERS

2 miles W of Swanage, on the B3069

Before tourism, the main industry around Swanage was quarrying the famous Purbeck stone that has been used in countless churches, cathedrals and fine houses around the country. **The Purbeck Stone Industry Museum** at Langton Matravers tells the story of Purbeck Marble, a handsome and durable material which was already being cut and polished back in Roman times. This sizeable village is also home to **Putlake Adventure Farm** where visitors are encouraged to make contact with a variety of friendly animals, bottle feed the lambs, or have a go at milking cows. There are pony and trailer rides, picnic and play areas, a farm trail, gift shop and tea room.

WORTH MATRAVERS

4 miles W of Swanage, off the B3069

In the graveyard of St Nicholas' Church is the grave of a local farmer, Benjamin Jesty, whose tomb inscription is worth quoting in full: An upright and honest man, particularly noted for having been the first person known that introduced the Cow Pox by inoculation, and who, from his great strength of mind, made the experiment from the cow on his wife and two sons in the year 1774. His family's "great strength of mind" might also have been noted since the inoculation was made using a knitting needle. The man usually credited with discovering inoculation, Edward Jenner, didn't make his first successful experiment until 1796 – twenty-two years after Benjamin's.

Standing high on the cliffs of St Aldhelm's Head, a couple of miles south of the village and accessible only by a bridleway, the **Chapel of St Aldhelm** stands alone. It is one of the oldest churches in Dorset, a low square building with a fine Norman doorway and one solitary window. Uniquely, the chapel has no east wall as the corners of the walls are aligned to the points of the compass. In its dank, dim interior the stonework is bare of decoration, just a central column from which eight ribs extend to the walls. According to legend, the church was built in 1140 by a local man in memory of his newly-married daughter and her husband. He was watching from this clifftop as the boat in which they were sailing to a new home was caught in a sudden squall and capsized. All on board perished.

CORFE CASTLE

5 miles NW of Swanage on the A351

One of the grandest sights in the country is the impressive ruin of **Corfe Castle** (National Trust), standing high on a hill and dominating the attractive grey stone village below. Once the most impregnable fortress in the land, Corfe dates back to the days of William the Conqueror, with later additions by King John and Edward I. The dastardly John threw 22 French knights into the castle dungeons and left them to starve to death. Later, Edward II was imprisoned here before being sent to Berkeley Castle and his horrible murder.

Although Corfe now stands in splendid ruin, you can see a smaller, intact version at the **Model Village** on the Square. This superbly accurate replica is built from the same Purbeck stone as the real thing and the detail of the

Corfe Castle remained important right up until the days of the Civil War when it successfully withstood two sieges before it fell into Parliamentary hands through treachery. A month later, Parliament ordered the castle to be 'slighted' – rendered militarily useless.

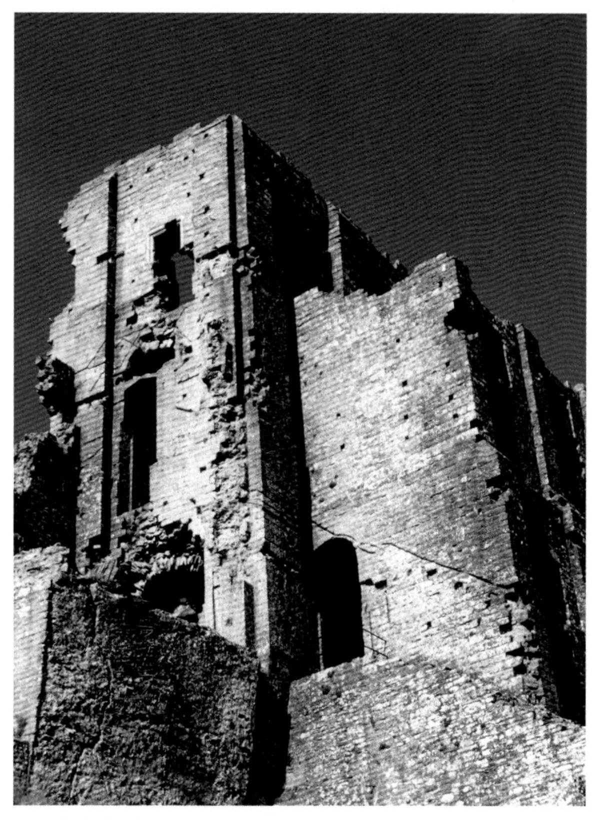

Corfe Castle

60 RED LION HOTEL

Wareham

Fine old hostelry with good food, excellent ales, quality accommodation and regular entertainment evenings.

see page 167

miniature medieval folk going about their daily business is wonderful. Surrounded by lovely gardens, this intriguing display is well worth a visit. You might also want to explore the local museum which is housed in the smallest Town Hall building in the country.

NORDEN

7 miles NW of Swanage, on the A351

About half a mile north of Corfe Castle, Norden Station is the northern terminus of the **Swanage Railway** and there's a regular bus service from the station to the castle. The hamlet of Norden itself is actually another mile further to the northeast, a delightful place surrounded by pine trees and heathland.

WAREHAM

Situated between the rivers Frome and Piddle, Wareham is an enchanting little town lying within the earthworks of a 10th century encircling wall. Standing close to an inlet of Poole Harbour, Wareham was an important port until the River Frome clogged its approaches with silt. Then, in 1726, a devastating fire consumed the town's timber buildings, a disaster which produced the happy result of a rebuilt town centre rich in handsome Georgian stone-built houses.

Wareham's history goes back much further than those days. Roman conquerors laid out its street plan: a stern grid of roads which faithfully follows the points of the compass. Saxons and Normans helped build the **Church of St Mary**, medieval artists covered its walls with devotional paintings of remarkable quality. It was in the grounds surrounding the church that King Edward was buried in AD 879 after his stepmother, Queen Elfrida, contrived his murder at Corfe Castle. Elfrida added insult to injury by having the late king buried outside the churchyard, in unhallowed ground.

Occupying the 12th century Holy Trinity Church near the quay, the Purbeck Information & Heritage Centre offers copious information about the town; while in East Street, the **Wareham Museum** has some interesting displays and artefacts illustrating the town's history.

In the Saxon St Martin's Church, notable for its early medieval wall paintings, there's a striking memorial to what appears at first glance to be a medieval crusader dressed in Arab robes, holding an Arab dagger and resting his head on a camel's saddle. This is a **memorial to TE Lawrence**, 'Lawrence of Arabia', who is actually buried at Moreton (qv).

Wareham boasts one building that is unique – the privately owned **Rex Cinema** which was built pre-1914 and is the only gas-lit cinema in the country. The original antique carbon arc projectors are still used to show the latest blockbusters.

An even more ancient survival is the custom of the Court Leet. In Norman times these courts were the main judicial institution in many parts of the country. On four evenings in November, strangely dressed men visit the town's inns to check the quality and quantity of the food and ale on offer. The officials include ale-tasters, bread weighers and 'carnisters' who sample the meat. Although they have no powers nowadays, it is a quaint tradition.

AROUND WAREHAM

FURZEBROOK

4 miles S of Wareham off the A351

If you are interested in natural curiosities, follow the brown and white signs for the **Blue Pool**. Here, in what was originally a clay pit, tiny particles of clay in the pool diffract light and create an astonishing illusion of colour, varying from sky blue to deepest azure. There's a tea house, shops and museum here and the tree-lined shore is a popular picnic place.

WINFRITH NEWBURGH

9 miles SW of Wareham off the A352

This charming little village stands on a minor road that leads to one of the county's best-known beauty spots, **Lulworth Cove.** An almost perfectly circular bay, the Cove is surrounded by towering 440ft cliffs. Over the centuries, the sea has gnawed away at a weak point in the limestone here, inadvertently creating a breathtakingly beautiful scene. Best to visit out of season, however, as parking places nearby are limited.

About a mile to the west of Lulworth Cove stands another remarkable natural feature which has been sculpted by the sea. **Durdle Door** is a magnificent archway carved from the coastal limestone. There's no road to the coast at this point, but you can reach it easily by following the South West Coast Path from Lulworth Cove. Along the way, you will also see another strange outcrop, a forest of tree-stumps which have become fossilised over the centuries.

A couple of miles inland, **Lulworth Castle** (English Heritage) looks enormously impressive from a distance: close-up, you can see how a disastrous fire in 1929 destroyed most of it. Amongst the remains, though, is a curious circular building dating from 1786: the first Roman Catholic church to be established in Britain since Henry VIII's defiance of the Pope in 1534. Sir Thomas Weld was given permission to build this unique church by George III. The king cautiously added the proviso that Sir Thomas' new place of worship should not offend Anglican sensibilities by looking like a church. It doesn't, and that's a great part of its appeal. The castle's other attractions include indoor and outdoor children's play areas; an animal farm; pitch & putt; woodland walks; café and shop.

BOVINGTON CAMP

6 miles W of Wareham off the A352

It was at Bovington Camp that TE Lawrence served as a private in the

61 BARBROOK BLUE POOL

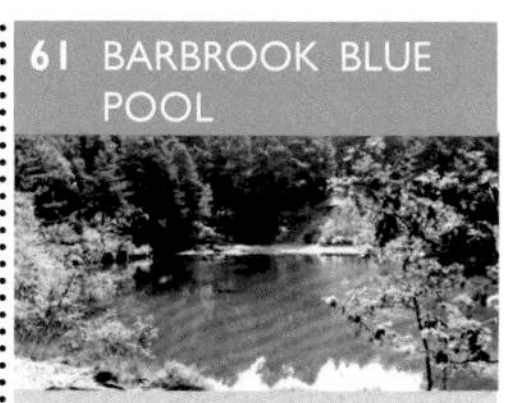

Furzebrook

The Blue Pool was once a clay pit and particles in the water cause dramatic colour changes. Museum, shops and tea room.

 see page 168

62 CLAVELL'S CAFÉ, BRADLE AND KIMMERIDGE FARMHOUSES

Kimmeridge Bay

Friendly cafe offering wholesome, freshly cooked lunches and cream teas all year round. Also sells produce from Kimmeridge Farm. The two farmhouses offer beautiful B&B accommodation.

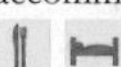 see page 169

63 THE CROMWELL HOUSE HOTEL

Lulworth Cove

Just 200 yards from Lulworth Cove, Cromwell House is a family run hotel with lots of character and outstanding cuisine available to all.

see page 168

64 LUCKFORD LAKE

West Holme, nr Wareham

Offering a wonderful means of escape, this country house provides everything a guest could want, with unbeatable hospitality, fine food and superb surroundings.

 see page 168

65 LUCKFORD WOOD HOUSE

East Stoke, nr Wareham

This delightful farmhouse provides comfortable accommodation. Nearby attractive pitches for camping and caravanning and activities for all.

see page 170

Royal Tank Corps. Today, the camp is home to the **Tank Museum** which has more than 150 armoured vehicles on display dating from World War I to the present day. Audio tours are available, there's a children's play area, restaurant and gift shop, and during the summer tanks take part in live action displays.

A very different kind of attraction, to the east of Bovington camp, is Monkey World whose 65 acres are home to more than 160 primates rescued from all over the world. Half-hourly Keepers' Talks reveal the stories behind the stars of TV's Monkey Business series, and provide insights into man's closest living relatives. The site also includes the largest children's adventure play area on the south coast, an education centre, woodland walk, pets corner, café, picnic areas and full disabled facilities.

BERE REGIS

7 miles NW of Wareham on the A35

Most visitors to the church at Bere Regis are attracted by its associations with Hardy's *Tess of the D'Urbervilles*. They come to see the crumbling tombs of the once-powerful Turberville family whose name Hardy adapted for his novel. It was outside the church, beneath the Turberville window, that Hardy had the homeless Tess and her family set up their 4-poster bed. A poignant fictional scene, but the church is also well worth visiting for its unique and magnificent carved and painted wooden roof. Large figures of the twelve Apostles (all in Tudor dress) jut out horizontally from the wall and there are a number of humorous carvings depicting men suffering the discomforts of toothache and over-indulgence. There's also a carving of Cardinal Morton who had this splendid roof installed in 1497. The church's history goes back much farther than that. In Saxon times, Queen Elfrida came here to spend the remainder of her days in penitence for her part in the murder of young King Edward at Corfe Castle in AD 979. Further evidence of the church's great age is the fact that around 1190 King John paid for the pillars of the nave to be "restored".

TOLPUDDLE

11 miles NW of Wareham on the A35

The small village of Tolpuddle is a peaceful little place today but in the early 19th century, Tolpuddle was far sleepier than it is now. Not the kind of place you would expect to foment a social revolution, but it was here that six ill-paid agricultural labourers helped lay the foundations of the British Trade Union Movement. In 1833, they formed the Friendly Society of Agricultural Labourers in an attempt to have their subsistence wages improved. The full rigour of the landowner-friendly law of the time was immediately invoked. All six were found guilty of taking illegal oaths and sentenced to transportation to New South Wales, Australia, for seven years. Even the judge in their case was forced to say that it was not for anything they had done, or intended to do, that he passed such a sentence, but "as an example to others". Rather surprisingly, public opinion sided with the illegal 'confederation'. Vigorous and sustained protests eventually forced the government to pardon the men after they had served three years of their sentence. They all returned safely to England in 1838, honoured ever afterwards in Trade Union hagiography as the Tolpuddle Martyrs. Only one, James Hammett (1811-1891), returned to Tolpuddle. His grave, with a headstone designed by Eric Gill, is in Tolpuddle churchyard. The **Martyrs' Museum** at Tolpuddle tells their inspiring story.

ORGANFORD

3 miles N of Wareham off the A35

The tiny village of Organford stands on the edge of the tree-covered expanses of Gore Heath. The settlement is so small it doesn't possess either a church or a pub, but it does have a Manor House which enjoys a wonderfully quiet and secluded position surrounded by woods. It's also home to **Farmer Palmer's** countryside theme park where children can feed lambs and goats, watch cows being milked, enjoy a wild trailer ride, drive pedal tractors or work off some energy in the bouncy castles and soft play zone.

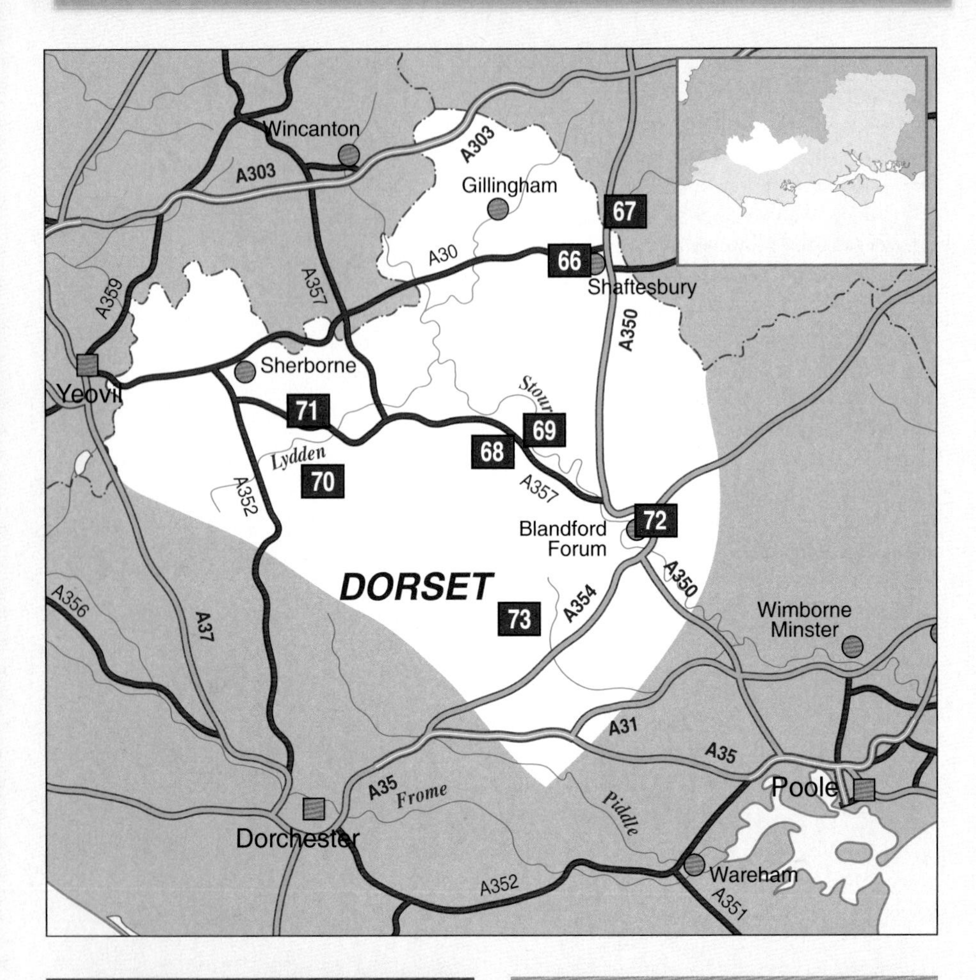

ACCOMMODATION

FOOD & DRINK

PLACES OF INTEREST

North Dorset

Largely agricultural, north Dorset represents rural England at its most appealing It's a peaceful, unspoilt area embracing half a dozen small market towns and many attractive villages. The area's most glorious building is Sherborne Abbey and the same small town also contains Sir Walter Raleigh's Sherborne Old Castle as well as several other striking medieval houses. Blandford Forum, the administrative centre of the district, has a pleasing town centre, mostly Georgian, and in Shaftesbury, Gold Hill became one of the most familiar streets in the county as a result of being featured in the classic TV commercial for Hovis bread.

Running along the northwestern border of the district, Blackmoor Vale is still much as Thomas Hardy described it in *Tess of the d'Urbervilles*, "The Vale of Little Dairies". The landscape here is on an intimate scale, tiny fields bordered by ancient hedgerows which have escaped the wholescale uprooting inflicted by agribusiness elsewhere.

North Dorset is a place to explore for its enchanting countryside and beguiling little towns. There are very few tailor-made tourist attractions. One of the rare exceptions to that rule, the Dorset Rare Breeds Centre near Gillingham, reflects the agricultural pre-occupations of the area.

66 SHAFTESBURY ABBEY MUSEUM & GARDEN

Shaftesbury

The site of a Saxon Benedictine Nunnery and a state-of-the-art museum.

see page 170

SHAFTESBURY

Set on the side of a hill 700feet high, Shaftesbury was officially founded in AD 880 by King Alfred who fortified the town and also built an abbey of which his daughter was first Prioress. A hundred years later, the King Edward who had been murdered by his stepmother at Corfe Castle was buried here and the abbey became a major centre of pilgrimage. A few remains of **Shaftesbury Abbey** have survived – they can be seen in the walled garden of the **Abbey Museum** which contains many interesting artefacts excavated from the site.

Abbey Walls & Gold Hill, Shaftesbury

Shaftesbury is a pleasant town to explore on foot. In fact, you *have* to walk if you want to see its most famous sight, **Gold Hill**, a steep, cobbled street, stepped in places and lined with 18th century cottages. Already well-known for its picturesque setting and grand views across the Vale of Blackmoor, Gold Hill became even more famous when it was featured in the classic television commercial for Hovis bread. Also located on Gold Hill is the **Shaftesbury Local History Museum** which vividly evokes the story of this ancient market town.

The 17th century Ox House, which is referred to in Thomas Hardy's *Jude the Obscure*, is just one of a number of interesting and historic buildings in the town. Others include the Church of St Peter, the Tudor-style Town Hall dating from the 1820s, and the Grosvenor Hotel, a 400-year-old coaching inn.

Shaftesbury boasts one of the liveliest arts centres in the country, the **Shaftesbury Arts Centre** which, remarkably, is completely owned by its membership and administered entirely by volunteers. The results of their efforts are anything but amateur, however. The centre's Drama Group is responsible for 3 major productions each year, performed in the well-equipped theatre which also serves as a cinema for the centre's Film Society, screening a dozen or more films during the season. One of the most popular features of the centre is its Gallery which is open daily with a regularly changing variety of exhibitions ranging from paintings, etchings and sculpture, to batiks, stained glass, embroideries and quilting.

AROUND SHAFTESBURY

ASHMORE

5 miles SE of Shaftesbury off the B3081

To the northwest of Ashmore is **Compton Abbas Airfield** which is generally considered to be the most picturesque airfield in the country. It is surrounded by an Area of Outstanding Natural Beauty and 50% of the airfield is organically farmed. One of the most popular displays is the collection of famous aeroplanes, special effects and memorabilia from film and television productions. For the more adventurous, flights are available with a qualified instructor for a trip over this scenic part of the county; training courses for a full pilot's licence are also conducted here. The airfield hosts regular events throughout the year, including aerobatic displays; there's a shop selling a range of stunt and power kites; a bar and restaurant. To the west of Ashmore are Fontwell and Melbury Downs, two estates that cover an important stretch of chalk downland cut by steep-sided valleys. Both areas are owned by the National Trust.

MARNHULL

7 miles SW of Shaftesbury on the B3092

The scattered village of Marnhull claims to be the largest parish in England, spread over a substantial area with a circumference of 23 miles. The village itself is well worth exploring for its part-Norman St Gregory's church with a fine 15th century tower, and who knows what you might find along Sodom Lane? This now-prosperous village appears in *Tess of the d'Urbervilles* as 'Marlott', the birthplace of the heroine. The thatched **Tess's Cottage** (private, but visible from the lane) is supposedly the house Hardy had in mind, while the Crown Inn (also thatched) is still recognisable as the "Pure Drop Inn" in the same novel.

STALBRIDGE

9 miles SW of Shaftesbury on the A357

The 15th century church here has a striking 19th century tower which provides a landmark throughout the Vale of Blackmoor. Perhaps even more impressive is the town's **Market Cross** standing 30feet high and richly carved with scenes of the Crucifixion and Resurrection. Just outside the town, **Stalbridge Park** (private) sheltered Charles I after his defeat at Marston Moor. The house (now demolished) was built by Richard Boyle, 1st Earl of Cork, and it was here that his 7th son, the celebrated physicist and chemist Robert Boyle carried out the experiments that eventually led to his formulation of Boyle's Law.

STURMINSTER NEWTON

10 miles SW of Shaftesbury on the A357

This unspoilt market town – the 'capital' of the Blackmore Vale – is

•

About 3 miles northwest of Shaftesbury, the Dorset Rare Breeds Centre harbours the county's largest collection of rare and endangered farm animals. They range from knee-high Soay sheep to mighty Suffolk Punch horses weighing a ton or more. All of these native breeds are at great risk and the centre hopes to alert animal lovers to the imminent threat.

•

67 BENETT ARMS

Semley

Traditional public house surrounded by beautiful scenery and lots of tourist attractions such as Stonehenge, Waldorf Castle and Compton Abbas Airfield. Great hospitable atmosphere.

see page 171

68 THE ROYAL OAK

Okeford Fitzpaine, nr Sturminster Newton

The Royal Oak is a traditional pub with a warm and friendly atmosphere and boasts good traditional food, all made with local produce.

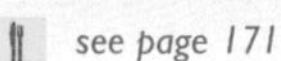

see page 171

69 THE SAXON INN

Child Okeford, nr Sturminster Newton

One of the most delightful and attractive country inns you'll ever come across, with outstanding food and drink and very comfortable B&B accommodation

see page 172

an essential stop for anyone following in Thomas Hardy's footsteps for it was at Sturminster Newton that he and his first wife Emma had their first real home together. From 1876 until 1878, they lived in "a pretty cottage overlooking the Dorset Stour, called **Riverside Villa**". Here, Hardy wrote *The Return of the Native* and he often referred later to their time at Sturminster Newton in his poems. It was, he said, "our happiest time". The house is not open to the public but is visible from a riverside footpath.

Until Elizabethan times, Sturminster and Newton were separate villages standing on opposite sides of the River Stour. Shortly after the graceful **Town Bridge** linked the two communities, a mill was built some 250 yards upstream. Once again restored to working order, **Newton Mill** offers guided tours explaining the milling process, and the delightful setting attracts many amateur and professional artists and photographers. Incidentally, the fine old 6-arched bridge still bears a rusty metal plaque carrying the dire warning: "Any person wilfully injuring any part of this county bridge will be guilty of felony and upon conviction liable to be transported for life by the court. P. Fooks".

LYDLINCH

13 miles SW of Shaftesbury on the A357

The small hamlet of Lydlinch in the Vale of Blackmore features in a poem by the Dorset dialect poet, William Barnes. He recalls as a young boy hearing the sound of Lydlinch church bells wafting across meadows to his home in nearby Bagber: *Vor Lydlinch bells be good vor sound, / And liked by all the neighbours round.* The five bells he heard still hang in the tower of the 13th century church.

EAST STOUR

4 miles W of Shaftesbury on the A30

East Stour's literary connections are not with Dorset's omnipresent Thomas Hardy but with the man who has been dubbed 'Father of the Novel', Henry Fielding. When he was 3 years old, Fielding's family moved to the Manor House here which stood close to the church. Fielding spent most of his childhood in the village before leaving to study at Eton and Leyden. He then spent a few years in London writing plays before returning to East Stour in 1734 with his new young wife, Charlotte Cradock, who provided the model for Sophia Western in his most successful novel, *Tom Jones*. By the time that book was published in 1749, Charlotte was dead, Fielding was seriously ill and he was to die just five years later while visiting Lisbon in an attempt to recover his health.

GILLINGHAM

4 miles NW of Shaftesbury on the B3081

The most northerly town in Dorset, Gillingham was once an important centre for the milling of silk and the manufacture of the distinctive Victorian red-hot bricks.

The parish church has a 14th century chancel but the rest of the building, like much of the town, dates from after the arrival of the railway in 1859. **Gillingham Museum** charts the history of the town and the surrounding villages from prehistoric times; an interesting exhibit here is a manual fire engine dating from 1790.

SHERBORNE

One of the most beautiful towns in England, Sherborne beguiles the visitor with its serene atmosphere of a cathedral city, although it is not a city and its lovely **Abbey** no longer enjoys the status of a cathedral. Back in AD 705 though, when it was founded by St Aldhelm, the abbey was the Mother Cathedral for the whole of southwest England. Of that original Saxon church only minimal traces remain: most of the present building dates back to the mid-1400s which, by happy chance, was the most glorious period in the

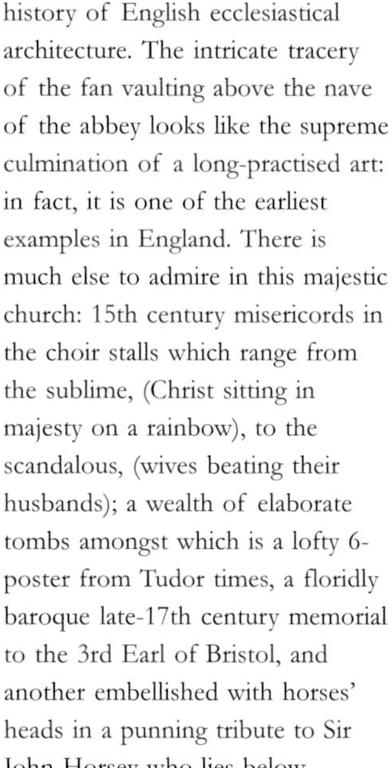

history of English ecclesiastical architecture. The intricate tracery of the fan vaulting above the nave of the abbey looks like the supreme culmination of a long-practised art: in fact, it is one of the earliest examples in England. There is much else to admire in this majestic church: 15th century misericords in the choir stalls which range from the sublime, (Christ sitting in majesty on a rainbow), to the scandalous, (wives beating their husbands); a wealth of elaborate tombs amongst which is a lofty 6-poster from Tudor times, a floridly baroque late-17th century memorial to the 3rd Earl of Bristol, and another embellished with horses' heads in a punning tribute to Sir John Horsey who lies below alongside his son.

In 2005 Sherborne celebrated 1300 years since St Aldhelm founded the Abbey with a great festival. A statue to St Aldhelm was commissioned and placed in a niche over the porch.

Perhaps the best-known

70 HALSEY ARMS

Pulham

The Halsey Arms is a family friendly pub which hosts live music and serves good hearty food.

see page 173

71 CAPHAYS HOUSE

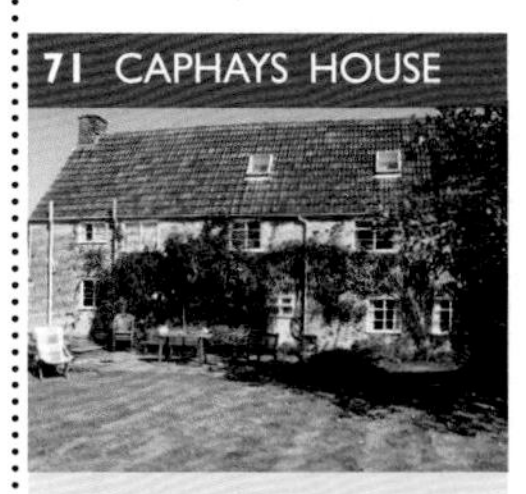

Caundle Marsh, nr Sherborne

A beautiful 17th Century house with magnificent views, this B & B is in a prime location.

see page 173

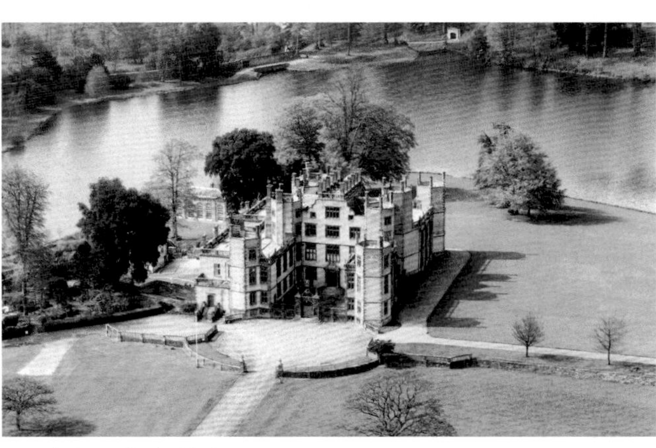

Sherborne Castle, Sherborne

•

As well as founding the Abbey, St Aldhelm is also credited with establishing Sherborne School which numbered amongst its earliest pupils the two elder brothers of King Alfred, (and possibly Alfred himself). Later alumni include the Poet Laureate Cecil Day-Lewis and the writer David Cornwell, better known as John le Carré, author of **The Spy Who Came in from the Cold** *and many other thrillers.*

•

resident of Sherborne however is Sir Walter Raleigh. At a time when he enjoyed the indulgent favour of Elizabeth I, he asked for, and was granted, the house and estate of **Sherborne Old Castle** (English Heritage). Sir Walter soon realised that the medieval pile with its starkly basic amenities was quite unsuitable for a courtier of his sophistication and ambition. He built a new castle alongside it, **Sherborne New Castle**, a strange three-storeyed, hexagonal structure which must rate, from the outside, as one of the most badly-designed, most unlikeable mansions to be erected in an age when other Elizabethan architects were creating some of the loveliest buildings in England. Inside Sir Walter's new castle, it is quite a different story: gracious rooms with elaborately-patterned ceilings, portraits of the man who single-handedly began the creation of the British Empire, and huge windows which at the time Sir Walter ordered them proclaimed a clear message that its owner had the wealth to pay the enormous cost of glazing such vast expanses. After Sir Walter's execution, the castle was purchased in 1617 by Sir James Digby and it has remained with his descendants ever since. They added exquisite gardens designed by 'Capability' Brown and in the late 1800s re-decorated the interior in Jacobean style. Amongst the castle's greatest treasures is the famous painting by Robert Peake depicting Elizabeth I on procession, being carried on a litter and surrounded by a sumptuously dressed retinue. The old cellar of the castle is now a museum housing an eclectic display of items, most gruesome of which is the skull of a Royalist soldier killed in the seige of 1645. A bullet is still lodged in his eye socket. Sherborne New Castle, incidentally, is one of several locations claiming to be the genuine setting for the old story of Sir Walter enjoying a pipe of tobacco and being doused with a bucket of water by a servant who believed his master was on fire. Sherborne Castle is open from April to October, and also offers visitors an attractive lakeside tearoom, a well-stocked gift shop, and various special events throughout the year.

This appealing small town with a population of around 8500 has much else to interest the visitor. The **Almshouse of Saints John the Baptist and John the Evangelist**, near the abbey, was founded in 1437 and the original buildings completed in 1448 are still in use as an almshouse, accepting both men and women. The almshouse chapel boasts one of the town's greatest treasures, a late-15th century Flemish altar tryptich which can be viewed on afternoons during the summer. Close by, the **Conduit House** is an attractive small hexagonal building from the early 1500s, originally used as a lavatorium, or washroom, for the abbey monks' ablutions. It was moved here after the Reformation and has served variously as a public fountain and a police phone box. The Conduit

House is specifically mentioned in Hardy's *The Woodlanders* as the place where Giles Winterborne, seeking work, stood here in the market place "as he always did at this season of the year, with his specimen apple tree". Another striking building is the former **Abbey Gatehouse** which frames the entrance to Church Lane where the **Sherborne Museum** has a collection of more than 15,000 items relating to local history. Particularly notable are two major photographic collections recording events and people in the town since 1880.

About 2 miles north of Sherborne, **Sandford Orcas Manor House** is a charming Tudor building with terraced gardens, topiary and herb garden. Since it was built in honey-coloured Ham Hill stone in the 1550s, only three different families have lived here. The present owner, Sir Mervyn Medlycott, whose family has lived here for more than 250 years, personally conducts guided tours that take in the manor's Great Hall, stone newel staircases, huge fireplaces, fine panelling, Jacobean and Queen Anne furniture and family portraits.

AROUND SHERBORNE

MELBURY OSMOND

6 miles SW of Sherborne off the A37

It was in the Church of St Osmund in this pretty village that Thomas Hardy's parents, Jemima Hand and Thomas Hardy, were married in 1839. At the northern end of the footpath through the churchyard is a thatched house where Hardy's mother is thought to have lived as a child. In Hardy's novels the village appears as Great Hintock which provides the setting for *The Woodlanders.* Melbury Osmond is still unspoilt and picturesque with many oak trees – find time to walk down from the church to the water splash, and beyond to some 17th century thatched stone cottages.

BLANDFORD FORUM

Blandford Forum, the administrative centre of North Dorset, is beautifully situated along the wooded valley of the River Stour. It's a handsome town, thanks mainly to suffering the trauma of a great fire in 1731. The gracious Georgian buildings erected after that conflagration, most of them designed by local architects John and William Bastard, provide the town with a quite unique and soothing sense of architectural harmony.

Two important ancient buildings escaped the fire of 1731: the **Ryves Almshouses** of 1682, and the splendid 15th century **Old House** in The Close which was built in the Bohemian style to house Protestant refugees from Bohemia. The old parish church did not survive the fire, but its 18th century replacement, the **Church of St Peter & St Paul**, crowned by

To the south of Sherborne, near the railway station, Pageant Gardens were established in 1905 using funds raised by a great pageant of that year celebrating the 1200th anniversary of the founding of the town by St Aldhelm.

72 SCRUPLES COFFEE HOUSE

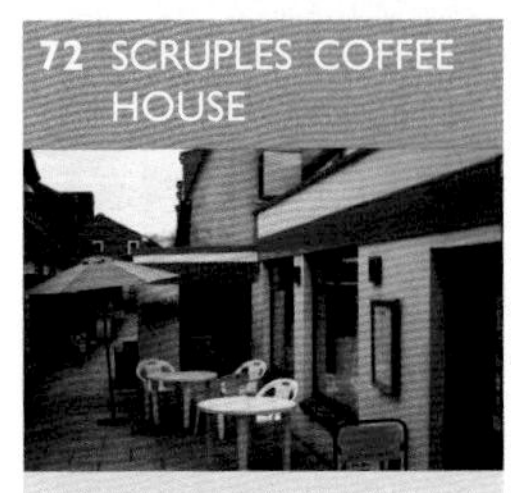

Blandford Forum

This charming coffee house offers great homemade food with warm and friendly service.

see page 174

Housed in Blandford in one of the town houses designed by the Bastard brothers, the Cavalcade of Costume Museum displays a fantastic collection of costumes from the 1730s through to the 1950s. Originally amassed by the late Mrs Betty Penny, the collection comprises more than 500 items. The museum also has a garden, shop and tea room. Open Thursday, Friday, Saturday and Monday.

an unusual cupola, now dominates the market-place. It's well worth stepping inside the church to see the box pews, an organ presented by George III, the massive columns of Portland stone, and the elegant pulpit, designed by Sir Christopher Wren, removed here from St Antholin's Church in the City of London.

In front of the church, the **Fire Monument** (known locally as Bastard's Pump) has a dual purpose – to provide water for fire fighting and as a public drinking fountain. Opposite the church, the **Blandford Museum** features a diorama of the Great Fire along with a wonderful collection of artefacts illustrating many aspects of life in and around Blandford over the years.

Just outside the town centre, at Blandford Camp, the **Royal Signals Museum** explores the arcane world of military communications with displays featuring spies, codes and code-breaking, the ENIGMA machine, Women at War and Dorset's involvement in the preparations for D-Day.

AROUND BLANDFORD FORUM

TARRANT HINTON

5 miles NE of Blandford Forum on the A354

This small village is the setting for the **Great Dorset Steam Fair**, held in late-August/early September. Occupying a huge 600-acre site, this is one of the world's largest international steam events, attracting some 200 steam engines and more than 220,000 visitors. The annual extravaganza includes working engine displays, an old-time steam funfair, demonstrations of rural crafts, displays of working Shire horses and live music.

CHETTLE

7 miles NE of Blandford Forum off the A354

A picturesque village with a charming manor house, **Chettle House,** designed by Thomas Archer in the English baroque style and completed in 1720. Archer's work includes the north front of Chatsworth and the Church of St John in Smith Square and his buildings are typified by lavish curves, inverted scrolls and their large scale, a style that owed much to the Italian architects Bernini and Borromini. Chettle House was bought in 1846 by the Castleman family who added an ornate ceiling. The house contains portraits of the Chafin family, earlier owners, and the beautifully laid out gardens include herbaceous border, a rose garden and croquet lawn.

BLANDFORD ST MARY

1 mile SW of Blandford Forum off the A354

The main attraction here is the **Hall & Woodhouse Brewery** of Badger Beer fame, which was founded at Ansty near Dorchester in 1777 but moved to its present site here beside the River Stour in 1899. The original brewery was founded by Charles Hill, a farmer's son who learnt the brewing art along with farming. The brewery expanded quickly thanks to a contract to supply ale to the Army during the Napoleonic Wars. It is still thriving and visitors can take a tour of the premises.

MILTON ABBAS

6 miles SW of Blandford Forum off the A354

This picture postcard village of thatched cottages was created in the 1770s by Joseph Damer, 1st Earl of Dorchester. The earl lived in the converted former abbey from which the village takes its name but he decided to demolish the medieval buildings, and build a more stately mansion surrounded by grounds landscaped by 'Capability' Brown. The earl's ambitious plans required that the small town that had grown up around the abbey would have to go, so more than 100 houses, 4 pubs, a brewery and a school were razed to the ground. The residents were moved more than a mile away to the present village for which Brown had made the preliminary plans. The earl's new mansion is now a private school and the only part of the abbey that survived is the **Abbey Church** which contains some wonderful Pugin glass and an extraordinary tomb to the earl and his wife Caroline designed by Robert Adam. Exquisitely carved by Agostino Carlini, the monument shows the earl propped up on one elbow gazing out across his beautiful wife.

MILBORNE ST ANDREW

9 miles SW of Blandford Forum on the A354

An attractive village in the valley of a tributary of the River Piddle, Milborne St Andrew was owned in medieval times by the Morton family. One of them gave his name to the expression 'Morton's Fork'. As Lord Chancellor to Henry VII (and Archbishop of Canterbury), John Morton devised a system of parting the rich, and the not-so-rich, from their money. He proposed the thesis that if a man was living in grand style he clearly had money to spare; if he lived frugally, then he obviously kept his wealth hidden away. This ingenious argument became known as Morton's Fork and many a citizen was caught on its vicious prongs. However, the system enriched and delighted the king who made Morton a Cardinal in 1493. Morton spent his remaining years spending lavishly on the building and restoration of churches, most notably in the magnificently carved and painted roof of Bere Regis church.

73 LUCCOMBE FARM

Milton Abbas, nr Blandford Forum

This working farm encompasses 650 acres of rolling countryside and offers sumptuous luxury in beautiful surroundings.

see page 175

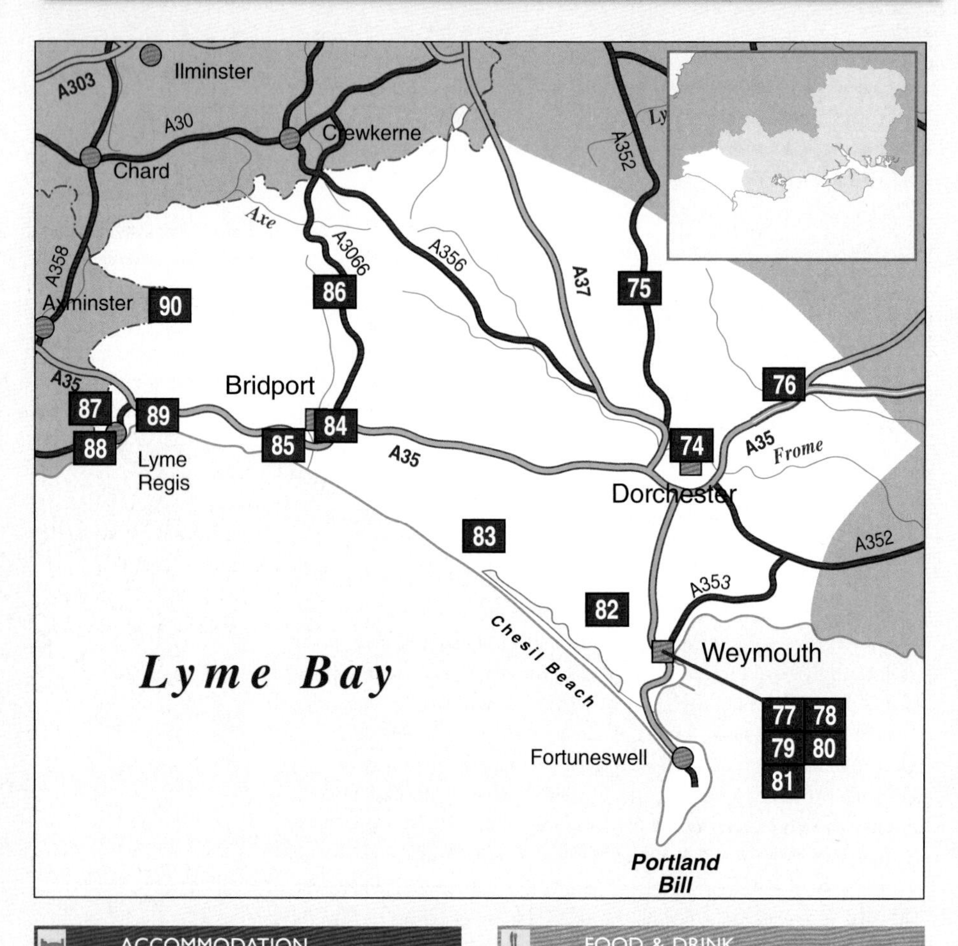

ACCOMMODATION

74	The Old Tea House, Dorchester	p 112, 174
75	Abbots, Cerne Abbas	p 115, 176
77	Wadham Guest House, Weymouth	p 120, 177
78	Edenhurst Guest House, Weymouth	p 120, 177
80	The Warwick, Weymouth	p 121, 179
81	Southville Guest House, Weymouth	p 121, 178
84	Lord Nelson Hotel, Bridport	p 125, 180
86	The Bridge House Hotel, Beaminster	p 126, 182
87	Talbot Arms, Uplyme, nr Lyme Regis	p 127, 184
88	Blue Sky B & B, Lyme Regis	p 127, 183

FOOD & DRINK

74	The Old Tea House, Dorchester	p 112, 174
75	Abbots, Cerne Abbas	p 115, 176
76	The Blue Vinny, Puddletown	p 118, 176
82	Turks Head Inn, Chickerell, nr Weymouth	p 123, 180
84	Lord Nelson Hotel, Bridport	p 125, 180
85	New Inn, Eype, nr Bridport	p 125, 183
86	The Bridge House Hotel, Beaminster	p 126, 182
87	Talbot Arms, Uplyme, nr Lyme Regis	p 127, 184
90	Bottle Inn, Marshwood, nr Bridport	p 129, 185

PLACES OF INTEREST

79	Weymouth Sea Life Park, Weymouth	p 120, 178
83	Abbotsbury, Abbotsbury	p 124, 181
89	Charmouth Heritage Coast Centre, Charmouth	p 128, 185

Dorchester & West Dorset

In West Dorset we really are in the heart of Thomas Hardy country. The great novelist and poet was born and grew up in the little village of Higher Bockhampton where his cottage is now a National Trust property. So too is the house in Dorchester, Max Gate, where he lived for more than 40 years before his death in 1928. As Casterbridge, this appealing town is featured in several of his novels, most extensively in *The Mayor of Casterbridge*. Other great writers also have strong connections with the area. Jane Austen and her family stayed at Lyme Regis – part of her novel *Persuasion* is set in the town; the Cobb provided a crucial location for *The French Lieutenant's Woman*, written by Lyme Regis resident John Fowles; and TE Lawrence lived for a while at Cloud's Hill near Moreton.

This beautiful area has surprisingly few grand buildings although Wolfeton House and Athelhampton are both absolute gems of Tudor and Elizabethan architecture, and Portland Castle is the best preserved of Henry VIII's string of coastal fortresses. Maiden Castle near Dorchester is one of the most impressive prehistoric sites in the country and the area also boasts the singular Chesil Bank, a 16-mile-long bank of pebbles 23feet high and up to 510feet wide that stretches from Portland to Abbotsbury.

74 THE OLD TEA HOUSE

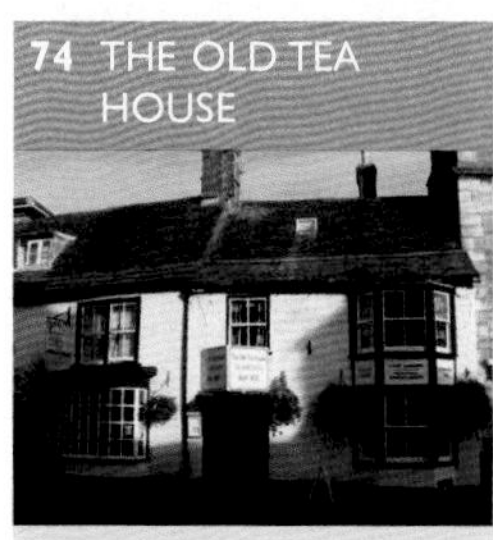

Dorchester

Packed full of history, the Old Tea House is a beautiful and comfortable place to stay whilst exploring the surrounding area.

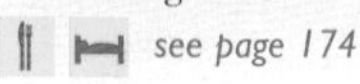

see page 174

DORCHESTER

One of England's most appealing county towns, Dorchester's known history goes back to AD 74 when the Romans established a settlement called Durnovaria at a respectful distance from the River Frome. At that time the river was much broader than it is now and prone to flooding. The town's Roman origins are clearly displayed in its street plan, in the beautiful tree-lined avenues known as **The Walks** which follow the course of the old Roman walls, at **Maumbury Rings**, an ancient stone circle which the Romans converted into an amphitheatre, and in the well-preserved **Roman Town House** behind County Hall in Colliton Park. As the town's most famous citizen put it, Dorchester "announced old Rome in every street, alley and precinct. It looked Roman, bespoke the art of Rome, concealed dead men of Rome". Thomas Hardy was in fact describing 'Casterbridge' in his novel *The Mayor of Casterbridge* but his fictional town is immediately recognisable as Dorchester. One place he describes in great detail is **Mayor Trenchard's House,** easily identified as what is now Barclays Bank in South Street and bearing a plaque to that effect. Hardy made his home in Dorchester in 1883 and two years later moved into **Max Gate** (National Trust) on the outskirts of the town, a strikingly unlovely 'two up and two down' Victorian villa designed by Hardy himself and built by his brother at a total cost of £450. Here Hardy entertained a roll-call of great names – Robert Louis Stevenson, GB Shaw, Rudyard Kipling and HG Wells amongst many others – to tea at 4 o'clock.

The most accessible introduction to the town and the county can be found at the excellent **Dorset County Museum** in High Street West. The award-winning museum houses a comprehensive range of exhibits spanning the centuries, from a Roman sword to a 19th century cheese press, from dinosaur footprints to a stuffed Great Bustard which used to roam the chalk uplands of north Dorset but has been extinct in this country since 1810. Founded in 1846, the museum moved to its present site in 1883, into purpose-built galleries with lofty arches of fine cast ironwork inspired by the Great Exhibition of 1851 at the Crystal Palace. The building was designed by GR Crickmay, the architect for whom Thomas Hardy worked in 1870. The great poet and novelist is

Poundbury Hill Fort, Dorchester

celebrated here in a major exhibit which includes a fascinating reconstruction of his study at Max Gate, his Dorchester home. The room includes the original furnishings, books, pictures and fireplace. In the right hand corner are his musical instruments, and the very pens with which he wrote *Tess of the d'Urbervilles, Jude the Obscure,* and his epic poem, the *Dynasts*. More of his possessions are displayed in the Gallery outside – furniture, his watch, music books, and some of his notebooks. Also honoured in the Writers Gallery is William Barnes, the Dorset dialect poet, scholar and priest, who was also the first secretary of the Dorset Natural History and Archaeological Society which owns and runs the museum.

Opposite the County Museum, the Antelope Hotel and the 17th century half-timbered building beside it (now a tea-room) were where Judge Jeffreys (1648-89) tried 340 Dorset men for their part in Monmouth's Rebellion of 1685. As a result of this 'Bloody Assize', 74 men suffered death by being hanged, drawn and quartered. A further 175 were transported for life. Jeffreys' ferociousness has been attributed to the agony he suffered from gallstones for which doctors of the time could provide no relief. Ironically, when his patron James II was deposed, Jeffreys himself ended up in the Tower of London where he died. A century and a half after the Bloody Assize, another infamous trial took place in the Old Crown Court nearby. Six farm labourers who later became known as the Tolpuddle Martyrs were condemned to transportation for their part in organising a 'Friendly Society' – the first agricultural trade union. The **Court and Cells** are now open to the public where they are invited to "stand in the dock and sit in the dimly-lit cells...and experience four centuries of gruesome crime and punishment".

At the **Dorset Teddy Bear Museum** in a quaint old house in Antelope Walk, visitors join Mr Edward Bear and his family of human-size bears as they relax around the house or busy themselves making teddies in the Old Dorset Teddy Bear Factory. Hundreds of the cuddly creatures are on sale in the exhibition's period shop. In High Street East, **Terracotta Warriors** is the only museum outside China dedicated to these astonishing figures, regarded as the 8th wonder of the ancient world. As well as the unique life-size museum replicas from China, the exhibition includes costumes, armour and multi-media displays.

Off High Street East, in Icen Street, is the **Dinosaur Museum**, where actual fossils, skeletons and life-size reconstructions combine with audio-visual and hands-on displays to inform and entertain. Also well worth a visit is **The Keep Military Museum** housed in an interesting, renovated Grade II listed building. Audio technology and interactive computerised displays tell the remarkable story of those who have served in the

•

Just outside the Dorset County Museum stands the Statue of William Barnes and, at the junction of High Street West and The Grove, is the Statue of Thomas Hardy. There are more statues outside St George's Church, a group of lifesize models by Elizabeth Frink representing Catholic martyrs who were hanged, drawn and quartered in the 16th century.

•

An oddity in Dorchester town is an 18th century sign set high up in a wall. It carries the information that Bridport is 15 miles distant and Hyde Park Corner, 120. Apparently, the sign was placed in this position for the convenience of stage-coach drivers, although one would have thought that they, of all people, would have already known the mileage involved.

regiments of Dorset and Devon. An additional attraction is the spectacular view from the battlements across the town and surrounding countryside.

There can be few churches in the country with such a bizarre history as that of **Our Lady, Queen of Martyrs, & St Michael**. It was first erected in Wareham, in 1888, by a Roman Catholic sect who called themselves the Passionists, a name derived from their obsession with Christ's passion and death. When they found that few people in Wareham shared their fixation, they had the church moved in 1907, stone by stone to Dorchester where it was re-assembled and then served the Catholic community for almost 70 years. By the mid-1970s the transplanted church had become too small for its burgeoning congregation. The Passionists moved out, ironically taking over an Anglican church whose communicants had become too few to sustain it. A decade later, their abandoned church was acquired by an organisation called World Heritage which has transformed its interior into the **Tutankhamun Exhibition**. It includes a reconstruction of the magnificent tomb of the boy-king including his famous golden mask, with "sight, sound and smell combining to re-create the world's greatest discovery of ancient treasure". With the help of a running commentary, visitors can follow the footsteps of the archaeologist Howard Carter who discovered the real tomb in 1922. The tour ends beside a life-size facsimile of the youthful Pharoah's mummy constructed from a genuine skeleton covered with organic-substitute flesh and animal skin.

Wolfeton Manor, Charminster

AROUND DORCHESTER

CHARMINSTER

1 mile N of Dorchester on the A52

An attractive town on the River Cerne, it has a 12th century church with an impressive pinnacled tower added in the 1400s. Inside are some striking memorials to the Trenchard family whose noble mansion, **Wolfeton House,** stands on the northern edge of the town. A lovely medieval and Elizabethan manor house, it is surrounded by water meadows near the meeting of the rivers Cerne and Frome. The house contains a great stone staircase, remarkable plaster ceilings, fireplaces and carved oak panelling – all Elizabethan – some good pictures and furniture. Opening times are restricted. There is also a cider house here from which cider can be purchased.

GODMANSTONE

4 miles N of Dorchester on the A352

Dorset can boast many cosy, intimate pubs, but the **Smith's Arms** at Godmanstone is in a class of its own, claiming to be the smallest inn in the country with a frontage just 11 feet wide. This appealing 14th century thatched building was originally the village smithy and, according to tradition, Charles II happened to stop here to have his horse shod. Feeling thirsty, the king asked for a glass of ale and was not best pleased to be told that as the blacksmith had no licence, no alcoholic drink was available. Invoking the royal prerogative, Charles granted a licence immediately and this tiny hostelry has been licensed ever since. Given the cramped interior, elbow-bending at the Smith's Arms can be a problem at busy times, but fortunately there is a spacious terrace outside.

PIDDLETRENTHIDE

6 miles N of Dorchester on the B3143

Mentioned in the *Domesday Book*, this village is named after the river beside which it stands and the '30 hides' of land for which it was assessed. A beautiful place in a beautiful location, Piddletrenthide is believed to have been the home of Alfred the Great's brother, Ethelred.

CERNE ABBAS

7 miles N of Dorchester on the A352

This pretty village beside the River Cerne takes its name from **Cerne Abbey**, formerly a major Benedictine monastery of which an imposing 15th century gatehouse, a tithe barn of the same period, and a holy well still survive, all well worth seeing. So too are the lofty, airy church with grotesque gargoyles and medieval statues adorning its west tower, and the old Market House on Long Street. In fact, there is much to see in this ancient village where cottages dating back to the 14th century still stand.

75 ABBOTS

Cerne Abbas

Abbots specialises in home cooked food using the best of local West Country suppliers. It also has 5 rooms available for B&B

see page 176

Pitchmarket House, Cerne Abbas

•
Although Thomas Hardy was cremated and his ashes buried in the Poets' Corner of Westminster Abbey, his heart was brought to Stinsford to be interred in a graveyard tomb here. According to a scurrilous local tradition, it is shared with the village cat which had managed to eat the heart before it was buried.
•

But the major visitor attraction is to be found just to the north of the village – the famous **Cerne Abbas Giant** (National Trust), a colossal 180feet-high figure cut into the chalk hillside, brandishing a club, naked and full-frontal. An ancient tradition asserts that any woman wishing to become pregnant should sit, or preferably sleep the night, on the giant's huge erect penis, some 22feet long. The age of this extraordinary carving is hotly disputed but a consensus is emerging that it was originally created by ancient Britons as a fertility symbol and that the giant's club was added by the Romans. (There are clear similarities between the giant and the representation of Hercules on a Roman pavement of AD 191, preserved at Sherborne Castle). As with all hill-carvings, the best view is from a distance, in this case from a layby on the A352. A curious puzzle remains. The giant's outlines in the chalk need a regular scouring to remove grass and weeds. Should this be neglected, he would soon fade into the hillside. In medieval centuries, such a non-essential task of conservation could only have been authorised by the locally all-powerful Abbots of Cerne. What possible reason did those Christian advocates of chastity have for carefully preserving such a powerful pagan image of virility?

MINTERNE MAGNA

9 miles N of Dorchester, on the A352

A couple of miles north of the Cerne Giant, Minterne Magna is notable for its parish church, crowded with memorials to Napiers, Churchills and Digbys, the families who once owned the great house here and most of the Minterne valley. The mansion itself, rebuilt in the Arts & Crafts style around 1900 is not open to the public but its splendid **Minterne Gardens** are. The gardens are laid out in a horseshoe below the house and landscaped in the 18th century style of Capability Brown. They contain an important collection of Himalayan rhododendrons and azaleas, along with cherries, maples and many other fine and rare trees. The gardens are open daily from March to early November. On Batcombe Hill, to the west of Minterne Magna, stands a stone pillar known as the Cross and Hand, thought to date from the 7th century. Its purpose is unknown, but in *Tess of the d'Urbevilles* Hardy relates the local legend that the pillar marks the grave of a criminal who was tortured and hanged there, and whose mournful ghost appears beside the column from time to time.

STINSFORD

1 mile NE of Dorchester, off the A35

It was in **St Michael's Church** at Stinsford that Thomas Hardy was christened and where he attended services for much of his life. He sang hymns to the accompaniment of the village band, (amongst whom were several of his relatives), which played from a gallery at the back of the church. The gallery was demolished in Hardy's lifetime, but many years later he drew a sketch from memory which showed the position of each player and the name of his instrument. A copy of this drawing is on display in the church, alongside a tablet commemorating the Hardys who took part.

Also buried in the churchyard is the Poet Laureate Cecil Day Lewis (1904-72). To the east of Stinsford, **Kingston Maurward Gardens** are of such historical importance that they are listed on the English Heritage Register of Gardens. The formal Edwardian gardens include a croquet lawn, rose garden, herbaceous borders and a large display of tender perennials, including the National Collections of Penstemons and Salvias. Here, too, is an animal park.

HIGHER BOCKHAMPTON

2 miles NE of Dorchester off the A35

In the woods above Higher Bockhampton, reached by a series of narrow lanes and a 10-minute walk, is a major shrine for devotees of Thomas Hardy. **Hardy's Cottage** is surrounded by the trees of Puddletown Forest, a setting he evoked so magically in *Under the Greenwood Tree.* The delightful thatched cottage and gardens are now owned by the National Trust and the rooms are furnished much as they would have been when the great novelist was born here in 1840. Visitors can see the very room in which his mother gave birth only to hear her child proclaimed still-born. Fortunately, an observant nurse noticed that the infant was in fact breathing and so ensured that such classics of English literature as *Tess of the d'Urbervilles* and *The Return of the Native* saw the light of day. This charming cottage was Hardy's home for the first twenty-two years of his life until he set off for London to try his luck as an architect. In that profession his record was undistinguished, but in 1871 his first novel, *Desperate Remedies,* was published. An almost farcical melodrama, it gave few signs of the great works that would

Hardy's Cottage, Higher Bockhampton

76 THE BLUE VINNY

Puddletown

A modern restaurant with old roots, The Blue Vinny provides a first-class dining experience in spectacular settings.

see page 176

follow but was sufficiently successful for Hardy to devote himself thereafter to writing full time.

PUDDLETOWN

5 miles NE of Dorchester off the A35

Originally called Piddletown ('piddle' is the Saxon word for 'clear water') the village's name was changed by the sensitive Victorians. It was here that Hardy's grandfather and great-grandfather were born. Renamed 'Weatherbury' it features in *Far From the Madding Crowd* as the place where Fanny's coffin was left out in the rain, and Sergeant Troy spends the night in the porch of the church after covering her grave with flowers.

Just to the east of Puddletown, **Athelhampton House** is a delightful, mostly Tudor house surrounded by a series of separate, 'secret' gardens. It's the home of Sir Edward and Lady du Cann and has the lived-in feeling that adds so much interest to historic houses. One of the finest houses in the county, Athelhampton's most spectacular feature is its magnificent Great Chamber built during the reign of Elizabeth I. In the grounds are topiary pyramids, fountains, the Octagonal Garden designed by Sir Robert Cooke in 1971, and an unusual 15th century circular dovecote. It is almost perfectly preserved, with its 'potence', or revolving ladder used to collect eggs from the topmost nests, still in place and still useable.

MORETON

7 miles E of Dorchester off the B3390

Thomas Hardy may be Dorset's most famous author, but in this small village it is another distinguished writer, (also a scholar, archaeologist and military hero), who is remembered. In 1935 T.E. Lawrence, "Lawrence of Arabia", left the RAF where he was known simply as Aircraftsman T.E. Shaw and retired to a spartan cottage he had bought in 1923. It stands alone on the heath outside Moreton village and here Lawrence lived as a virtual recluse, without cooking facilities and with a sleeping bag as his bed. He was to enjoy this peaceful, if comfortless, retreat for only a few weeks. Lawrence loved speeding along the Dorset lanes on his motor-cycle and one sunny spring day his adventurous driving led to a fatal collision with two young cyclists. The King of Iraq and Winston Churchill attended the hero's burial in the graveyard at Moreton, where a tree was planted and later a stone memorial. The home Lawrence occupied for such a short time, **Cloud's Hill** (National Trust), is now open to the public. Lawrence remains a fascinating figure, and at an auction in 2008 letters in which he writes how well his Brough Superior motor-cycle is running (he owned several down the years) and of his love of books were sold for £10,000. He wrote the letters to an RAF flight sergeant while stationed on the Isle of Wight in 1932/33.

WINTERBORNE CAME

2 miles SE of Dorchester off the A352

This tiny hamlet is a place of pilgrimage for admirers of Dorset's second most famous man of letters who is buried in the graveyard here. William Barnes was Rector of Winterborne Came from 1862 until his death in 1886 and in the old Rectory (not open to the public) he entertained such luminaries of English literature as Alfred Lord Tennyson and Hardy himself. Although Barnes was highly respected by fellow poets, his pastoral poems written in the distinctive dialect of the county never attracted a wide audience. At their best, though, they are marvellously evocative of the west Dorset countryside:

The zwellen downs, wi' chalky tracks
A-climmen up their zunny backs,
Do hide green meads an zedgy brooks...
An' white roads up athirt the hills.

OWERMOIGNE

6 miles SE of Dorchester off the A352

Just north of the village is a dual attraction in the shape of **Mill House Cider Museum** and the **Dorset Collection of Clocks**. Housed in a mill that featured in Hardy's *The Distracted Preacher* (he called the village Nethermoynton), the Cider Museum has a collection of 18th and 19th century cider-making mills and presses, reflecting the importance of cider as a main country drink in bygone days. The Collection of Clocks showcases numerous timepieces ranging from longcase clocks to elaborate turret clocks displayed in date order. Visitors get the opportunity to see the intricate movements that are usually hidden away in the large clocks found on churches and public buildings.

MAIDEN CASTLE

2 miles SW of Dorchester off the A35

Maiden Castle is one of the most impressive prehistoric sites in the country. This vast Iron Age fortification covering more than 45 acres dates back some 4000 years. Its steep earth ramparts, between 60 and 90 feet high, are nearly 2 miles round and together with the inner walls make a total of 5 miles of defences. The settlement flourished for 2000 years until AD 44 when its people were defeated by a Roman army under Vespasian. Excavations here in 1937 unearthed a war cemetery containing some 40 bodies, one of which still had a Roman arrowhead embedded in its spine. The Romans occupied the site for some 30 years before moving closer to the River Frome and founding Durnovaria, modern Dorchester. Maiden Castle was never settled again and it is a rather forbidding, treeless place but the extensive views along the Winterborne valley by contrast are delightful.

WINTERBOURNE ABBAS

4 miles W of Dorchester

The village of Winterbourne Abbas stands at the head of the Winterborne valley, close to the river which is notable for running only during the winter and

Winterborne Came's unusual name, incidentally, derives from the fact that in medieval times the village was owned by the Abbey of Caen in France.

77 WADHAM GUEST HOUSE

Weymouth

Spacious Georgian house close to the Old Harbour offering quality en suite accommodation.

 *see page 177*

78 EDENHURST GUESTHOUSE

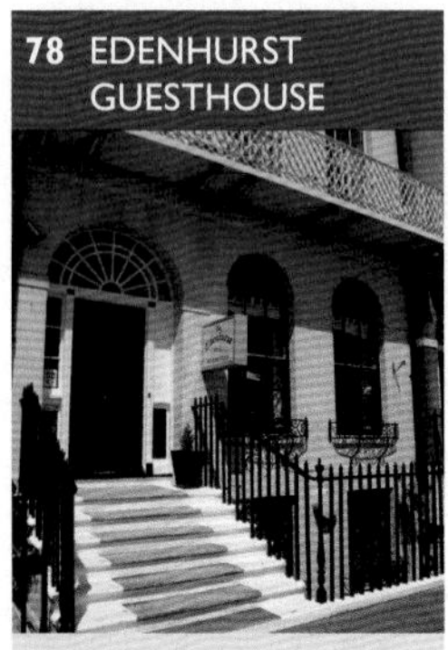

Weymouth

Sea-front family-run guest house close to all the town's major attractions; some rooms with sea view and balcony.

 *see page 177*

79 WEYMOUTH SEA LIFE PARK

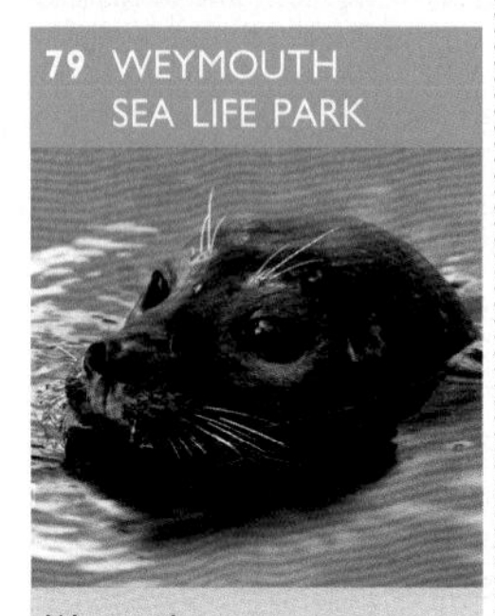

Weymouth

Facinating wildlife park offering visitors a chance to view some interesting sea life.

 *see page 178*

becoming a dry ditch in summer. The second part of the name, Abbas, comes from having been owned by the abbots of Cerne. The village is surrounded by ancient barrows, amongst which are the **Nine Stones**, Dorset's best example of a standing stone circle. Not the best location, however. The circle lies beside the busy A35, isolated from the village to the west and surrounded by trees. Despite the constant din of passing traffic, the circle somehow retains an air of tranquillity of its own.

WEYMOUTH

No wonder the good citizens of Weymouth erected a **Statue of George III** to mark the 50th year of his reign in 1810. The troubled king had brought great kudos and prosperity to their little seaside resort by coming here to bathe in the sea water. George had been advised that sea-bathing would help cure his 'nervous disorder' so, between 1789 and 1805, he and his royal retinue spent a total of 14 holidays in Weymouth. Fashionable society naturally followed in his wake. The imposing statue is unusual in being painted. Not far away, at the head of King Street, his grand-daughter Victoria's own 50th year as queen is commemorated by a colourful **Jubilee Clock** erected in 1887. Nearby, the picturesque harbour is always busy – fishing boats, paddle steamers, pleasure boats, catamarans servicing the Channel Islands and St Malo in France and, if you're lucky, you may even see a Tall Ship or two.

One of the town's premier tourist venues is **Brewers Quay**, an imaginatively redeveloped Victorian brewery offering an enormous diversity of visitor attractions within a labyrinth of paved courtyards and cobbled streets. There are no fewer than 22 different establishments within the complex, ranging from craft shops and restaurants through a fully automated Ten Pin bowling alley to the **Timewalk Journey** which promises visitors that they will "See, Hear and Smell over 600 years of Weymouth's spectacular history".

From Brewers Quay, a path leads through **Nothe Gardens** to **Nothe Fort**, built between 1860 and 1872 as part of the defences of the new naval base being established on Portland. Ten huge guns face out to sea; two smaller ones are directed inland. The fort's 70 rooms on three levels now house the **Museum of Coastal Defence** which has many interesting displays illustrating past service life in the fort, history as seen from the Nothe headland, and the part played by the people of Weymouth in World War II. Nothe Fort is owned and operated by the Weymouth Civic Society which also takes care of **Tudor House,** just north of Brewers Quay. One of the town's few remaining Tudor buildings, the house originally stood on the edge of an inlet from the harbour and is thought to have been a merchant's house. It's now furnished in the style of an early-17th century middle class home and the guided tour gives some fascinating insights into life in those days.

Only yards from the waters of Weymouth Bay, **Lodmoor Country Park** is another popular attraction. Access to most of the park is free and visitors can take advantage of the many sport and recreation areas, wander around the footpaths and nature reserve, or enjoy a picnic or barbecue. Set within the park and surrounded by beautiful gardens complete with a bird aviary, **Model World** is a quite unique attraction which has been more than 25 years in the making. Back in 1972, Colin Sims conceived the idea of creating a model village and during the course of the next nine years constructed hundreds of finely detailed hand-made models from a variety of materials: stone, concrete, specially treated wood and plastics to withstand all kinds of weather. All built to a scale of 1:32 of life size, together the models create a complete world in miniature.

Another major family attraction is **Deep Sea Adventure,** opened in 1988 by Princess Anne, and with two separate attractions under one roof. Deep Sea Adventure tells the story of underwater exploration and marine exploits from the 17th century through to the modern day. This entertaining and educational exhibition fills three floors of an imposing Victorian grain warehouse with a wealth of animated and interactive displays recounting compelling tales of shipwreck survival and search & rescue operations, a 'Black Hole' in which you can experience what it is like to be a deep sea diver, and a unique display which tells the epic story of the *Titanic* in the words of the officers, crew and survivors, along with the original *Titanic* signals and one of the largest models of the doomed ship in the world. Sharky's Play & Part Warehouse is a huge, all-weather adventure play area with slides, ball pools and four floors of fun.

OSMINGTON

3 miles NE of Weymouth on the A353

There are several 'White Horses' carved into hillsides around the country, but the **White Horse** near Osmington, apart from being one of the largest, (354feet high and 279feet wide), is the only one which also has a rider. The horse was created in 1807; the rider was added about 3 years later. Wearing a tall cocked hat and carrying a whip, the horseman represents George III. The king was a frequent visitor to nearby Weymouth and his royal patronage naturally attracted many free-spending courtiers to the town. The town fathers of Weymouth decided to express their appreciation by paying the local militia to add the royal rider. The result was an unrecognisable, if undoubtedly loyal, tribute to His Majesty. Like all the other White Horses in England, it looks much better when seen from a few miles away; close up, it is meaningless.

80 THE WARWICK

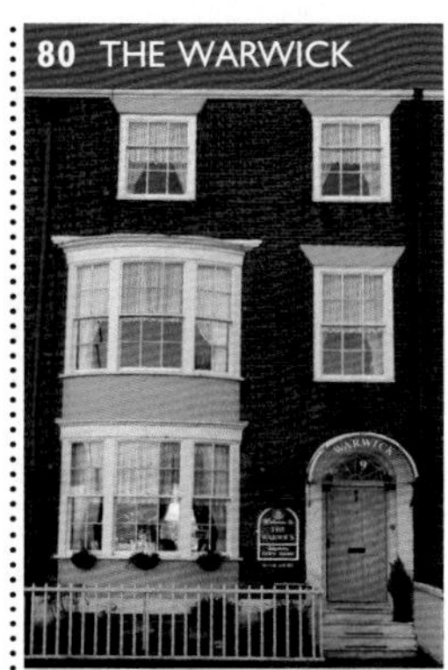

Weymouth

Grade II* listed building just 20 metres from the beach offering excellent en suite B&B accommodation.

see page 179

81 SOUTHVILLE GUEST HOUSE

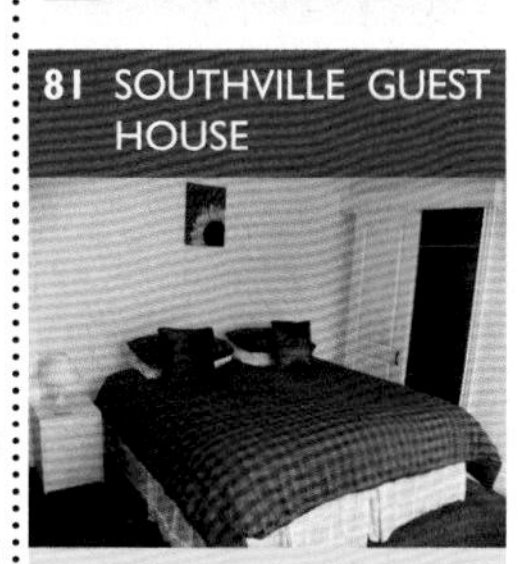

Weymouth

Family run guest house offering quality en suite accommodation and breakfasts based on local Dorset produce.

see page 178

Burning Cliffs Ringstead Bay, nr Osmington Mills

•
On the highest point of Isle of Portland is Verne Citadel which was a base for troops defending Portland and Weymouth. It became a prison in 1950.
•

A mile south of Osmington, at Osmington Mills, the area's notorious history in trading contraband liquor lingers in the name of The Smugglers Inn. Unlike many similarly-named hostelries, this one really was a regular haunt for smugglers. Dating back to the 13th century, this former fisherman's cottage enjoyed a secluded position and the nearby beach provided safe landing. The inn's landlord in the early 1800s was Emmanuel Carless who, together with his French partner, Pierre Latour or 'French Peter', ran a thriving business importing thousands of gallons of brandy each year. Unfortunately, the liquor was so inferior locals refused to drink it and the spirit had to be carried inland on stage coaches, disguised as luggage, to be distilled again.

ISLE OF PORTLAND

4 miles S of Weymouth, on the A354

Portland is not really an island at all, but a 4.5 mile long peninsula, well known to devotees of shipping forecasts and even more famous for the stone from its quarries. It is a Unesco World Heritage Site, a Site of Special Scientific Interest, and a European Special Area of Conservation, all of which might not stop the excavation of a new quarry to acquire Portland Stone to restore buildings damaged by World War II bombs. Numerous buildings in London are constructed of Portland stone, among them the Cenotaph, St Paul's Cathedral, Inigo Jones' Banqueting Hall in Whitehall, and Buckingham Palace, and the stone was also favoured by sculptors such as Henry Moore. (The stone was also used for the graves of British servicemen killed in both World Wars; the stone used for these graves proved vulnerable to erosion and in 1998 the Commonwealth War Graves Commission began to use a type of marble instead.) In the **Tout Quarry Sculpture Park** some 50 pieces in the local stone are on display – watch out for Anthony Gormley's figure of a man falling down the rock face!

The island's most famous building is **Portland Castle** (English Heritage), one of the finest of Henry VIII's coastal fortresses. Its active role lasted for 500 years, right up to World War II when it provided a D-Day embarkation point for British and American forces. Oliver Cromwell used the castle as a prison and in Victorian times it was the residence of Portland's governors. Visitors can try on the armour, meet 'Henry VIII' in the Great Hall, and enjoy the special events that are held regularly throughout the year. The battlements overlook superb views of Portland Harbour whose breakwaters were constructed by convict labour to create the second largest man-made harbour in the world.

At the southernmost tip of the island, the Bill of Portland, the first lighthouse to be built here is now a base for birdwatchers. The current Portland Bill Lighthouse offers guided tours during the season and also has a visitor centre. Nearby are some particularly fascinating natural features: the tall, upright Pulpit Rock which can be climbed, and some caves to explore.

The Isle provides some good cliff-top walks with grand views of **Chesil Beach**, a vast bank of pebbles worn smooth by the sea which stretches for some 10 miles to Abbotsbury. Inexplicably, the pebbles are graded in size from west to east. Fishermen reckon they can judge whereabouts on the beach they are landing by the size of the pebbles. In the west they are as small as peas and usually creamy in colour; at Portland they have grown to the size of cooking apples and are more often grey. The long, narrow body of water trapped behind the beach is known as **The Fleet.** It is now a nature reserve and home to a wide variety of waterfowl and plants, as well as fish that can be viewed by taking a trip in a glass-bottomed boat.

CHICKERELL

3 miles NW of Weymouth off the 3157

A pretty village of thatched cottages, Chickerell is best known for its **Water Gardens** which were created in 1959 by Norman Bennett. He began by growing water lilies in the disused clay pits of a brickworks and the gardens are now home to the National Collection of Water Lilies. Within the gardens is a museum telling the story of the village which featured in the *Domesday Book.*

PORTESHAM

6 miles NW of Weymouth on the B3157

On the Black Downs northeast of Portesham stands **Hardy's Monument** (National Trust) which commemorates not Thomas Hardy, the great novelist of Wessex, but Sir Thomas Hardy, the flag-captain of *HMS Victory* at Trafalgar to whom the dying Lord Nelson spoke the immortal words, "Kiss me, Hardy", (or possibly, "Kismet, Hardy"). Sir Thomas was born in Portesham and, like his novelist namesake, was descended from the Hardys of Jersey. After Trafalgar, he escorted Nelson's body back to London and soon afterwards was created a baronet and, eventually, First Sea Lord. Sir Thomas's stunningly graceless memorial has been variously described as a 'huge candlestick', a ''peppermill', and most accurately as a 'factory chimney wearing a crinoline'. But if you stand with your back to it, there are grand views over Weymouth Bay.

•

At Southwell, near the tip of Portland Bill, St Andrew's Avalanche church was built in 1879 chiefly as a memorial to those who perished when the clipper **Avalanche** ***sank off the Portland coast at the beginning of a passage to New Zealand. Also in Southwell is the Portland Museum which was founded by the birth control pioneer Marie Stopes who lived on the island. Housed in a charming pair of thatched cottages, the museum tells the story of life on the island from smuggling and shipwrecks to traditions and customs.***

•

82 TURK'S HEAD INN

Chickerell, near Weymouth

Charming inn with olde worlde character, a superb restaurant and well chosen wine list.

see page 180

83 ABBOTSBURY

Abbotsbury

A delightful English village, home to the Swannery, the Sub-Tropical Gardens and the Tithe Barn and Childrens Farm

see page 181

In Portesham itself an unusual attraction, the **Great Dorset Maize Maze,** challenges visitors to 'crack' the world-class maze with its fiendishly intricate design. Popular with families, the site also gives youngsters the opportunity to mingle with farm animals, and to have fun on the trampolines and pedal go-carts, or in the indoor fun barns. Hot refreshments are available and plans are under way to add Frisbee golf and a golf driving range.

ABBOTSBURY

8 miles NW of Weymouth on the B3157

Surrounded by hills, picturesque Abbotsbury is one of the county's most popular tourist spots and by any standards one of the loveliest villages in England. Its most striking feature as you approach is the 14th century **St Catherine's Chapel,** perched on the hill-top. Only 45feet by 15feet, it is solidly built to withstand the Channel gales with walls more than 4feet thick. St Catherine was believed to be particularly helpful in finding husbands for the unmarried and in medieval times spinsters would climb the hill to her chapel chanting a dialect jingle which concludes with the words *"Arn-a-one's better than Narn-a-one"* – anyone is better than never a one.

Abbotsbury takes its name from the important Benedictine Abbey that once stood here but was comprehensively cannibalised after the Reformation, its stones used to build the attractive cottages that line the village streets. What has survived however is the magnificent **Great Abbey Barn**, 247feet long and 31feet wide, which was built in the 1300s to store the abbey's tithes of wool, grain and other produce. With its thatched roof, stone walls and a mightily impressive entrance it is one of the largest and best-preserved barns in the country.

About a mile south of the village is the famous **Abbotsbury Swannery**, established in Saxon times to provide food for the abbey during the winter months. More than 600 free-flying swans have made their home here and visitor figures rocket from the end of May to the end of June – the baby swans' hatching season.

Just to the west of the village, **Abbotsbury Sub-Tropical Gardens** enjoy a particularly well-sheltered position and the 20 acres of grounds contain a huge variety of rare and exotic plants and trees. Other attractions include an 18th century walled garden, beautiful lily ponds and a children's play area.

BRIDPORT

With its broad streets, (inherited from the days when they were used for making ropes), Bridport is an appealing little town surrounded by green hills and with a goodly number of 17th and 18th century buildings. Most notable amongst these are the stately Georgian **Town Hall**, and the pleasing collection of 17th century houses in the street running south from the Town Hall. An even older survivor is the medieval **Prior's House.** If you visit the town on a Wednesday or Saturday you'll find its three main streets chock-a-block with dozens of stalls participating in the regular Street Market. The Town Council actively encourages local people who produce goods at home and not as part of their regular livelihood to join in. So there's an extraordinary range of artefacts on offer, anything from silk flowers to socks, fossils to fishing tackle. Another popular attraction is **Palmers Brewery** in West Bay Road. Established in 1794, part of the brewery is still thatched. During the season, visitors are welcomed on Tuesdays and Wednesdays for a tour of the historic brewery, the charge for which includes a commemorative certificate and also a glass or two of beer.

Bridport Museum is good on local history and family records and also has an interesting collection of dolls. You can also learn about two distinguished visitors to the town. One was Joan of Navarre who landed at Bridport in 1403 on her way to become queen to Henry IV; the other, Charles II who arrived in the town after his defeat at the Battle of Worcester in 1651. He was fleeing to France, pretending to be the groom in a runaway marriage. As he attended to his horses in the yard of an inn, an ostler approached him saying "Surely I know you, friend?" The quick-thinking future monarch asked where the ostler had been working before. When he replied "In Exeter", Charles responded "Aye, that is where we must have met". Charles then excused himself and made a speedy departure from the town. If the ostler's memory for faces had been better, he could have claimed the £1,000 bounty for Charles' capture and subsequent English history would have followed a very different course.

WEST BAY

1 mile S of Bridport off the A35

When Bridport's own harbour silted up in the early 1700s, the townspeople built a new one at the mouth of the River Brit and called it West Bay. During the 19th century, hundreds of ships docked here every year, and West Bay had its own shipbuilding industry until 1879. The little town never became a fashionable resort but the beach, backed by 100feet high sandstone cliffs, is much enjoyed by holiday-makers, and there's still a stall at the little harbour where you can treat yourself to a tub of cockles. From the harbour you can take a mackerel boat round the bay or go for the deeper waters in search of cod, conger, skate or pollock – and keep a lookout for one of the playful dolphins.

Close to the harbour is the Bridport Arms Hotel, a historic old thatched building that in parts dates back as far as the 1500s. The inn's picturesque qualities earned it two roles in the BBC-TV series *Harbour Lights* starring Nick Berry and Tina Hobky. The inn appeared as both The Piers Hotel and the Bridehaven public house.

84 LORD NELSON HOTEL

Bridport

Close to the Jurassic Coast, this pub/B&Bl is a perfect base for tourists and visitors to the area.

see page 180

85 NEW INN

Eype

A real local in the heart of the Jurassic coast, and offering a friendly and homely atmosphere, the New Inn is not to be ignored.

see page 182

86 THE BRIDGE HOUSE HOTEL

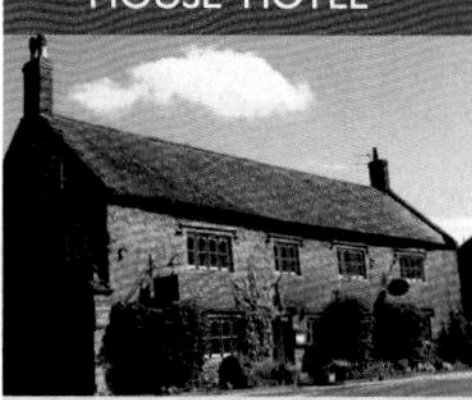

Beaminster

Atmospheric town centre hotel with 13th century origins, 3-star accommodation rated restaurant and brasserie.

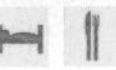  *see page 183*

BEAMINSTER

5 miles N of Bridport on the A3066

In Hardy's novel, when Tess Durbeyville arrives in Beaminster, (Emminster in the novel), she finds a delightful little market town. Visitors today will find that remarkably little has changed. The whole of the town centre is a conservation area and contains an astonishing 200 listed buildings. The 17th century almshouse, the majestic church tower in gold-tinted Hamstone, the 16th century Pickwick's Inn, and the charming Market Square with its stone roofed market cross are all much the same as Hardy knew them. What have disappeared are the many small industries that thrived in those days – rope and sailcloth, embroidered buttons, shoes, wrought ironwork and clockmaking were just some of the artefacts produced here. Housed in the former Congregational Chapel of 1749, **Beaminster Museum** displays objects relating to the life of the town from medieval times to the present day

Visitors to Beaminster's imposing 15th century church tend to be overwhelmed by the grandiose, over-lifesize sculptures of the Strode family who lived at **Parnham House**, a gem of Tudor architecture about a mile south of the town. The splendidly restored interior hosts exhibitions of cutting edge contemporary work in glass, wood, textiles and ceramics. The house is now owned by John Makepeace and much of the modern furniture is created by him and his students at the John Makepeace Furniture Workshops that he runs from here. His wife Jennie has undertaken the restoration of the gardens within whose14 acres are some unusual plants, a lake rich in wildlife, delightful woodland walks, children's play area, picnic areas and even a croquet lawn. There's also a licensed tea room and craft shop.

MAPPERTON

5 miles NE of Bridport off the A3066

It's not surprising to find that the house and gardens at **Mapperton** have featured in three major films – *Tom Jones, Emma* and *Restoration.* Home of the Earl and Countess of Sandwich, this magnificent Jacobean mansion set beside a lake is stunningly photogenic. The Italianate upper gardens contain some impressive topiary, an orangery, dovecote and formal borders descending to fish ponds and shrub gardens. The house stands in an area of outstanding natural beauty with some glorious views of the Dorset hills. The

Mapperton Gardens, Beaminster

gardens are open during the season; tours of the house only by appointment.

LYME REGIS

Known as the Pearl of Dorset, Lyme Regis is a captivating little town enjoying a setting unrivalled in the county, an area of outstanding natural beauty where the rolling countryside of Dorset plunges to the sea. The town itself is a maze of narrow streets with many charming Georgian and Regency houses, and the picturesque harbour will be familiar to anyone who has seen the film *The French Lieutenant's Woman*, based on the novel by Lyme resident, John Fowles. The scene of a lone woman standing on the wave-lashed Cobb has become one of cinema's most enduring images.

The Cobb, which protects the harbour and the sandy beach with its clear bathing water from south-westerly storms, was first recorded in 1294 but the town itself goes back at least another 500 years to Saxon times when there was a salt works here. A charter granted by Edward I allowed Lyme to add 'Regis' to its name but during the Civil War the town was staunchly anti-royalist, routing the forces of Prince Maurice and killing more than 2000 of them. Some 40 years later, James, Duke of Monmouth, chose Lyme as his landing place to start the ill-fated rebellion that would end with ferocious reprisals being meted out to the insurgents by the notorious Judge Jeffreys.

Happier days arrived in the 18th century when Lyme became a fashionable resort, famed for its fresh, clean air. Jane Austen and her family visited in 1803 and part of her novel *Persuasion* is set in the town. The **Jane Austen Garden** commemorates her visit.

A few years after Jane's visit, a 12-year-old girl called Mary Anning was wandering along the shore when she noticed bones protruding from the cliffs. She had discovered the first ichthyosaur to be found in England. Later, as one of the first professional fossil collectors, she also unearthed locally a plesiosaur and a pterodactyl. The 6-mile stretch of coastline on either side of Lyme is world famous for its fossils and some fine specimens of local discoveries can be seen at the award-winning **Lyme Regis Museum** in Bridge Street and at **Dinosaurland & Fossil Museum** in Coombe Street which also runs guided 'fossil walks' along the beach.

Just around the corner from Dinosaurland, in Mill Lane, you'll find one of the town's most interesting buildings. It was in January 1991 that a group of Lyme Regis residents got together in an effort to save the old **Town Mill** from destruction. There has been a mill on the River Lim in the centre of the town for many centuries, but most of the present buildings date back to the mid-17th century when the mill was rebuilt after being burned down during the Civil War siege of Lyme in 1644. Today, back in full working order, Town Mill is

87 TALBOT ARMS

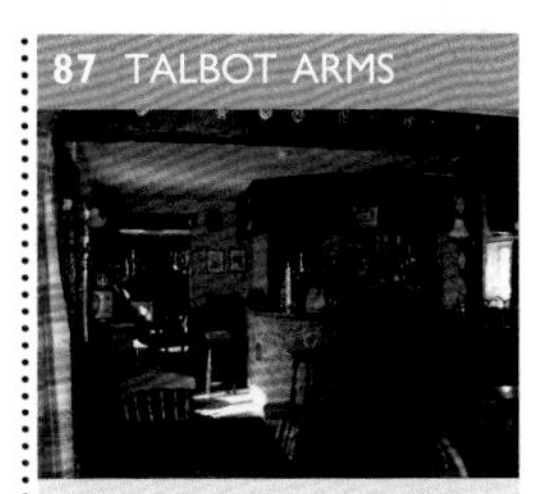

Uplyme

Beautifully decorated free house and bed and breakfast close to the famous River Cottage. Visit this property for a memorable weekend away, or just for a lovely pub lunch.

see page 184

88 BLUE SKY B & B

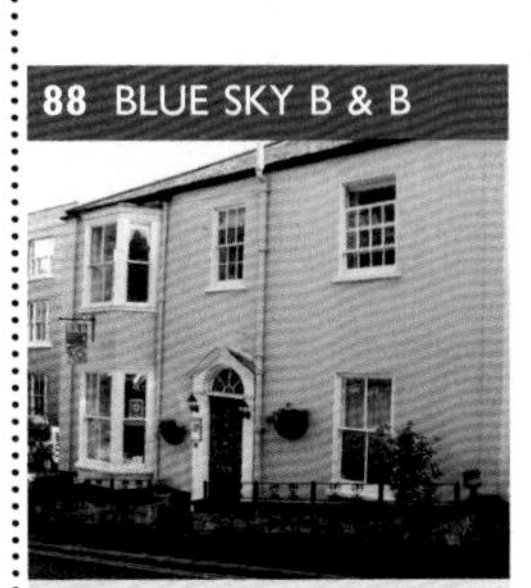

Lyme Regis

This comfortable B & B is a prime place for amateur fossil hunters to stay a night or two.

see page 182

•

For its size, Lyme Regis has an extraordinary range of activities on offer, too many to list here although one must mention the famous week-long Regatta and Carnival held in August. Bands play on the Marine Parade, there are displays by Morris Men and folk dancers.

•

•

If you enjoy walking, the South West Coast Path passes through Lyme: if you follow it eastwards for about 5 miles it will bring you to Golden Cap (617feet), the highest point on the south coast with spectacular views from every vantage point. Or you can just take a pleasant stroll along Marine Parade, a traffic free promenade stretching for about a mile from the Cobb.

•

one of Lyme's major attractions, incorporating two Art Galleries which stage a wide range of exhibitions, concerts, poetry readings and other live performances. There is also a stable building which houses craft workshops.

Lyme has maintained a **Town Crier** for over a thousand years without a break and the current incumbent in his colourful 18th century costume can be seen and heard throughout the town during the summer months.

CHARMOUTH

2 miles NE of Lyme Regis off the A35

What better recommendation could you give the seaside village of Charmouth than the fact that it was Jane Austen's favourite resort? "Sweet and retired" she called it. To quote Arthur Mee, "She loved the splendid sweep of country all round it, the downs, the valleys, the hills like Golden Cap, and the pageantry of the walk to Lyme Regis". Charmouth remains an attractive little place with a wide main street lined with Regency buildings, and a quiet stretch of sandy beach that gradually merges into shingle. This part of the coast has yielded an amazing variety of fossils, many of which can be seen at the **Charmouth Heritage Coast Centre**. Two large aquariums house a variety of local marine life, while a computerised display enables you to 'dive' into Lyme Bay and explore the secrets of the underwater world. The centre is run by three wardens who, throughout the season, organise a series of guided fossil-hunting walks along this scenic stretch of the Jurassic Coast.

WHITCHURCH CANONICORUM

4 miles NE of Lyme Regis off the A35

Clinging to the steep hillside above the valley of the River Char, Whitchurch Canonicorum is notable for its enchanting setting and for its **Church of St Candida and the Holy Cross**. This noble building with its Norman arches and an

89 CHARMOUTH HERITAGE COAST CENTRE

Charmouth

One of the country's leading coastal geological visitor centres with a host of displays.

see page 185

Cobb Harbour, Lyme Regis

imposing tower built around 1400 is remarkable for being one of only two churches in England still possessing a shrine to a saint. (The other is that of Edward the Confessor in Westminster Abbey). St Candida was a Saxon woman named Wite – the Anglo-Saxon word for white, which in Latin is Candida. She lived as a hermit but was murdered by a Viking raiding party in AD 831. During the Middle Ages a major cult grew up around her memory. A large shrine was built of golden Purbeck stone, its lower level pierced by three large ovals into which the sick and maimed thrust their limbs, their head or even their whole body, in the hope of being cured. The cult of St Wite thrived until the Reformation when all such "monuments of feigned miracles" were swept away. That might have been the end of the story of St Wite but during the winter of 1899-1900 the foundations of the church settled and cracked open a 13th century tomb chest. Inside was a lead casket with a Latin inscription stating that "Here rest the relics of St Wite" and inside the casket the bones of a small woman about 40 years old. The shrine still attracts pilgrims today, the donations they leave in the openings beneath the tomb now being devoted to causes which aid health and healing.

BROADWINDSOR

9 miles NE of Lyme Regis on the B3163

Just to the south of this pretty terraced village is a trio of hill forts, Pilsdon Pen, Lambert's Castle and Coney's Castle (all National Trust). They are connected by a network of paths and all provide magnificent views out across Marshwood Vale to the sea. William Wordsworth took a house on Pilsdon Pen for a while and declared that there was no finer view in England.

FORDE ABBEY

11 miles N of Lyme Regis off the B3162

About as far west as you can get in Dorset, **Forde Abbey** enjoys a lovely setting beside the River Axe. Founded as a Cistercian monastery more than 800 years ago, it is now the home of the Roper family. The abbey church has gone but the monks of those days would still recognise the chapter house, dormitories, kitchen and refectories. The Upper Refectory is particularly striking with its fine timbered roof and carved panelling. After the Dissolution of the Monasteries, the abbot's residence became a private house and was greatly extended in 1649 by Cromwell's Attorney-General, Sir Edmond Prideaux. The mansion's greatest treasures are the superb Mortlake tapestries of around 1630 which are based on cartoons by Raphael and have borders probably designed by Rubens. Gardens extending to 30 acres and with origins in the early 1700s, are landscaped around this enchanting house – a suitably peaceful place to bring our tour of the county to an end.

90 BOTTLE INN

Marshwood

The site of the world famous Annual Sting Nettle Eating Championships is in an ideal location and supplies good food and drink in a warm and welcoming atmosphere.

see page 185

Accommodation, Food & Drink and Places of Interest

The establishments featured in this section includes hotels, inns, guest houses, bed & breakfasts, restaurants, cafes, tea and coffee shops, tourist attractions and places to visit. Each establishment has an entry number which can be used to identify its location at the beginning of the relevant chapter or its position in this section.

In addition full details of all these establishments and many others can be found on the Travel Publishing website - **www.travelpublishing.co.uk**. This website has a comprehensive database covering the whole of Britain and Ireland.

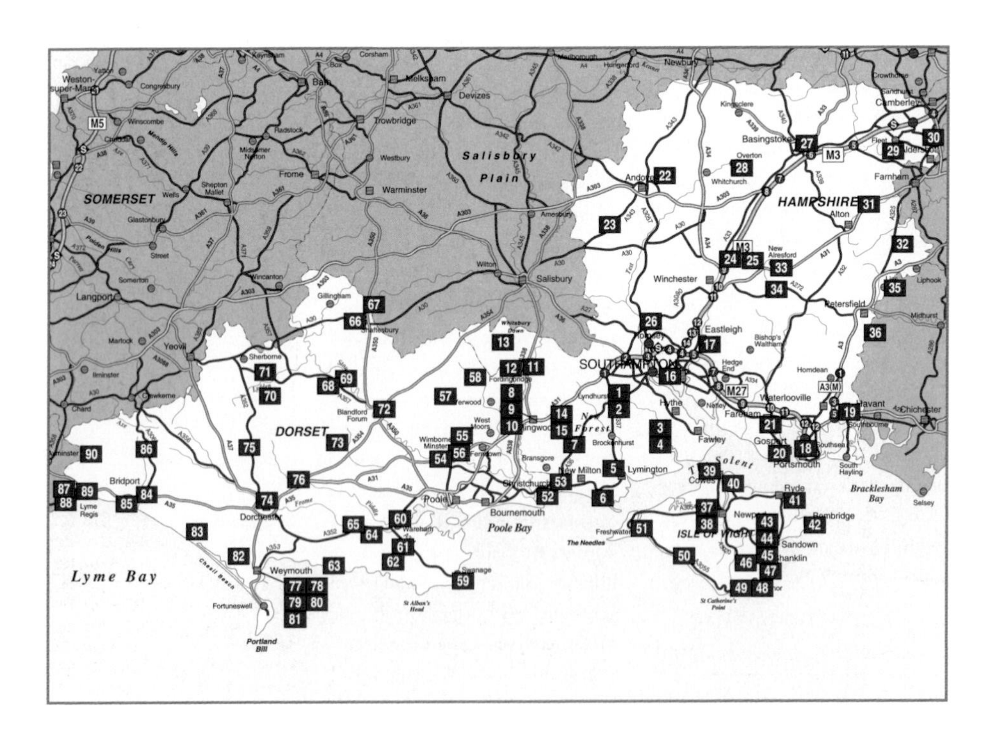

ACCOMMODATION

FOOD & DRINK

PLACES OF INTEREST

1 UNDER THE GREENWOOD TREE

65 High Street, Lyndhurst,
Hampshire SO43 7BE
Tel: 02380 282463
e-mail: david-r-brooks@hotmail.com
website: www.underthegreenwoodtree.com

Owned since 2003 by David and Sue, **Under the Greenwood Tree** used to be a fire station and is a traditional building with lovely high ceilings and a modern, contemporary décor. The surrounding buildings on the high street are Tudor in look - black and white frontings with classic bow windows. The restaurant is a decent size, and features a mixture of tables with chairs and coffee tables with soft seating, offering seating choices for all occasions. David has more than 30 years experience in the catering industry working in senior management positions and that experience shines through.

Thousands of people visit Lyndhurst every year and The Greenwood Tree has a wide and varied menu to suit every taste. Using local produce, the menu provides options for breakfasts, morning coffee, lunches, snacks and afternoon teas. Features of the menu include the huge range of home made cakes and scones, gourmet sandwiches, and fresh home made waffles with sweet and savoury toppings. The unusual name is inspired by the novel 'The Children of the New Forest' by Frederick Marryat. Under The Greenwood Tree is open seven days a week from 9am to 5pm.

2 CAFÉ PARISIAN

64 High Street, Lyndhurst,
Hampshire SO43 7BJ
Tel: 02380 284546

Café Parisien - a little taste of France at the heart of the New Forest in the town of Lyndhurst - is a welcoming café whose continental service provides a great dining experience for everyone. It is brightly decorated with a light, airy and friendly atmosphere provided by large windows at the front and a back garden where dogs are allowed to come and enjoy the company of their owners while they have a lovely coffee or lunch.

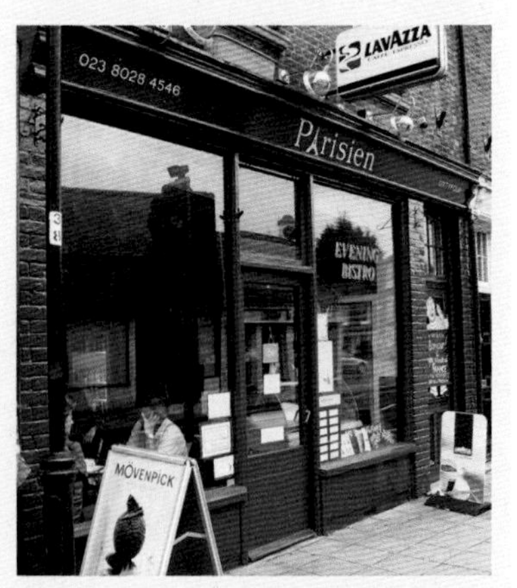

The menu is a definite highlight - filled fresh baguettes, baked on the premises as well as lovely pastries, jacket potatoes, omelettes and salads. An English, French or veggie breakfast is served all day. There are some French snacks and a special menu for the little ones.

With such a variety and quality in the menu, a visit to Café Parisien is a must.

Café Parisien has been open more than 20 years now and is open 7 days a week between 8am and 5pm with take-aways available.

3 THE ROYAL OAK

Hilltop, Beaulieu, Hampshire SO42 7YR
Tel: 01590 612228

Dating back some 300 years, **The Royal Oak** is a fine old traditional hostelry, complete with beamed ceilings and replete with charm and character. It has a large garden with plenty of seating, a play area for children and beautiful views across the forest heath. There's even a paddock where riders can leave their mounts while savouring the excellent cuisine on offer here. Dogs on leads are also welcome.

Chef Lee Hurst offers a menu with lots of old favourites such as rib eye steak, breaded plaice & chips, homemade chilli with wild basmati rice and cheesy nachos, as well as vegetarian options such as a vegetable lasagne with garlic bread and side salad. In addition to the regular menu, there are daily specials often featuring unusual dishes such as kangaroo, crocodile or wild boar. Lee also specialises in fish dishes and there are special Fish Nights on the first and third Fridays of the winter months. Food is served from noon until 3pm, and from 6pm to 9pm, Monday to Friday; and from noon until 9pm on Saturday and Sunday.

4 BEAULIEU NATIONAL MOTOR MUSEUM

Beaulieu, Brockenhurst,
Hampshire SO42 7ZN
Tel: 01590 612345 Fax: 01590 612624
e-mail: info@beaulieu.co.uk
website: www.beaulieu.co.uk

The **National Motor Museum**, in the grounds of Lord Montagu's estate, houses over 250 vehicles. Among the exhibits - the oldest dates from 1896 - are world landspeed record-breakers *Bluebird* and *Golden Arrow*, Damon Hill's championship winning Formula 1 Williams Grand Prix car, an Outspan Orange car, Ariel and Vincent motorcycles and much more. Special attractions include the exhibition of James Bond cars, including the Jaguar XKR Roadster from *Die Another Day* and the world record jumping boat from *Live and Let Die*. The exhibition also includes examples of Q's gadgetry and some of the villains' trademarks, notably Jaws' steel teeth. One of the many permanent displays is an accurate reconstruction of a 1938 garage complete with forecourt, servicing bay, machine shop and office.

Many Montagu family treasures are now on display in **Palace House**, formerly the Great Gatehouse of Beaulieu Abbey, where visitors can meet characters from Victorian days, among them the butler, housemaid and cook, who will talk about their lives. The old monks' refectory houses an exhibition of monastic life, and embroidered wall hangings designed and created by Belinda, Lady Montagu, depict the story of the Abbey from its earliest days. The glorious gardens are an attraction in their own right, and there are plenty of rides and drives for young and old alike - including a monorail that runs through the roof of the Museum in the course of its tour of the estate. Open every day 10am-5pm (6pm in summer)

5 FISHERMANS REST

All Saints Road, Lymington,
Hampshire SO41 8FD
Tel: 01590 678931
e-mail: fishermansrest@fullers.co.uk

The Fisherman's Rest is a traditional pub that welcomes many visitors to Lymington and its marinas. Whether you're seeking out a quiet, relaxing pint, or a place to enjoy a great meal, the Fisherman's Rest has a good deal to offer. During winter, the rustic interior is bathed in candlelight creating a wonderfully, cosy atmosphere.

Situated between the New Forest and the Solent Coast line, Fisherman's Rest boasts an extensive menu to satisfy all appetites. Enjoy everything from a two-course lunch, to an evening menu. In summer, fish is bought in from local fishing boats; you can experience fresh lobster or crab in the new alfresco dining area. A typical dish: pan-fried fillets of local seabass on stir-fried vegetables with a sweet chilli glaze. Local produce features strongly on the seasonal menus and the Fisherman's Rest is proud to be part of the New Forest Marque, allowing them to offer their clientele award winning cheeses from Loosehanger cheese while helping to sustain the rural economy.

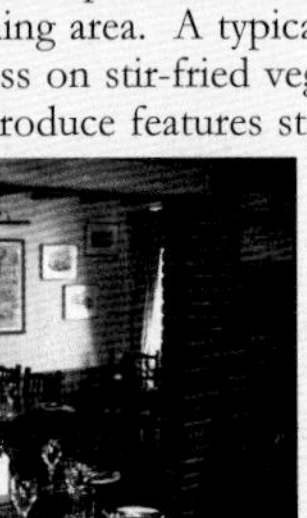

Outstanding cask conditioned ales; great wines and exemplary service complete the picture at this superb local pub that is open all year round.

6 POLLY'S PANTRY

46 High Street, Milford-on-Sea, Lymington,
Hampshire SO41 0QD
Tel: 01590 645 558

The main high street in Milford-on-Sea is lined with typical village shops and a unique teapot themed tearoom called **Polly's Pantry**. This mid 19th Century building has been a tearoom for over 100 years and has been Polly's Pantry since 1994; needless to say, it has got the art of providing traditional cream teas down to a 'T'! The unique theme is down to the array of teapots available to purchase or simply browse around this quaint tearoom.

Offering 'traditional quality and value' Polly's Pantry has an extensive menu, featuring Full English Breakfasts, light lunches, home made daily specials, delicious home made cakes, cream teas and baguettes & sandwiches made freshly to order.

Milford-on-Sea is a delightful village, protected from development on the outskirts by a green belt of land, there are magnificent views available; on a clear day the Needles off the Isle of Wight are visible. With the New Forest on its doorstep and the large towns of Bournemouth and Lymington not too far away, Milford-on-Sea is a great day out.

Polly's Pantry is open between 8.30am – 4.30pm on Monday to Saturday and 11am – 3pm on Sundays, during the summer months.

7 STATION HOUSE AT HOLMSLEY

Holmsley, Burley, Ringwood,
Hampshire BH24 4HY
Tel: 01425 402 468
e-mail: info@stationhouseholmsley.co.uk
website: www.stationhouseholmsley.co.uk

Surrounded by hundreds of acres of ancient woodland, heath and grassy plains, you'll discover that **The Station House at Holmsley**, a 19th century former railway station, has been lovingly and sympathetically converted into what many say is the finest tea house in the New Forest. The station was the reason for the village thriving, built in 1847, the station has seen some famous faces over the years. Prince Edward, the oldest son of Queen Victoria, used the railway to visit his property in Bournemouth, Kaiser Wilhelm and his cabinet are believed to have used the railway in 1907 to visit Highcliffe Castle and General Eisenhower during the preparations for the D-Day landings. The station is also the setting of the fictional station 'Browndean' in Robert Louis Stevenson's novel 'The Wrong Box'. The station's finest hour though was in World War II, when its position was ideal as a drop off point for equipment and supplies for the newly built Holmsley Aerodrome. Further information on the history of the station can be found on the excellent website.

Owners Steve and Mary have done a grand job creating an 'Oasis in the Forest', offering the famous 'tea in the forest' cream teas, the deserving winner of many awards through the years as well as delicious breakfasts, a wide ranging lunch menu, daily specials and lighter bites - all made from fresh and locally sourced produce, something that the local New Forest excels in. The main menu is extensive, the Station House succeeding in offering the best of the traditional fayre with more contemporary dishes. That's why you'll not only find popular dishes like Steak and Kidney Pie, or Sausage and Mash, but more avant-garde offerings such as Lamb and Mint Suet Pudding, Whole Sea Bass baked 'en papillotte' with Lemon and Dill, or Aubergine Parmigiano with slow roasted Tomatoes and baby Leeks. Also available all day long is a vast menu of sandwiches, baguettes, cakes & pastries and light lunches, and being licensed, your delicious meal can be washed down with a nice Rosé, a cup of tea, or a pint of Ringwood Best.

The Station House is open 7 days a week, from 10am – 5pm, serving food all day every day. Breakfast is available between 10am – 11.15am, lunch is available between 11.45am – 2.15pm and afternoon teas & light lunches are served all day long. Please visit the website for up to date information on opening times.

8 THE LAMB INN

2 Hightown Road, Ringwood,
Hampshire BH24 1NN
Tel: 01425 473 721
website: www.lambinnringwood.co.uk

With the beautiful New Forest on its doorstep and the beaches of Bournemouth within easy reach, **The Lamb Inn** is an ideal place to stay for a few nights. It is believed that there has been a Lamb Inn in Ringwood for hundreds of years and the history is available on the website. All 5 rooms are en-suite and are comfortable, clean and spacious with colour televisions and tea & coffee making facilities. The pub downstairs is a popular one, traditionally decorated with flag stone floors, it has a well stocked bar and pool table.

10 BETTLES GALLERY

80 Christchurch Road, Ringwood,
Hampshire BH24 1DR
Tel: 01425 470410
website: www.bettles.net

Bettles Gallery is housed in a 300-year-old building with oak beams, low ceilings and an inglenook fireplace. The gallery specialises in British studio ceramics and contemporary paintings and over the years has built up a first-class reputation for the quality of the work on display. The eight or nine solo or group exhibitions held each year attract collectors from far afield. Work from leading potters and promising newcomers is always available and interesting ceramic jewellery and carefully selected paintings, mostly by artists from the South of England with leanings towards impressionistic and the abstract, are also on display.

9 WHITE HART INN

171 Southampton Road, Ringwood,
Hampshire BH24 1HU
Tel: 01425 483 123

Geoff and Tracy have been the managers of the **White Hart Inn** for 3 years now, and between them they have over 50 years experience in the trade and that shines through in this delightful pub. The pretty building has been here for 350 years and retains a lot of character - slate roof, hanging baskets and window boxes. Inside, the story remains the same, comfortable leather chairs, ingle nook fireplace and wooden floors create a warm welcoming atmosphere, which goes very well with the great food and drink on offer.

Situated right on the edge of the New Forest, the White Hart Inn attracts a lot of holiday makers - walkers, cyclists and families on a day out. This is not to say that it is not popular with the locals, the pub is rarely empty and the locals have a wealth of knowledge about the surrounding area, which they are happy to impart.

The food is a traditional, home cooked affair which is available all week long and they can also provide take-aways. The pub also has lots to do - there is a pool table, a darts board, quiz nights and they can cater for large groups either in the pub or elsewhere.

12 ALDERHOLT MILL

Sandleheath Road, Alderholt,
Fordingbridge, Hampshire SP6 1PU
Tel: 01425 653130
Fax: 01425 652868
e-mail: alderholt-mill@zetnet.co.uk
website: www.alderholtmill.co.uk

Set amidst lovely Dorset countryside, **Alderholt Mill** is a picturesque working water mill offering both bed & breakfast and self-catering accommodation. The mill stands on an island formed by the River Allen, a small tributary that joins the River Avon at the nearby town of Fordingbridge. The mill has a large garden with plenty of water features, a wildlife pond, bog garden and a stream where wildlife abounds. Kingfishers and herons are frequent visitors. Private fishing is available with grayling and trout the predominant species. Owners of the mill, Sandra and Richard Harte can supply a bait fridge and a lock-up for fishing tackle.

For those guests staying on a bed & breakfast basis, the accommodation is provided in former workers' cottages and comprises 3 double and 1 twin-bedded room, all with en suite shower rooms; and 1 single room with wash-hand basin, private toilet and shared bathroom. At breakfast time, guests can sample the bread made from the mill's freshly milled flour which comes from locally grown wheat.

If you prefer self-catering, the mill has 3 charming flats available - 2 on the ground floor, each sleeping 2 people, and one 1st/2nd floor flat sleeping 4/6. All the properties are comprehensively equipped, including colour TV, video, DVD and CD player, and each has its own garden where, on warm summer nights, guests have the option of barbecue-ing by the river. Alternatively, Sandra and Richard can recommend a number of very good hostelries in the region.

Alderholt Mill regrets that it is unable to take children under 8 years old because of the proximity of the river. Well-behaved dogs are accepted by prior arrangement.

At weekends, from 2pm to 6pm, the mill is open for cream teas and the sale of bread, flour etc., and milling demonstrations take place at 3pm on Sundays between Easter and October.

Providing an ideal retreat in which to unwind and really relax, Alderholt Mill is also a convenient base from which to explore not only Dorset but also West Hampshire, Salisbury, the Wiltshire Downs and, of course, the New Forest. It is within easy reach of the south coast and just a short drive from Bournemouth and Poole.

11 NEW FARM COTTAGE

South Gorley, Fordingbridge,
Hampshire SP6 2PW
Tel: 01425 625499

Located in the heart of the New Forest National Park, just inside Fordingbridge, **New Farm Cottage** offers self-catering accommodation in 2 properties. The 16th century cottage sleeps 6 people, and has a lounge with colour TV, dining room, kitchen and bathroom. Also available is 'Melville', a turn of the century property sleeping 4. It has a lounge with open fire and colour TV, dining room, kitchen and bathroom. Outside there's a very large garden, part of which is fenced off and can be used for a pony with permission.

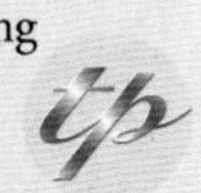

13 ROSE & THISTLE

Rockbourne, Fordingbridge,
Hampshire SP6 3NL
Tel: 01725 518236
e-mail: enquiries@roseandthistle.co.uk
website: www.roseandthistle.co.uk

Located in the idyllic village of Rockbourne, on the edge of the New Forest, the **Rose & Thistle** is a quintessential English country pub serving delicious home cooked meals. With its thatched roof, white-washed walls, hanging baskets and tubs of flowers, it is perfect picture postcard material. The interior is just as appealing - low ceilings, ancient beams, open fires and wooden benches all add to the magic.

Mine host, Kerry Dutton, took over here in June 2008 after moving from London. She is a great believer in good quality service and that's something you will certainly find at the Rose & Thistle. And good food - the menu is based on fresh seasonal ingredients from local suppliers and is served every lunchtime from noon until 2.30pm, and from 7pm to 9.30pm, Monday to Saturday. Such is the popularity of the food served here, booking is essential at weekends. Children are welcome; dogs are allowed in the bar and all major credit cards are accepted.

And for history lovers, a visit to the Rose & Thistle can be easily combined with a trip to the nearby Rockbourne Roman Villa.

14 WAYSIDE COTTAGE

27 Garden Rd, Burley,
Hampshire BH24 4EA
Tel: 01425 403 414
e-mail: jwest@waysidecottage.co.uk
website: www.wayside-cottage.co.uk

Janet and John have created the perfect haven for a relaxing and comfortable weekend or a longer stay in the New Forest. **Wayside Cottage** is a charming wisteria covered Edwardian cottage in the New Forest village of Burley. A fantastic location, Burley is close to the attractive small towns of Lyndhurst, Brockenhurst, Ringwood and Lymington, Lymington offers a ferry across to the Isle of Wight for an exciting day out. Slightly longer drives away are the larger towns of Bournemouth, Southampton and Salisbury; with such a vast array of things to do, it is good to have a base from which to launch your expeditions and Wayside Cottage is perfect.

There are six rooms available in this delightful Bed & Breakfast, and a lovely personal touch is that they are all named after Puccini Heroines. All of the rooms are en-suite, with the exception of La Fanciulla del West, which has its own private bathroom. And they all have colour televisions, clock radios, tea & coffee making facilities and 2 easy chairs. Wayside Cottage offers lots of amenities, such as a lovely patio area for sitting, an ancient croquet set for use and a guest sitting room with an open fire and choice of board games. The local village has lots to do - there are 3 pubs to frequent, lots of little shops, tea rooms, cycle hire shop and riding stables. At the weekend it is possible to catch a game of cricket on the local green or enjoy a wagon ride through the forest. And of course the entire New Forest is right on the cottage's doorstep for exploring.

A full English breakfast is available for guests every morning or there is a choice of specials, cooked by Janet using fresh, local produce wherever possible. Janet has had a long standing interest in catering having run a catering company in the past as well as teaching people how to cook. She provides a full traditional English breakfast of local bacon, sausages to a local butchers own recipe, tomatoes, free range eggs, mushroom and beans, together with a full buffet of cereals, fruit, yoghurts and toasts. Janet will also cater for other diets if requested in advance - just ask the night before and she will have something prepared. Dinner can also be prepared, a reservation is required for a minimum of four people so that the food can be ordered in advance.

Also available is Bakery Cottage and Hawthornes offering beautiful self-catering accomodation for all the family. The Bakery Cottage has 2 bedrooms, parking for one car, living room, wood burning stove, bathroom and fully fitted modern kitchen and south facing gardens. The 2 bedroomed Hawthorne Cottage has a kitchen/diner, bathroom, living room with open fire and a shelterd garden to the front and rear.

15 THE OLD FARMHOUSE RESTAURANT & TEA ROOM

The Cross, Burley, Ringwood,
Hampshire BH24 4AB
Tel: 01425 402 218
e-mail: info@oldfarmhouseinburley.co.uk
website: www.oldfarmhouseinburley.co.uk

The **Old Farmhouse Restaurant** is a charming 16th Century building found in the picturesque New Forest village of Burley. Peter and Cathy Cutler offer friendly service, good quality food and a warm welcoming atmosphere. Split into 4 dining rooms, each seating around 20 people, the Old Farmhouse Restaurant lends itself to private party dining perfectly. Each room is traditionally decorated, with a wonderful inglenook fireplace in one of the dining rooms. The Cutler name is well known in the New Forest; Peter's Grandfather, Father and Brothers have spent and continue to spend their working lives in and around this beautiful area.

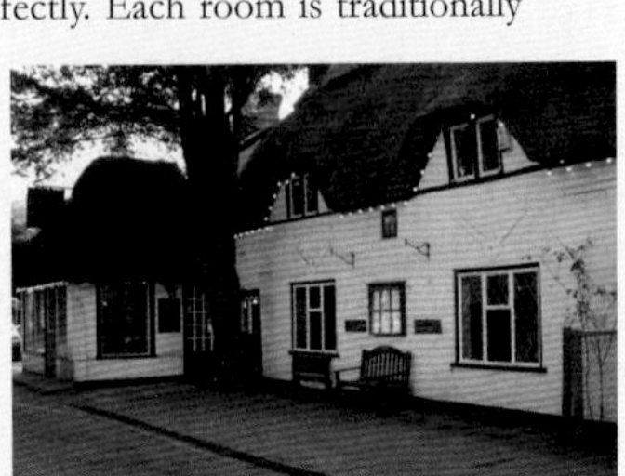

Peter's wealth of experience comes from 20 years spent as head chef in a local hotel. The experience shines through in the menu, which features old pub favourites and lighter dishes created with only the finest of local ingredients. Highlights include Fresh Ratatouille with Goats Cheese, Roasted Lamb Shank and Creamy Fish Pie. Between 9am – 11am there is a breakfast menu available and the Old Farmhouse Full English Breakfast is certainly not for the faint hearted! The lunch menu is available 12pm – 3pm every day and an excellent evening menu is available on Friday and Saturday nights.

16 SOUTHAMPTON CITY ART GALLERY

Civic Centre,Southampton SO14 7LP
Tel. 023 8083 2743
e-mail: art.gallery@southampton.gov.uk
website: www.southampton.gov.uk/art

Southampton City Art Gallery is the most outstanding gallery in the South of England and is internationally renowned for its impressive collection and temporary exhibitions programme. Housed within a beautiful example of 1930's municipal architecture, the Gallery is fortunate in possessing a rich and varied collection of fine art. It's located in the Civic Centre, adjacent to Watt's Park and within easy walking distance of the City's shopping area. The visitor facilities are excellent and it's fully wheelchair accessible, including the Gallery Shop. The shop stocks a wide range of greetings cards, stationery, wrapping paper, postcards and crafts. Entrance to the Gallery is free of charge. Opening times: Tues – Sat 10am-5pm and Sun 1-4pm, closed on Mondays.

18 PORTSMOUTH HISTORIC DOCKYARD

College Road, HM Naval Base,
Portsmouth, Hampshire PO1 3LJ
Tel: 023 9286 1533 Fax: 023 9229 5252
e-mail: mail@historicdockyard.co.uk
website: www.historicdockyard.co.uk

Portsmouth Historic Dockyard is home port to three of the greatest ships ever built, but has many other attractions. The latest of these is the blockbusting Action Stations, where visitors can test their skills and abilities through a series of high-tech interactive displays and simulators.

The most famous of the ships is undoubtedly *HMS Victory*. From the outside it's a majestic three-master, but inside it's creepily claustrophobic except for the Admiral's and Captain's spacious, mahogany-panelled quarters. Visitors can pace the very same deck from which Nelson masterminded the decisive encounter with the French navy off Cape Trafalgar in 1805. Standing on the deck arrayed in his Admiral's finery, Nelson was an easy target for a keen-eyed French sniper; the precise spot where he fell and the place on the lower deck where he later died (knowing that the battle was won) are both marked by plaques.

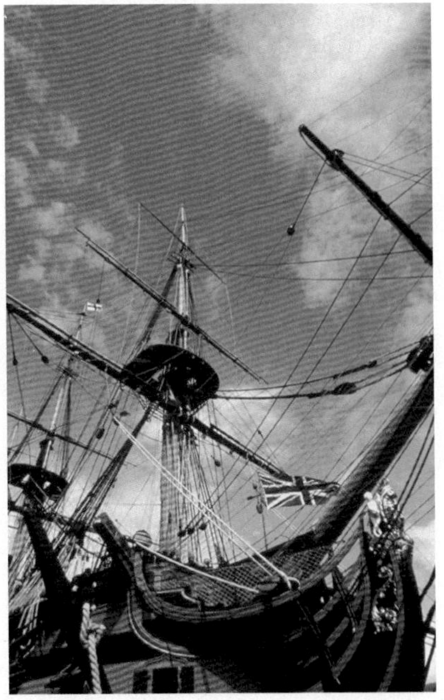

The *Mary Rose*, the second largest ship in Henry VIII's fleet, was putting out to sea, watched proudly by the King from Southsea Common, when she suddenly heeled over and sank. All 700 men on board lost their lives. More than 400 years later, in 1982, the ship was raised in an amazingly delicate operation from the seabed. The impressively preserved remains of the ship are now housed in the timber-clad Mary Rose Museum. (One of the tombs in Portsmouth Cathedral is that of one of the Mary Rose's crew.) *HMS Warrior* was the Navy's first iron-clad warship and the most formidable fighting ship the world had seen in 1860: bigger, faster and more heavily armed than any warship afloat, built of iron and powered by both sail and steam. Her size and might proved to be a deterrent to potential enemies and she never actually had to go to war.

Boat trips round the harbour give a feel of the soul of the city that has been home to the Royal Navy for more than 800 years, and the most attractive part, picturesque Old Portsmouth, can be seen to advantage from the little ferry that plies the short route to Gosport.

The Royal Naval Museum is the most fascinating of its kind, with a marvellous exhibition of the life and deeds of Nelson, and the interactive Dockyard Apprentice Exhibition explains the skills and crafts of 1911 that went into the building of the world's finest fighting ships, the Dreadnoughts. A relatively new addition is Action Stations, an exciting insight into the modern high-tech Royal Navy of today. Five interactive areas offer physical or electronic challenges and a ride on the 19 seat simulator is an experience not to be missed.

17 EASTLEIGH MUSEUM

25 High Street, Eastleigh,
Hampshire SO50 5LF
Tel: 02380 643026
website: www.hants.gov.uk

Eastleigh Museum is the ideal place to discover what life was like in the town in the past. Visitors can meet Mr and Mrs Brown, a local engine driver and his wife, and see the re-creation of their home including the living room, scullery, back yard and outhouse. Also re-created is part of the Southern Railway locomotive works and a steam engine footplate. The museum always offers something new to see with special exhibitions, including art, crafts, photography, local history and natural history, as well as the work of local artists and societies. Refreshments are served in the Whistle Stop Café.

19 THE ROBIN HOOD

6 Homewell, Havant, Hampshire PO9 1EE
Tel: 02392 482779

The Robin Hood inn has been described as "an unexpected gem in the centre of Havant". It stands in the old historic area of the town, opposite the Church and dates back to the early 1700s. The interior is full of charm and character with low beams, wooden floors, open fires and local memorabilia displayed around the walls. Hearty, good quality pub food is served at lunchtimes with the regular menu supplemented by daily specials. Fullers real ales are served, and smokers are provided with the convenience of a heated patio area.

20 EXPLOSION! THE MUSEUM OF NAVAL FIREPOWER

Priddy's Hard, Gosport,
Hampshire PO12 4LE
Tel: 023 9250 5600 Fax: 023 9250 5605
e-mail: info@explosion.org.uk
website: www.explosion.org.uk

Explosion! the Museum of Naval Firepower, is a hands on, interactive Museum set in the historic setting of a former gunpowder and munitions depot at Priddy's Hard, on the Gosport side of Portsmouth Harbour.

Telling the story of naval warfare from the days of gunpowder to modern missiles, the two hour tour of the museum includes a stunning multi media film show set in the original 18th century gunpowder vault, with the latest technology and interactive touch screens that bring the presentations to life.

There's a fascinating social history too, including the story of how 2,500 women worked on the site during its peak in World War II. It describes the role that Priddy's Hard played in naval operations worldwide for over 200 years, as well as its importance to the local Gosport community, which not only armed the Navy but also fed and watered it.

Explosion! has a Gift Shop and Waterside Coffee Shop area that are open to non-visitors, so please stop by and sample some of our traditional homemade lunches on the Camber Dock overlooking the stunning views of the harbour.

21 THE CROFTON

48 Crofton Lane, Hill Head, Fareham,
Hampshire PO14 3QF
Tel: 01329 314 222

Ian and Jenny Readman have been proud employees of the publican's trade for 20 years and their experience really shines through when you visit **The Crofton**. This light and airy establishment provides bags of character with a welcoming fire and friendly chatter coming from the wooden skittle alley.
Situated in the charming village of Hill Head, the Crofton is a 10 minute walk away from the local beach and Titchfield Haven Nature Reserve, making it the ideal pit stop during a day-out.

The bar hosts six well kept real ales and the pub has had the distinction of being featured in CAMRA's Real Ale Guide. The quality does not stop with the bar though, the food is cooked to a high standard and the menu is packed full of home cooked favourites with a continental flavour. Being so close to the coast, fresh fish specials occur daily and vegetarians and children are superbly catered for. The definite highlight of the week is the Sunday roast; a traditional roast dinner with all the trimmings is just the ticket after a day at the beach! Dogs are more than welcome and the Readmans even offer free biscuits to keep their 4-legged visitors happy.

The pub is open between 11am and 11pm all week long and food is served all day Saturday and Sunday.

22 FINKLEY DOWN FARM PARK

Andover, Hampshire SP11 6NF
Tel: Enquiries/Bookings: 01264 324141
Tel: (24 Hour Information): 01264 352195
website: www.finkleydownfarm.co.uk

Finkley Down Farm Park is a family run children's farm with all the character of a traditional farm but in a safe, friendly environment. It's an exciting day out that the whole family will love. Generations of children have enjoyed feeding the lambs and grooming the ponies during the activities, which take place throughout the day, or you can wander around and pet the animals at your leisure. A happy combination of education and fun, Finkley boasts a large adventure playground with a good old fashioned tree house and trampolines. A tea room serves a selection of snacks and drinks and the gift shop has a large array of toys and gifts.

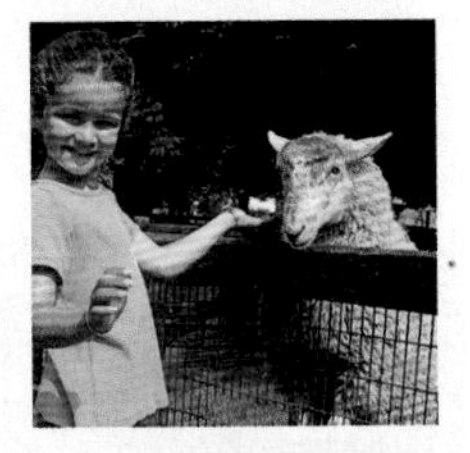

23 MUSEUM OF ARMY FLYING

Middle Wallop, Hampshire SO20 8DY
Tel: 01980 674421 Fax: 01264 781694
e-mail: enquiries@flying-museum.org.uk
website: www.flying-museum.org.uk

The Museum of Army Flying, housed on a former Battle of Britain airfield, tells the history of military aviation from kites and gliders to the very latest combat helicopters through a series of imaginative dioramas and static displays. Here, too, is a children's science centre, gift shop and an excellent café, which overlooks the airfield where aeroplanes and helicopters can be seen taking off and landing. The museum is open daily 10am-4.30pm.

24 THE CHESTNUT HORSE

Easton, Winchester,
Hampshire SO21 1EG
Tel: 01962 779257 Fax: 01962 779037
website: www.thechestnuthorse.com

Although only a 5 minute drive from junction 9 of the M3, the idyllic village of Easton in the Itchen Valley is about as delightful an English village as you are ever likely to find. It also boasts what is probably the best pub in Hampshire. **The Chestnut Horse** is a charming 16th century hostelry representing old English heritage character in abundance. Here you can enjoy a business lunch, family lunch, romantic evening meal or just a drink with friends. Award-winning English beers can be enjoyed in the bar or in the garden, over a discussion on the day's fly fishing perhaps.

Having managed The Chestnut Horse for the previous 7 years, on July 11th 2006 mine host Karen Wells took a six year tenancy of the inn. "This has never been just a job to me, it is a way of life, and even more so now that it is mine. I want my team to be recognised by the general public for making The Chestnut Horse what it is today – one of the best country pub/restaurants in Hampshire."

The food served here is definitely a major attraction. Chef Neil Beckett won the Hampshire Chef of the Year Award in 2006, this is reflected in every aspect of his work. Having worked in several well known hotels on the south coast he joined the team in 2005 to take the inn's culinary status to another level. He and his brigade take great pride in sourcing fresh local produce. Typical dishes include a tomato and mozzarella feuillette amongst the starters; pan-fried mackerel, penne pasta with roasted vegetables and tomato sauce, or the inn's famous fish and chips as main courses. For lighter appetites, sandwiches are available.

The decked area at the rear of the pub enables you to enjoy the afternoon or early evening amongst the blooming flowers in the tranquillity of the Itchen Valley countryside. You can also book an outdoor table to have a meal.

The Chestnut Horse can be a wonderful setting for a function - traditional English 16th Century pubs are hard to find. The smaller of the two restaurants lends itself to holding private functions for up to 20 people, whilst the pub in its entirety can be hired (with no hire charge) for weddings, birthdays or business functions for up to one hundred people. As Karen says "We will organise the event from start to finish with the exception of paying the bill!"

25 AVINGTON PARK

Winchester, Hampshire SO21 1DB
Tel: 01962 779260 Fax: 01962 779864
e-mail: enquiries@avingtonpark.co.uk
website: www.avingtonpark.co.uk

One of the finest stately homes of England, **Avington Park** is a family home of great distinction that is open to the public at certain times for visits and is also available for hire as the perfect atmospheric setting for a grand event - reception, wedding, private party - or a conference. William Cobbett, author of *Rural Rides*, called it 'one of the prettiest places in the county', an assessment that still holds true. The site of the original building goes back many centuries, perhaps even to Roman times, as Roman wine jars were found during work on the old cellar in 1927.

The banqueting hall, of which little survives, was built in the 16th century where the Orangery now stands; under the auspices of Charles ll, a frequent visitor to Winchester, the building was enlarged in 1670 by the addition of two wings and a classical portico and by enclosing the earlier part with a façade of the same brickwork. The State Rooms on view include the Ballroom, the Red Drawing Room and the Library, and each has its own unique attractions and points of interest. The main hall was decorated by Clermont in about 1780, and at the foot of the main staircase is a memorial to the Hon. Charles Rolls, who was killed in a ballooning accident in Bournemouth in 1911. The Ballroom, or Great Saloon, has a truly magnificent gold plasterwork ceiling, painted wall panels depicting the four seasons and many other remarkable paintings, as well as some imposing mirrors. Among the features in the Library are original Delft tiles, painted panels of centaurs, a George lll round table, an 18th century samovar and a Dutch model of a man-of-war - and about 2,000 books.

In the grounds, the iron bridge over the River Itchen is a rare feature dating from the 18th century. Avington Park is usually open 2.30 to 5.30 on Sundays and Bank Holidays from May to September. St Mary's Church, one of the finest Georgian churches in Hampshire, replaced a Saxon church that stood on the site and may be visited.

For private functions, the Library can be transformed into an intimate dining room for 90 diners or a reception room for 175 buffet-style. For more information about visiting times and private hire contact Sarah Bullen. Avington Park is located a short distance northeast of Winchester: leave the B3047 opposite the Trout Inn at Itchen Abbas and turn right through the iron park gates after the hump bridge.

26 RANVILLES FARMHOUSE ★★★★★

Pauncefoot Hill, Romsey,
Hampshire SO51 6AA
Tel: 023 80 814481
e-mail: info@ranvilles.com
website: www.ranvilles.com

Secluded, self-contained "love nest" or family retreat, **Ranvilles Farm House** 5 star accomodation caters for all even your pet! Whether you are simply looking for somewhere to relax and unwind or need a touring base from which to explore Hampshire's numerous attractions, including the cathedral cities of Winchester and Salisbury or The New Forest, Ranvilles House couldn't be better placed.

Nestled within five acres of attractive gardens and paddock, this lovely house comprises a spacious and charming Grade II* listed property of considerable character, with five en-suite bedrooms all wonderfully furnished with antiques.

Alternatively seek out serenity in the self-contained, beautiful and recently converted barn suite with its own garden. Guests can find a delicious food basket full of wonderful treats in the fully equipped kitchen. Other luxurious furnishings include a super king-size bed, 32" flat screen TV with Sky and the 'wow' factor bathroom. Recognised as a five star accommodation by Enjoy England you can expect truly exceptional facilities with a wealth of luxury.

Steeped in history, Ranvilles Farm dates from the 14th Century when Richard de Ranville came from Normandy and settled here with his family. Visit the website and take a virtual tour which gives an informative insight into the farmhouse. The tour is designed to give guests a chance to view, both the inside of the house, including all the bedrooms and the exterior of the house.

27 MILESTONES

Leisure Park, Churchill Way West,
Basingstoke, Hampshire RG21 6YR
Tel: 01256 477766 Fax: 01256 477784
e-mail: stensethhouse@aol.com
website: www.milestones-museum.com

This is Hampshire's living history museum, where the county's heritage comes to life in cobbled streets with shops, factories, interactive areas, staff in period costume and superb exhibits relating to industrial and everyday life. Among the many highlights are the Tasker and Thorneycroft collections of agricultural and commercial vehicles, and the renowned AA collection. Disabled access and audio guides are available and a gift shop sells souvenirs. A café serves teas, coffees and light snacks and there is a Victorian public house.

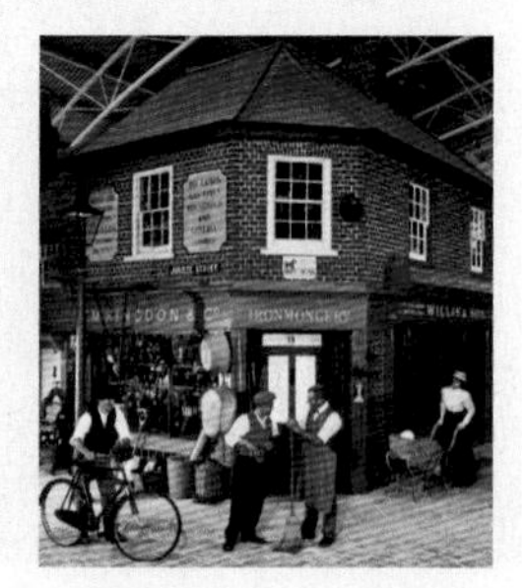

29 THE WYVERN

75 Aldershot Road, Church Crookham,
Fleet, Hampshire GU52 8JY
Tel: 01252 624772
e-mail: wyvern@talktalkbusiness.net

The Wyvern is a friendly community pub located in the village of Church Crookham. As it is in the only pub here, it acts as the heart of the village, offering good food, real ales and a tremendous social atmosphere. The traditional red brick building has ample seating, both for dining and high bar stools for a more casual approach. There is parking available here and children are more than welcome until 8pm. There is also a beer garden, perfect for the warmer months.

28 THE HONEY POT TEAROOMS & RESTAURANT

19 Winchester Street, Overton,
nr Basingstoke, Hampshire RG25 3HR
Tel: 01256 771771

The Honey Pot Tearooms & Restaurant were established in 2001 by Teresa Ruth, a charming lady with some 25 years experience in the hospitality business. Teresa is passionate about good food and everything on her extensive menu is home-cooked and based on top quality fresh local produce. Among the starters you'll find a home-made Soup of the Day, Butterfly Sardine Fillets served on croutons, and tasty filled mushrooms. For the main course, the options include Beef Wellington, Honey Pot Chicken and fish dishes such as Poached Salmon Florentine. Vegetarians are well catered for with a choice that includes Mushroom Stroganoff and Aubergine and Walnut Bake. The menu also offers an English All Day Breakfast, Home-made Pie of the Day and lighter options such as jacket potatoes, ploughman's and hot and cold sandwiches.

In addition to the regular menu, daily specials are also available. Tea-time treats include some delicious cakes, a Cream Tea and toasted tea cakes.

Thursday and Friday evenings are Pie Nights, and the Honey Pot also offers a takeaway menu of fish and chips at lunchtime, Tuesday to Saturday, and evenings from Thursday to Saturday.

30 PARK LODGE

74 Park Road, Farnborough,
Hampshire GU14 6LU
Tel: 01252 540651 Fax: 01252 404212
e-mail: martin@parklodgeguesthouse.com
website: www.parklodgeguesthouse.com

Martin and Gill would like to warmly welcome you to **The Park Lodge,** a contemporay guesthouse suitable for all, even the family dog. Offering competitive prices, there are 9 stunningly decorated rooms, all with tea and coffee making facilities, TV, free wi-fi internet and display images by fine art photographer David Fowler. Every room has it's own private ensuite bathroom. You can enjoy a continental breakfast during your stay, or a full English breakfast, which is sourced locally from Bethanies butcher, located just around the corner, serving award-winning sausages.

If you are interested in having a lazy day and don't wish to venture outside for something to eat, then why not dine 'at home' using the guests kitchenette? The kitchen has a sink, microwave and fridge and is available to guests all day. Open all year around, check in is at 2pm and all rooms must be vacated by 10am. There is off road parking at this property.

31 THE HEN AND CHICKEN

Upper Froyle, Alton,
Hampshire GU34 4JH
Tel: 01420 22115
e-mail: info@henandchicken.co.uk
website: www.henandchicken.co.uk

The **Hen and Chicken** is a historic building, which hasn't changed a great deal since it was built in the 17th Century. Originally a Chaise house, stagecoaches used to stop here whilst the horses rested and passengers refreshed themselves. Today the original inglenook fireplace is still in use and a huge feature of the pub. The décor is traditional, with exposed beams travelling throughout and smooth cream walls. With its charming surroundings, this pub is popular with locals and tourists as the location is close to Jane Austin's house.

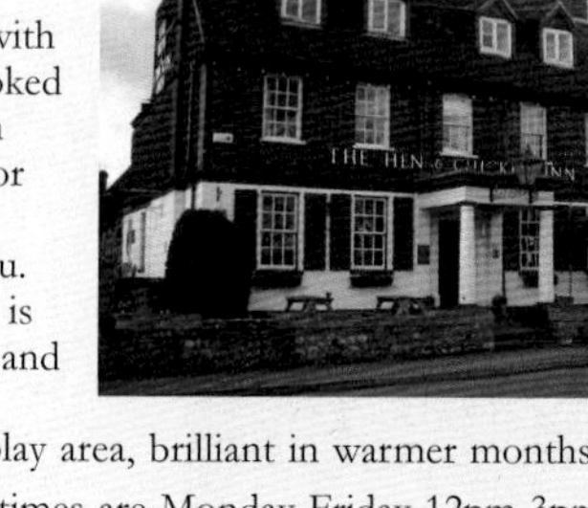

The food served here is of restaurant quality, with dishes such as pheasant casserole and poached smoked haddock gracing the menu. The food is so good in fact, that the head chef has received much praise for his mouth-watering menu. The premises is child friendly and has a large garden with play area, brilliant in warmer months.

Opening times are Monday-Friday 12pm-3pm and 6pm-11.30pm, Saturdays from 12pm-11.30pm and Sundays from 12pm-9pm. Food is available daily but note that food stops being served approximately 2 hours before pm closing times.

32 THE CROWN INN

Arford, Headley, Hampshire GU35 8BT
Tel: 01428 712150

In the beautiful hamlet of Arford, set in the Hampshire countryside lays **The Crown Inn.** In what can only be described as a stunning setting, this traditional pub caters for all, including the locals, cyclists and avid walkers. This 16th Century 'pub on the corner' is how pubs should be, exposed beams and a wooden bar, with lots of charm.

The owner Simon is a trained chef and has been cooking in pubs for 18 years. His passion for the trade is reflected in the beautiful menu available here, which is served during the times of 12am-2.15pm, Monday-Sunday, 6.30pm-9.30pm Monday-Saturday and 7pm-9.30pm on Sundays. On top of this there are 4 real ales to try and an extensive wine list.

The Crown Inn is set in the Headley village, mentioned in the *Doomsday Book* and is surrounded by many National Trust Heritage Sights and additional outdoor activities, making it the perfect place to either warm you up before an outing, or relax after inhaling the crisp country air. There is plenty of ample parking close to the premises and it is suitable for wheelchairs or those with limited mobility.

33 HAYGARTH BED & BREAKFAST

82 Jacklyns Lane, Alresford,
Hampshire SO24 9LJ
Tel: 01962 732715
Mob: 07986 372895

The owner of **Haygarth Bed & Breakfast**, Valerie Ramshaw, has lived in the pretty Georgian town of Alresford for some 40 years. After retiring from the NHS where she was a catering manager, Valerie opened her B&B in 1996. She is a keen gardener and guests are welcome to relax in the garden. Haygarth's 3-star accommodation comprises 3 attractively furnished and decorated rooms, two of which are en suite. A hearty breakfast served between 7am and 10am is included in the tariff, and Valerie is happy to cater for vegetarian and other diets.

34 HINTON AMPNER GARDENS

Bramdean, Alresford,
Hampshire SO24 0LA
Tel: 01962 771305

The **Hinton Ampner** of today is largely the creation of Ralph Dutton, the 8th and last Lord Sherborne. Born here in 1898, he inherited the house in 1936 and set about remodelling the house and garden in a carefully considered marriage of modern gardening, neo-Georgian building and neo-Classical furnishings. His plan for the garden was to lead visitors gently from mood to mood; the design is formal but the planting informal, and he created delightful walks with unexpected vistas by the thoughtful siting of trees and statues.

The lily pond, which he laid out on his father's croquet lawn, is home to nine different varieties of water lily and a good number of golden orfe and goldfish. The Sunken Garden, the first area planned by Dutton, boasts some of the wonderful topiary that is such an identifying feature of Hinton Ampner.

The Long Walk is a perfectly straight path linking the east and west extremities of the garden and featuring an avenue of 30 clipped Irish yews. The Dell, the Philadelphus Walk, the Yew Garden and the Temple - built as a folly, gazebo and resting place - are other highlights of this quite superb garden.

Ralph Dutton also greatly altered the house, more or less demolishing his grandfather's gloomy Victorian mansion and restoring the Georgian style that he much preferred. In 1960 a fire badly damaged the house and its contents, and in its subsequent rebuilding Dutton made further changes and set about collecting Regency furniture and Italian paintings to replace those lost in the fire. On his death in 1985, there being no heir, Ralph Dutton bequeathed the house, the gardens and the hamlet of Hinton Ampner to the National Trust. The furniture and paintings are on display.

35 THE FLYING BULL INN

London Road, Rake, Liss, Hampshire GU33 7JB
Tel: 01730 892285 Fax: 01730 892282
e-mail: info@theflyingbull.co.uk
website: www.theflyingbull.co.uk

Located in the delightful village of Rake, **The Flying Bull Inn** is a friendly pub and restaurant where mine hosts, Chris and Andy Bayliss, assure visitors of a warm welcome and the highest standards of customer service.

The well-stocked bar offers a wide selection of lagers, spirits, wines and ales, including 3 cask beers - Ringwood Fortyniner, Ringwood Best Bitter, and Banks's Original. The bar has a cosy, friendly atmosphere and is perfect for socialising with friends and family, or simply enjoying a quiet drink by yourself. The inn has a bright and airy restaurant offering an extensive menu of freshly prepared, home-cooked food every lunchtime and evening. All dishes are made to order and are based on local produce wherever possible. There's a good selection of continental and traditional English dishes, plus some mouth-watering desserts.

The Flying Bull also offers very comfortable accommodation, with a choice of double, twin and family rooms. All rooms are tastefully decorated, attractively furnished and equipped with en suite bath or shower, alarm clock, television, hairdryer and hospitality tray. A full English or lighter Continental style breakfast is included in the tariff.

36 THE WHITE HART INN

The Street, South Harting,
West Sussex GU31 5QB
Tel: 01730 825355
e-mail: thewhitehartinn@tiscali.co.uk

This family run business is located on the main street of South Harting, a sleepy village on the edge of the South Downs. Popular with not only the locals but also walkers and cyclists on their journeys, **the White Hart Inn** is a beautifully renovated property, which dates back to the 16th century.

Grand both inside and out, the Inn is stunningly decorated, with exposed wooden beams and original oak flooring. There is also a wood burning fire located in the snug bar, which provides a warm and hospitable atmosphere.

All of the food served here is home made and locally sourced, including the free-range meats. The property is suitable for children and there is a large garden at the rear, with a pond and swings overlooking the downs. There is a car park at the rear of the building and opening times are 11am to 11pm, 7 days a week. Food is served 12-2.30 Monday to Saturday and till 3pm on Sundays when there is a traditional menu.

37 THE EIGHT BELLS

31 High Street, Carisbrooke,
Isle of Wight PO30 1NR
Tel: 01983 825501

The Eight Bells Inn is a listed building in the village of Carisbrooke, surrounded by the beautiful countryside. Extremely popular with families, walkers and cyclists, this public house is a beautiful premises, serving great food and great company. The village itself is famous for Carisbrooke Castle, making the Eight Bells the perfect location to visit after a historical outing or brisk walk in the nearby areas. The property is traditional, withholding many original features, such as the lovely beams adorning the ceiling. There is exposed brickwork throughout the pub, creating a rustic feel to the building, however the lighting provides a very homely atmosphere.

There is a great restaurant here, with covers for 100 inside, and 100 outside in the beautiful garden. The garden is tremendous and features a children's play area and a delightful duck pond, making it the perfect setting to eat on a warm summers day. There is also a balcony overlooking the garden and during warmer months, seating is provided here as well.

The food served here is hearty and delicious, using local produce wherever possible. The menu is extensive and has lovely dishes such as beef in creamy pepper sauce made with generous chunks of tender braising steak, spicy chicken and vegetarian options such as quorn and cashew korma served with poppadoms and rice, which is lovely. There is a separate menu available for children, favourites in child-sized portions at tremendous value. There are also snacks available at the bar throughout the day for those who prefer a lighter and more informal bite. Breakfast is served at this public house from 8.30, when the property opens, until 11.30am and it really is great. All meals are served daily from 8.30am and there is a carvery on a Sunday, which is a great hit with locals and visitors alike.

There is adequate parking at the Eight Bells and the property also has wheel chair access, making it suitable for everyone. This pub really is a pleasure to visit and in the summer months, the garden is absolutely beautiful. There are a bountiful number of ducklings that bathe in the outside pond, which is a great hit with children and the atmosphere really is top notch. This is a brilliant business by owner Dawn Webster.

38 CARISBROOKE CASTLE

Carisbrooke, Isle of Wight PO30 1XY
Tel: 01983 522107

Dating from Saxon times, **Carisbrooke** is the Isle of Wight's foremost castle. Once prison to Charles I and home to Princess Beatrice, the castle is also famous for the donkeys that work in the well house. Throughout the summer costumed guides and colourful events bring the castle alive and its remarkable history is told in the museum and castle exhibitions. Open daily except 24-26 December and 1 January.

40 BARTON MANOR

Whippingham, East Cowes,
Isle of Wight PO32 6LB
Tel: 01983 528989 Fax: 01983 528671

The estate of Barton is first mentioned in the Doomsday Book of 1086, and after a period as an Augustinian oratory was run as a farm until the 19th century. When Queen Victoria and Prince Albert bought Osborne House, **Barton Manor** became their home farm. In 1902, after the Queen's death, King Edward VII made a gift of Osborne to the nation and kept Barton Manor until 1922 when it was sold into private hands. The gardens are a real delight, with the rhododendron walk, the splendid rose maze, a water garden, a secret garden and the national collections of Watsonia and red hot pokers. The estate is open on special days in the year in aid of the local Earl Mountbatten Hospice.

39 RAWLINGS RESTAURANT HOTEL

30 Sun Hill, Cowes, Isle of Wight PO31 7HY
Tel: 01983 297507 Fax: 01983 281701
e-mail: rawlingshotel@onwight.net
website: www.rawlings-hotel-cowes.co.uk

Rawlings Restaurant Hotel is situated at the heart of the lively town of Cowes, world renowned for yachting and Rawlings certainly can cater for the yachting crowd. The hotel is a two minute walk from the hustle and bustle of the town, the property is secluded with a heated swimming pool, paved terrace and well tended gardens offering shelter. The hotel boasts 16 clean and comfortable en-suite rooms, ranging from singles to family, the family rooms could also be used for yacht crews!

Rawlings Restaurant is open for homecooked lunches and evening meals, all food is as much as possible Isle of Wight and British grown. Rawlings now provides a 'ring ahead' service so that your order can be ready when you are. The restaurant can cater for functions, the function room will seat 30 or 100 people in a buffet style, perfect for private parties, meetings and conferences.

The hotel has some impressive facilities, the swimming pool is heated and open between May and September, all the rooms have internet access and the bar is stocked with a wide variety of beverages. There is even a barbeque area for those balmy summer evenings after a hard day's sail. At your request we can organise special short stay breaks i.e deep sea fishing and visits to Jurassic Island and Osbourne House etc etc.

42 WIGHT COAST & COUNTRY COTTAGES

13 High Street, Bembridge,
Isle of Wight PO35 5SD
Tel: 01983 873163 Fax: 01983 872279
e-mail: mail@wcandcc.co.uk
website: www.wcandcc.co.uk

Situated on the beautiful Isle of Wight, **Wight Coast & Country Cottages** specialises in self-catering holiday homes and are renowned for finding the perfect destinations for self- catering family holidays, where you are never far from the sea or picturesque Isle of Wight scenery. Whether looking for a character cottage, modern bungalow or period home with swimming pool and /or tennis court, the varied collection of self-catering homes are all unique and provide parties of 2 to 15, with all the particulars of your individual requirements.

Primarily based in the Bembridge area, but also in Cowes (the sailing capital of the UK), they are very close to the great sandy beaches of the East side of the Isle of Wight and the many visitor attractions on offer. The cottages provide a prime base from which to explore the bountiful wonders of the Isle of Wight, whether by car, on foot or cycling.

Wight Coast & Country Cottages, formerly known as Bembridge Holiday Homes, is a long established holiday agency, with many years experience in providing property owners with an efficient and professional booking and management service for their properties, whilst at the same time offering holidaymakers a friendly and personal approach to finding the right property to suite their requirements. Their portfolio of properties is spreading rapidly, which is why they have changed their name to encompass the entire Isle of Wight.

The website is very good, easy to navigate around and enables the user to find what they are looking for with ease; by entering a requisite number of bedrooms and location, a list of properties is displayed, each with colour picture and generous description. The description includes exact location, local attractions, amenities and activities, as well as a rating from a well established tourist board. Securing your self-catering holiday and the perfect vantage point from which to explore the diverse character, unspoilt landscapes and welcoming hospitality the Isle of Wight offers, has never been easier.

41 SEAVIEW WILDLIFE ENCOUNTER

Seaview, Isle of Wight PO34 5AP
Tel: 01983 612261
e-mail: mailto:fp@iowight.com
website: www.flamingoparkiw.com

A unique wildlife encounter awaits you at **Seaview Wildlife Encounter**. As one of the Island's leading attractions this nature haven specialises in hands-on feeding which encourages everyone to participate in feeding an abundance of wildlife including Humboldt Penguins, Macaws and Parrots, Koi and Giant Mirror Carp plus thousands of domestic and exotic waterfowl tame enough to feed by hand. Exciting new projects include Beaver Island, Pelican Bay, Owl Country, Red Squirrels and the Rainbow Experience where visitors can step inside a World of Colour and surround themselves with a dazzling display of free-flying birds in every colour of the rainbow!

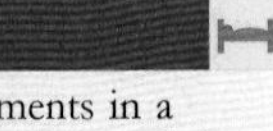

43 HAZELWOOD APARTMENTS

19 Carter Street, Sandown,
Isle of Wight PO36 8BL
Tel: 01983 402536
e-mail: wighthaz@btinternet.com /
pwrighthaz@btinternet.com

P Wright has created two great apartments in a lovely Victorian house situated in the centre of the seaside town of Sandown, Isle of Wight. **Hazelwood Apartments** consists of two self catered apartments, newly refurbished to a high standard, within walking distance of the sea. The large 19th century house hosts a large garden filled with unusual plants and the charm and quaintness of the property shines through.

The one bedroom apartment has just been revamped to a high standard, is beautifully decorated, and boasts a large kitchen and living room; the other apartment can host a small family and is decorated in a similar manner. The apartments then are certainly very comfortable and provide an excellent base from which to explore the island, these apartments would be perfect for walkers, especially those who 'walk the Wight'or cyclists.

Sandown is a lively town which offers lots for the visitor, the blue flag beach with a traditional pier, the Isle of Wight Zoo which specialises in breeding endangered animals and the Dinosaur Isle museum is very popular with kids. Hazelwood Apartments welcomes children and has ample off road parking available.

44 ALENDEL HOTEL

1 Leed Street, Sandown,
Isle of Wight PO36 9DA
Tel: 01983 402967
e-mail: paul@puppydogeclipse.co.uk

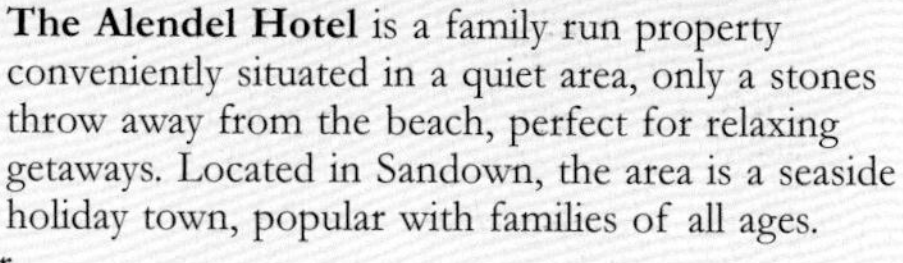

The Alendel Hotel is a family run property conveniently situated in a quiet area, only a stones throw away from the beach, perfect for relaxing getaways. Located in Sandown, the area is a seaside holiday town, popular with families of all ages. There are many attractions close by, suitable for children, including those young at heart.

The hotel itself is lovely and has a beautifully decorated interior. The building is Victorian and of a large size, housing 10 bedrooms, 7 of which are en-suite. The charming hotel has traditionally decorated rooms, with all the amenities you would expect to find at a modern hotel and the dining room is large and well lit, providing an enjoyable and sociable experience. Home cooked meals are served here from breakfast through to dinner and there is also seasonal entertainment, providing a tremendous atmosphere during your stay.

The Alendel really reflects the friendship of the town and you will arrive as a guest and leave as a friend. The staff are friendly and will ensure a great stay. There is ample car parking on site at this hotel.

45 MOUNT BROCAS GUEST HOUSE

15 Beachfield Road, Sandown,
Isle of Wight PO36 8LT
Tel: 01983 400276 Fax: 01983 406276
e-mail: mountbrocas@btconnect.com
www.mountbrocasguesthouse.co.uk

Located in the seaside resort of Sandown in the Isle of Wight, **Mount Brocas Guest House** is a Victorian building run by Mr Stone and offers home from home bed and breakfast accommodation. Close to all the local amenities and plenty of local interests such as the Isle of Wight zoo, this bed and breakfast is popular with families, couples, walkers and cyclists looking to have a quiet getaway. The big white building here is well maintained and has neutral décor, making it suitable for all. There are two family rooms, four double rooms and one twin, all with ensuite facilities and all are equipped with hair dryer, colour tv, complimentary tea and coffee and drinks fridge.

Rates are from £23 to £29 per person, per night, per room, based on two sharing and 4-12 years can stay for 50% of the rate. Included in this rate is a Full English breakfast, served with toast, cereal and preserves.

Please note that the arrival time is from 2pm and departure from rooms is 11am.

46 ST GEORGES HOUSE HOTEL

2 St Georges Road, Shanklin,
Isle of Wight PO37 6BA
Tel: 01983 863691 Fax: 01983 861597
website: www.stgeorgesiow.com

St Georges House is a family run property with 9 rooms available. Located in a quiet road between the town centre and the cliff top walk of Shanklin, this seaside resort is popular with all- including avid walkers and cyclists. Built in 1870 the building has many original features, combined with a modern twist, which is warm and inviting. The rooms are light and airy and are decorated traditionally and tastefully.

Owned by Michael and Jan Dawson, who have many years of experience in the hospitality trade, it is their aim to provide a comfortable and relaxing atmosphere, ensuring visitors return again and again.

The food served here is an important focus and there is a sunny dining room seating up to 30 people. All food is home cooked and is of a quality that you would only expect to find in a highly acclaimed hotel. Prices range from £28 per night in low season, to £38 per night in high season. Cheaper rates are available if staying for a week.

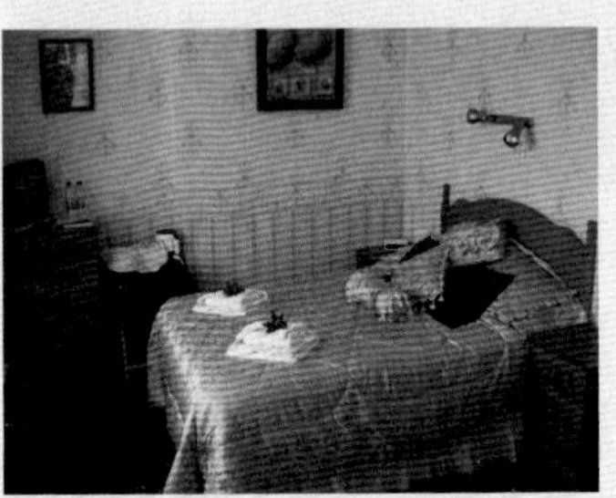

47 SAFFRONS

29 North Road, Shanklin,
Isle of Wight PO37 6DE
Tel: 01983 861589
e-mail: saffronsshanklin@yahoo.co.uk
website: www.saffronsshanklin.com

This property is simply splendid and extremely popular with the locals in and around Shanklin in the Isle of Wight. **Saffrons** is a tremendous restaurant, just off the main street in Shanklin and is only 5 minutes away from the beach. Sian Kirk manages here and the restaurant is doing very well. Having been here for 30 years, Saffrons has had beautiful write ups in papers and is often recommended for the delicious food that is served. Both Chefs working here have 80+ years experience between them, have both cooked throughout Europe, mostly Spain and Portugal and one of the chefs even had the pleasure of cooking for Royalty in the 1960's.

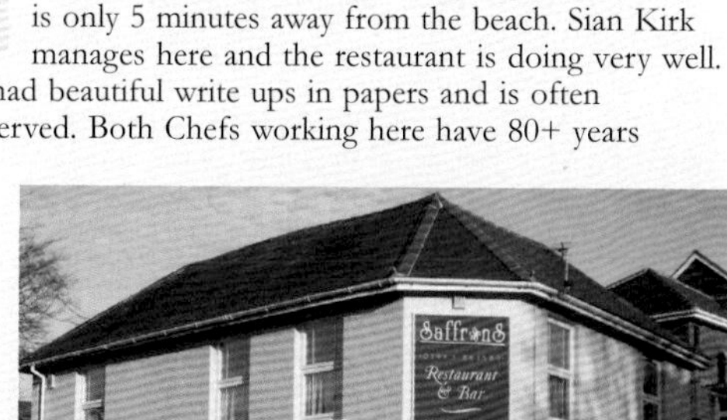

The food here is scrumptious and uses only fresh produce, which is sourced locally whenever possible. Fish dishes are a speciality and the fish is bought daily from the local fishmonger. Other dishes on the menu include Pan roasted duck breast with roasted garlic mash, Slow roasted belly of Pork and a Pot roasted Corn fed Chicken dish. Saffrons also provide brilliant Vegetarian dishes such as Hummus with roasted Vegetables and a balsamic reduction and Portobello Mushrooms topped with bean stuffing, tomato and Mozarella cheese. The restaurant is even waiting to hear if they have won an award for their spectacular meals. The décor within the building is beautiful. It is light and beautifully modern, with a relaxed atmosphere. There is plenty of exposed wood, Oak flooring throughout and beech furniture, which give the property a warm and welcoming feel. This property really is classy; the façade of the building is eye catching and features blue awnings and low-lit lighting.

Open from Monday to Saturday 6pm until late, Sunday meals are by reservation only and Saturday and Sunday lunch times are also by reservation. Saffrons is a family run establishment, which provides a memorable and welcoming experience for all. Children are very much welcome and catered for. Events take place here regularly and can be enjoyed by everyone, no matter what age. Visit Saffrons to experience an ever-changing menu including new Vegetarian/Non meat dishes. Being a neighbourhood restaurant, it is important to Saffrons to give locals the type of food they wish to eat. They are always happy to get feedback on their dishes in order to improve. Saffrons is a Vegetarian Society Food & Drink Guild awarded restaurant.

48 WINTERBOURNE COUNTRY HOUSE

Bonchurch, Ventnor,
Isle of Wight PO38 1RQ
Tel: 01983 852535 Fax: 01983 857529
e-mail: info@winterbournehouse.co.uk
website: www.winterbournehouse.co.uk

Winterbourne Country House is a magnificent 17th century house set amongst the idyllic scenery of the Isle of Wight. In 1960 the house was extended to accommodate a new wing and it succeeded in continuing the luxurious quality available; the gardens are beautifully kept and offer spectacular views over a horseshoe bay and access to the small shingle and sand beach. The garden also overlooks Bonchurch church, built in the memory of St. Boniface and restored in 1070, the church is said to be one of the oldest in the country.

The village of Bonchurch was originally a fishing hamlet and is said to be one of the prettiest on the island with its picturesque pond and lush greenery. Bonchurch gained popularity in the 19th century following the arrival of Queen Victoria to the island and boasts a healthy number of fine country residences. There are several activities available just a short walk or car journey from Winterbourne Country House; a swim from the private beach or swimming pool, riding, fishing, tennis, bowls or just exploring the island, this is the ideal base.

Winterbourne Country House is certainly a special base; providing a very high standard of luxury and comfort, all the bedrooms boast private bathrooms and most of the rooms have magnificent sea views. Guests can enjoy a breakfast room, two spacious lounges, a secluded terrace and swimming pool landscaped into the contours of the beautiful gardens. All the rooms are decorated to an extremely high standard and the lounges are very comfortable with lovely old fireplaces.

Winterbourne Country House enjoys a special reputation as a favourite holiday home of Charles Dickens, who worked on his great autobiographical novel, *David Copperfield*. He was shown the house and grounds and instantly fell in love with the place; this is shown in the letter he wrote to his wife that evening:

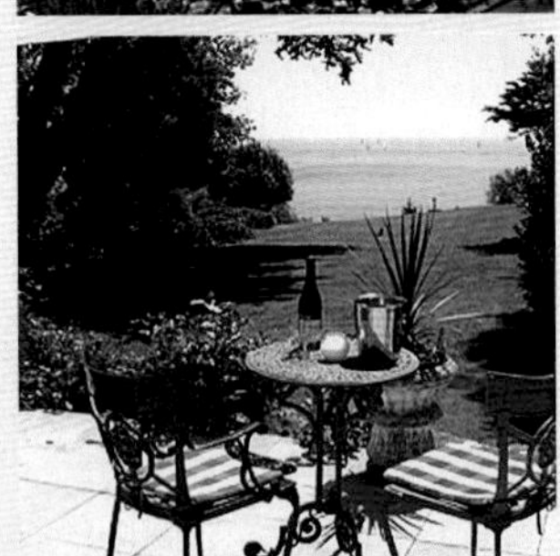

"My Dear Kate, I have not a moment – just got back, and post going out. I have taken a most delightful and beautiful house belonging to White at Bonchurch – cool, airy, private, bathing, everything delicious."

Dickens delighted in the peace and happiness he found at Winterbourne, he made it a rule that he be 'invisible' until two every day while he worked on his novel and then the rest of the day was taken up with a hectic social calendar; Dickens entertained many literary luminaries of the day: Thackery, Tennyson, Carlyle and Mark Lemmon.

49 EL TORO CONTENTO TAPAS BAR

2 Pier Street, Ventnor,
Isle of Wight PO38 1ST
Tel: 01983 857600
e-mail: lorri@plaestany.net
website: www.eltorocontento.co.uk

This wonderful tapas bar is located right in the centre of Ventnor and is a great place to come and experience the taste of Spain. **El Toro Contento Tapas Bar** has been trading since December 2006 and is doing fantastically well. 99% of visitors return again and again to enjoy beautifully homemade, traditional Spanish dishes. Lorraine Coste, a partner for this business, works alongside Serafin and Neil to provide a warm, hospitable welcome and overall great service.

The building is eye catching from the façade, especially in the evening when it is well lit. Decorated in red and green, the building has a quirky character not only from the décor but also from the gloriously traditional curved Victorian window, which is extremely unique. The property brings a smile to your face upon entering and the Spanish music puts you in the mood for a memorable visit. The food served here suits those visiting for a light bite or those who are a little more hungry. Tapas is a range of small Spanish dishes, which are designed to be shared, making this a fantastic sociable environment. Tapas dishes include light bites such as prawn fritters; artichokes with a spiced sauce; razor clams and a selection of Spanish cured meats and cheeses. There are also main dishes available such as sardines or roast duck. Paella is also extremely popular here and is cooked from scratch for between 4 and 16 people. Served with salad, lots of fresh crusty bread and washed down with good Spanish wine, the paella can have either a classic mix of meat and fish, just seafood or even a vegetarian option. In order to have paella, it is advised to book for groups at least one day in advance.

El Toro Contento Tapas Bar is a brilliant place to visit and it really is recommended when visiting the Island. Popular with the locals of Ventnor, many people reminisce of their Spanish holidays, as the food is so authentic. This property is suitable for people of all ages and caters for families with children extremely well.

Numerous events take place at this bar and feature evenings such as Mexican Mondays and wicked Wednesdays, where there is a spicy buffet from around the world for only £10 per person.

Open Monday - Saturday from 1pm - 8pm (last orders) Booking is recommended.

50 DINOSAUR FARM MUSEUM

Military Road (A3055), nr Brighstone,
Isle of Wight PO30 4PG
Tel/Fax: 01983 740844

Dinosaur Farm Museum came into being following the unearthing in 1992 of the skeleton of a brachiosaurus, the island's largest and most spectacular dinosaur discovery. Billed as 'The Working Museum in the Heart of Dinosaur Country', this unique attraction follows the tale - still unfolding - of the original skeleton and of the exciting fossil discoveries that are still being made on the island.

It is the only museum in Britain where visitors can see the bones of giant dinosaurs in the process of being identified, preserved and catalogued. Visitors are invited to bring their own fossils for identification, and to chat to the resident experts about dinosaurs and fossils.

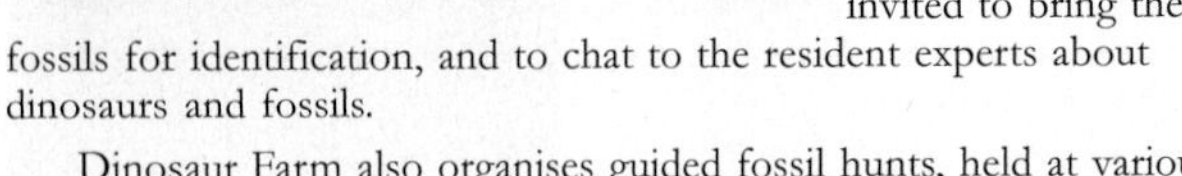

Dinosaur Farm also organises guided fossil hunts, held at various locations on the island, which can be pre-booked when visiting the museum. The museum shop is stocked with dinosaur-themed souvenirs and locally collected fossils, and refreshments are provided in an attractive tea room housed in a converted 17th century farmhouse. This fascinating museum is open Sundays and Thursdays from mid-April to the end of September, also Tuesdays and Fridays in July and August.

51 THE ROYAL STANDARD

15 School Green Road, Freshwater,
Isle of Wight PO40 9AJ
Tel: 01983 753227
e-mail: rshfreshwater@googlemail.com
website: www.theroyalstandardhotel.com

Steven Pettengell, the owner of **The Royal Standard Hotel,** has been in the hotel trade for 25 years, running hotels, pubs and restaurants all over the southeast and Europe. Steven's experience really shines through all through the hotel, from the comfortable rooms with little personal touches to the home cooked food available in the restaurant. The Royal Standard Hotel is a lovely building, dating from the early Victorian period; the Georgian style façade with white sash windows oozes charm and character. Inside the charm continues, traditional features are enhanced by modern benefits such as central heating and internet access.

All 10 rooms have en-suite facilities and are decorated in a comfortable and contemporary manner. Priced from £45 a night, the rooms represent great value for money in an Area of Outstanding Natural Beauty. The in-house Tennyson Restaurant serves great breakfasts from 8.30am to 9.30am and packed lunches are available for those looking to explore the area. Tennyson's restaurant is also open for evening meals Tuesday to Saturday 6.30pm to 10.30pm (last sitting 10.15pm) and for Sunday lunch between 12 noon and 3pm serving the best of locally sourced produce whenever possible; head chef Sam has created a fantastic menu. Lunch is served between 12noon and 3pm from Tuesday to Saturday in the Robert Hooke Bar; the bar is also available to relax in at the end of the day and colourful locals are on hand to dispense local folklore!

The Royal Standard is situated in the picturesque village of Freshwater, surrounded by open countryside; Freshwater has safe bathing beaches and spectacular coastal scenery. It is an area popular with walkers, horse riders, water sports enthusiasts and those looking for a more relaxed lifestyle. There is a modern sports centre, four banks, three post offices, an excellent medical centre and enough shops to make the village almost self sufficient.

A large percentage of Freshwater Parish is designated as an Area of Outstanding Natural Beauty. Within the AONB is Afton Marsh, which is a site of special scientific interest and also has local nature reserve status. The reserve is close to the village and is very popular with birdwatchers and botanists who wish to study the local flora and fauna.

52 THE MUSEUM OF ELECTRICITY 

The Old Power Station, Bargates,
Christchurch, Dorset BH23 1QE
Tel: 01202 480467 Fax: 01202 480468

Only five minutes walk from the centre of Christchurch, in the setting of a genuine Edwardian Power Station, the **Museum of Electricity** is a must for all ages. Everything here is electric, from an old Bournemouth tram to a pair of boot warmers! There really is something to interest everyone, with hands-on exhibits and the demonstrations for children tie in with the national curriculum. Car parking is free on site and picnic tables are available.

53 THE AMBERWOOD

154 Ringwood Road, Walkford,
Christchurch BH23 5RQ
Tel: 01425 272627 Fax: 01425 273231
e-mail: mcewen.amberwood@talktalk.net
website: www.theamberwood.co.uk

Customers visiting **The Amberwood** can be sure of a warm welcome from mine hosts Gill and John McEwen and their team. A former Coach House, the inn is conveniently located just off of the A35 at Walkford, near Christchurch,

The Amberwood prides itself not only on its excellent food and wine choices, but on its traditional local pub atmosphere. It offers traditional home-cooked food, served either in the Amberwood restaurant with full table service and a capacity of 80 covers, or in the comfortable and welcoming bar, both with easy level access. Family or business functions can be catered for either in our restaurant or in a smaller semi-private area (see photo).

Regularly changing menus and special boards include fresh fish dishes, and a traditional (and very popular) Sunday roast. Also available from Monday to Saturday is a 2-Course Lunchtime Special at a great value price, or you can create your own favourite with the Pick'n'Mix Snack Menu. In the bar, you'll find award-winning Hall & Woodhouse real ales as well as a good selection of fine wines.

The Amberwood hosts weekly live music on Fridays, Quiz Nights on Mondays, a Chess Club on Wednesdays, and jazz with the Bernie Farrenden on the 1st and 3rd Tuesdays of each month.

55 THE STOCKS INN

Furzehill, Wimborne, Dorset BH21 4HT
Tel: 01202882481
e-mail: goodfood@thestocksinn.com
website: www.thestocksinn.com

The Stocks Inn is an absolutely charming property located just outside of Wimborne. Deriving its name from the old village stocks that were situated just outside of the building many years ago, its thatched roof is stunning and overflowing with character. Surrounded by grassy areas and picnic tables, the pub will take you back to your childhood. The stocks themselves still remain and it has been rumoured that they were installed next to the pub in order for the bar maids to provide water for the people being incarcerated in them, sometimes for days at a time. To add to the history of the property, the local smuggler Isaac Gulliver who was known for smuggling gin, silk, lace and tea, is believed to have stashed his illegal contraband in the cellar beneath the pub, which is reason enough to visit.

Close by to the model town at Wimborne's Minster, the country mansion at Kingston Lacy and Honeybrook farm, the Stocks Inn is popular for its fantastic food, which has been carefully sourced within Dorset for its meat, chutney, bakeries, fisheries and wines. The owners Cherry and Steve Dyer, together with the resident managers aim to support local farmers and suppliers wherever possible and use only the freshest ingredients in order to produce dishes such as mushroom and courgette stroganoff, lasagne, whitebait and a beautiful lamb shank. The dishes here are made on the premises by the head chef Russell and are seasonal, seeing the menu change from the summer and winter months. There are also traditional Sunday roasts served weekly at an extremely affordable price, £8.50 per adult and £6.25 per child. Furthermore, the puddings available here are fantastic and will satisfy even the sweetest tooth. The goal here is to restore the true flavour of a local Dorset pub and to create a warm and welcoming atmosphere that is suitable for all.

The Stocks Inn is open 365 days a year, enabling customers to enjoy the homely feel of the interior during colder months and the shaded patio area during the summer. This fantastic pub is open from 11am till 11pm Monday to Saturday and 12pm till 11pm on Sunday. Food is served here from 12pm-2pm Monday to Thursday. 12pm-2.30pm Friday and Saturdays. 6pm to 9pm Monday to Saturday and Sundays from 12pm to 9pm.

54 ANGELS CAFÉ

10 East Street, Wimborne,
Dorset BH21 1DS
Tel: 01202 849 922

In June 2008, Margaret Philp took over an attractive property with a courtyard overlooking a river - the **Angels Café** offers wholesome freshly prepared meals at reasonable prices.

Angels Café is situated along the Stour River in the historic market town of Wimborne; the glory of the town is Wimborne Minster, which has recently celebrated 1300 years of ministry. Along the high street is the Museum of East Dorset Life, which re-creates 400 years of history in a series of rooms. After the sightseeing it would be difficult to pass up a meal and the Angel Café is perfect for hungry travellers.

The menu caters for modern tastes, hosting gluten free and dairy free menus. This along side the delicious weekly specials means you will have great difficulty in choosing! Should you prefer something lighter there is a selection of scrumptious homemade cakes, scones and teacakes, as well as a choice of surroundings, there is a riverside terrace or a courtyard terrace along with the main eating area.

The café is open from 8am – 4pm daily and from 8am – 11.30am offering a selection of breakfasts.

57 DROVERS INN

Gussage All Saints, Wimbourne,
Dorset BH21 5ET
Tel: 01258 840 084
e-mail: jason.anthony@btopenworld.com

The Cranbourne Chase area of Dorset has a reputation for being an Area of Outstanding Natural Beauty and this is the setting for the village of Gussage All Saints where **The Drovers Inn** can be found. This 17th Century traditional Dorset Cob building offers stunning views of the surrounding countryside as you enjoy the seasonal cooking. Inside, the bar, with sagging beamed ceilings supported by wooden pillars, is warmed by the great open fireplace fed with wood from the chimney nook. The décor is very much a traditional country look with oak and quarry tile flooring.

The food is all traditional British fare made with all local produce including a very popular Steak & Kidney Pie; the menu even includes home reared specials from animals kept on site.

The Drovers Inn attracts a diverse set of clientele for many reasons, walkers, cyclists, shoot parties, photographers and simply food and drink lovers. Dogs on leads and children are welcome for food served between 12pm – 2pm and 6pm – 9pm seven days a week.

56 HORNS INN

Burts Hill, Wimborne, Dorset BH21 7AA
Tel: 01202 883557
e-mail: mhastings050@aol.com

Horns Inn is a fine old-style traditional hostelry set in a semi-rural location surrounded by fields and opposite a peaceful woodland burial ground. Once inside you'll be greeted by attentive hosts Martine and Martin Hastings, a friendly and welcoming couple who have some 20 years experience in the hospitality business. They took over here in early 2008 with the aim of catering for both local trade and the family market, and that is exactly what they have accomplished - the mouth-watering menu concentrates on freshly prepared, traditional family food and there's a family-friendly play area where children can amuse themselves in safe surroundings whilst the adults enjoy a relaxing drink.

The Horns Inn also offers discounted meals for senior citizens and also welcomes dogs. There is an outdoor seating area where you can enjoy a meal and a drink in those warmer summer evenings. With there being an abundance of rolling fields nearby, why not enjoy a bite to eat in the Horns Inn followed by a picturesque walk.?

The inn is just one mile from the centre of Wimborne and with its famous Minster and Model Village it's a great place to explore if you have a few hours spare. It's also about 8 miles from historic Poole and a mere 4 miles from Bournemouth Airport if you are visiting the area from further afield. If you are looking for freshly prepared dishes, a welcoming atmosphere to enjoy a pint or just somewhere that your dog can accompany you, then a visit to the Horns Inn is a must.

58 FLEUR-DE-LYS

5 Wimbourne Street, Cranbourne,
Dorset BH21 5PP
Tel: 01725 517 282

The **Fleur-de-Lys** is a handsome 16th century Grade II listed building easy to spot on the A3078 on the way into Cranbourne. Hazel & Graham Thomas and their staff have a friendly greeting for all of their customers who can look forward to some of the best food in the region. All the food is sourced locally where possible and meals are served lunchtimes and evenings. Badger Gold and a guest seasonal ale are always available to quench thirsts throughout the day.

Cranbourne is a very pleasant place, well worth taking the time to explore, in a beautiful setting by the River Crane. Among the places to see are the Manor House, on the site of a royal hunting lodge built for King John, and a fine church with some superb 14th century wall paintings, not to mention the very popular garden centre and beautiful designated walks across the Cranbourne estate.

59 BROOK TEA ROOMS

15 The Parade, Swanage,
Dorset BH19 1DA
Tel: 01929 422 061

Peter White and his family have been supplying the Swanage area with goods from their bakery in Langton Matravers since 1866. Thirty years ago **The Brook Tea Rooms** was opened by the White family. This has been expanded as a restaurant supplying locally sourced, and traditional home cooked food at very competitive prices. The premises which are warm and welcoming, have a friendly, homely atmosphere, and are well located with breathtaking views over Swanage Bay and the magestic Isle of Wight.

The popular breakfast menu is available between 9am - 11.30am and it is well worth getting up for offering large Fisherman's and English breakfasts as well as vegetarian and children's options. The restaurant is open all day, offering specials such as lobster and crab salad, and roast dinners, all using locally sourced meat and fish. Freshly made sandwiches are always available. Dorset cream teas are very popular as are the variety of homemade cakes. Pastries and pies are served piping hot from the oven.

The beautiful setting and delicious food attracts a whole host of visiting walkers and cyclists and coach parties as well as the locals. Bookings can be made for that special occasion.

The Brook Tea Rooms are a really traditional experience and a truly hidden treasure within the lovely Purbecks.

60 THE RED LION HOTEL

North Street, Wareham,
Dorset BH20 4AB
Tel: 01929 552843

Located in the heart of this popular seaside resort, **The Red Lion Hotel** is an impressive 3-storey building with a spacious patio at the front with picnic tables where customers can settle down and watch the busy passing scene. This fine old hostelry is independently owned and run by brothers Geoffrey and Roger Letts, two local lads who took over here in 2004 and quickly established a reputation for providing good food, excellent ales and quality accommodation.

Their regular menu includes a good selection of traditional pub dishes such as steaks, home-made cottage pie, fish & chips, ham & eggs or chicken dishes, along with pasta choices and a vegetarian 3-cheese pasta & broccoli bake with salad garnish and garlic bread. To accompany your meal, there's a good choice of wines from around the world, available by the bottle or by the glass. Food is served from noon until 3pm, and from 5.30pm to 8.30pm, Monday to Saturday; and from noon until 6pm on Sunday when a superb roast dinner takes pride of place on the menu. The Red Lion is also noted for its outstanding breakfasts, served from 8am until noon. The extensive choice includes a full traditional English breakfast; an equally hearty vegetarian alternative, and lighter options such as eggs or beans on toast, or bacon or sausage roll.

The hotel is also well known for its lively entertainment. On Thursday evenings there's a Quiz Night with prizes up to £50; Sunday is karaoke evening; and there's other entertainment on Friday and Saturday evenings.

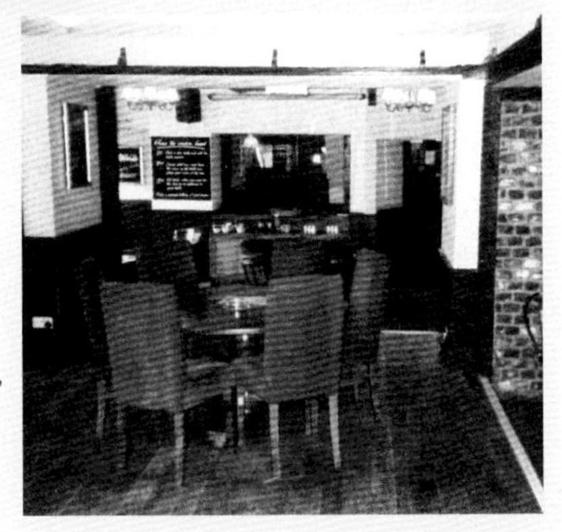

If you are planning to stay in this scenic part of the county, the Red Lion also offers bed & breakfast accommodation. There are 14 guest bedrooms, all smartly furnished and decorated, and most with en suite facilities.

Wareham itself is a delightful place to explore. It was once an important port but its harbour is now thronged with pleasure craft. Amongst its attractions, the town boasts a striking medieval church, an excellent museum – and the only gas-lit, privately owned cinema in the country!

61 BARBROOK BLUE POOL

The Blue Pool, Furzebrook,
nr Wareham, Dorset BH20 5AT
Tel: 01929 551408 Fax: 01929 551404

Tea house, shops and museum - an oasis of peace which has been attracting visitors since 1935. The **Blue Pool** itself, once a clay pit, retains particles of clay which cause a kaleidoscope of colour changes, and the 25 acres that surround it offer calm and gentle exercise among the heather, gorse and pine trees. Rare flora and fauna can be glimpsed, and after their stroll visitors can enjoy excellent home baking in the tea house.

64 LUCKFORD LAKE

West Holme, Wareham,
Dorset BH20 6AQ
Tel: 01929 551254 Fax: 01929 551254
e-mail: luckford@btinternet.com
website: www.luckfordlake.co.uk

Luckford Lake offers an escape from the 'stresses and strains' of everyday life in a superb country house, set in the picturesque countryside of the Isle of Purbeck. Tom and Sinead welcome bed and breakfast guests to their family home on the edge of Wareham. Each of the three, en-suite bedrooms has a television (video on request), beverage tray, is fitted with antique and contemporary furniture and some have spectacular views over the gardens and the Isle of Purbeck. A hearty farmhouse breakfast starts the day, served using local produce wherever possible - A real "Taste" of Dorset! Sinead is also happy to prepare evening meals and packed lunches on request.

63 THE CROMWELL HOUSE HOTEL

Lulworth Cove, Dorset BH20 5RJ
Tel: 01929 400 253
e-mail: catriona@lulworthcove.co.uk
website: www.lulworthcove.co.uk

A mere 200 yards from glorious Lulworth Cove and commanding outstanding views, **Cromwell House Hotel** is a comfortable family-run hotel where Catriona and Alistair Miller and their dedicated staff create a friendly and relaxed atmosphere in the style of a small country house.

Since they came to the hotel in 1991, Catriona and Alistair have steadily enhanced the standard of comfort provided. There are 25 rooms available including 1 with full disability access as well as two self-catering cottages which share the hotel facilities. In the older part of the house are three character bedrooms, which are particularly suitable for special occasions such as a honeymoon. All the rooms are equipped with colour TV, direct dial telephone and hospitality tray; radios can be provided on request. More than half the bedrooms and all the reception rooms enjoy superb sea views. Guests have the use of a comfortably furnished sitting room with satellite TV, a separate bar with open fire for afternoon tea, extensive gardens and a heated swimming pool.

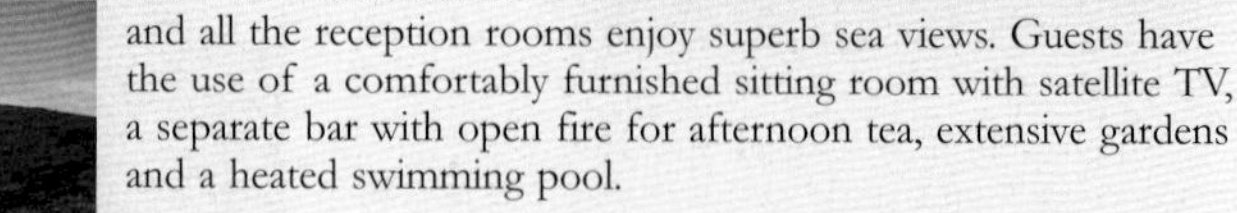

Catriona is an accomplished cook and the restaurant, which is open to non-residents, hosts a style of cuisine based on a tradition of good home cooking. Freshly prepared, varied and plentiful, her menu is complemented by an extensive choice of wines.

62 CLAVELL'S CAFÉ, KIMMERIDGE FARMHOUSE & BRADLE FARMHOUSE

Kimmeridge Bay, Wareham,
Dorset BH20 5PE
Tel: 01929 480 701
e-mail: info@clavellscafe.co.uk
website: www.clavellscafe.co.uk

CLAVELL'S CAFÉ

Kimmeridge, Wareham, Dorset BH20 5PE
Tel: 01929 480701

Clavell's Café was opened in May 2008 by Annette, Emma and Gillian Hole and has proved to be a great sucess in its first year. The farm shops sells local produce as well as everyday groceries. All the meat comes staight from the Hole family farm who have farmed here in Purbeck for over 45 years. The Café serves breakfast, lunches, cream teas, and evening meals using our own meat and local produce. We are open daily, and from May to September serve dinners in the evening.

KIMMERIDGE FARMHOUSE B&B

Kimmeridge, Wareham, Dorset BH20 5PE
Tel 01929 480990 Mrs Annette Hole
website: www.kimmeridgefarmhouse.co.uk

Kimmerage Farmhouse is a well-established and ideal place to stay for guests who are interested in walking the paths along the Jurassic Coast, an Area of Outstanding Natural Beauty. The paths start just a short distance from the house. Many lovely beaches, such as Studland, Lulworth and Durdle Door, are just a short car journey away. The farmhouse itself dates back to the 16th century and is built in lovely Purbeck stone. It nestles against the tiny parish church of Kimmeridge and is surrounded by a walled garden. The farmhouse has 3 attractively furnished guest bedrooms, all with en suite facilities. A hearty home-cooked breakfast is included in the tariff and is served in the period dining room. The farmhouse currently holds an english tourism 4 star rating and a gold award.

BRADLE FARMHOUSE

Bradle, Wareham, Dorset BH20 5NU
Tel: 01929 480712 Mrs Gillian Hole
e-mail: info@bradlefarmhouse.co.uk
website: www.bradlefarmhouse.co.uk

Bradle Farmhouse is another stunningly picturesque building in local Purbeck stone with superb views of Corfe Castle and has been providing quality acccommodation since 1982. It has also been awarded 4 stars by the Tourism board and a gold award. The interior of the farmhouse is large and spacious and is equipped with modern facilities blending with the traditional features of the house. The 3 guest bedrooms are all decorated to a high standard and all have en-suite facilities. There is a large garden at the front of the house which guests are welcome to use, and they are also free to wander around the farm. There are many walks direct from the farm and our land extends to the highest point in Purbeck with great views. A perfect base for exploring this glorious part of the county.

65 LUCKFORD WOOD HOUSE

Church Lane, East Stoke, Wareham, Dorset BH20 6AW
Tel: 01929 463098 Mobile: 07888 719002
e-mail: luckfordleisure@hotmail.co.uk
website: www.luckfordleisure.co.uk

Luckford Wood House near Lulworth, offers bed and breakfast and pitches for camping or caravanning in peaceful surroundings close to many beauty spots, beaches and places of historical interest. Ably managed by John & Lesley, the accommodation features farm views, large and tastefully decorated rooms and comfortable facilities. The main farmhouse is constructed in the Sussex house style with overhanging tiles, Georgian windows and bags of character. The well kept lawns match the attractive gardens and hanging baskets.

The six well appointed rooms all have farmland views and are decorated in a comfortable, charming and contemporary fashion. The caravan park is open with some woodland areas. Both are a short distance from Monkey World, Tank Museum and the World Heritage Site, the Jurassic coast, which provide fabulous surroundings to pitch a tent or try the hospitality offered at Luckford Wood. It is top notch! On arrival complementary refreshments are provided; the breakfast menu is enormous, from a simple continental breakfast through to kippers. There is something for everybody!

The sheer amount of activities available is mind boggling. Arrangements can be made for, to name but a few, deer stalking, fishing (in season), horse riding, clay pigeon shooting, gliding. The list is endless!

66 SHAFTESBURY ABBEY MUSEUM & GARDEN

Park Walk, Shaftesbury, Dorset SP7 8JR
Tel: 01747 852910
website: www.shaftesburyabbey.co.uk

Visitors can explore the site of Saxon England's foremost Benedictine nunnery, founded by King Alfred, who installed his daughter as the first prioress. The excavated remains of the original abbey church lie in a peaceful walled garden, and a nearby state-of-the-art museum, decorated in dramatic medieval colours chosen to reflect the original colours of the church, houses a fascinating collection of carved stonework, medieval floor tiles and other excavated objects. There's also an interactive touch-screen exhibition and a gift shop.

67 BENETT ARMS

Semley, Shaftesbury, Dorset SP7 9AS
Tel: 01747 83022

Come to Semley, in Wiltshire and you will find the ever so traditional **The Benett Arms.** A 16th century building, this public house still has all of its charm. Awaiting your visit is good company and good, home cooked food. Madelaine Moseley has been involved in the pub trade for many years, but it was the character of the Benett Arms, which ultimately won her heart and made her the new owner here.

Set back in a quiet village, the pub is surrounded by beautiful scenery and good country air, which is popular with both locals and tourists alike. This building is set over two levels, with casual seating area and adjoining lower level, which sports a roaring log fire, becoming the hub of the public house.

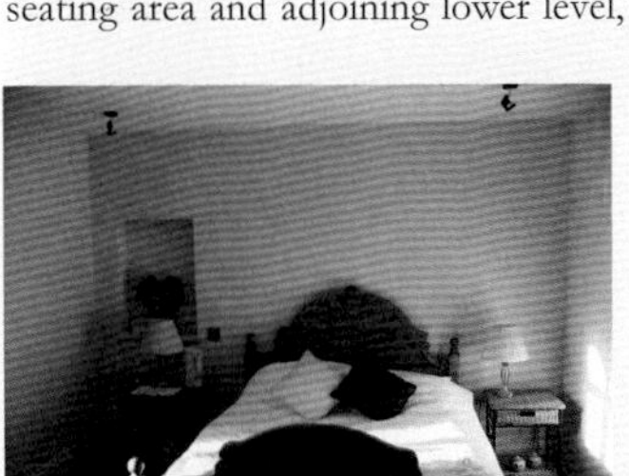

Not only is there an array of good local beers, there is also a great menu available, using all local produces, including local game. In addition to the pub, there are 5 rooms to let, all with ensuite bathrooms, starting at £42 for a single inclusive of breakfast to £85 for a family. Opening times are 12-3 weekdays, 5-11 evenings and open all day at the weekends. Food is served from 12-2 and 7-9.

68 THE ROYAL OAK

Lower Street, Okeford Fitzpaine,
Blanford Forum, Dorset DT11 0RN
Tel: 01258 861 561
e-mail: theroyaloak@newcastlefans.net

The Royal Oak is situated at the heart of Okeford Fitzpaine, well known for its walks and picturesque hills surrounding it, the village also hosts one of the few green telephone boxes left in Great Britain. This traditional pub with a warm and friendly atmosphere, run by George and Sharon boasts good traditional food, all made with local produce.

A full bar menu including panini, baguettes and jacket potatoes are just some items available lunch times and evening, from Tuesday to Sunday. The inn welcomes children and dogs, as well as cyclists, common due to there being a camp site just five minutes away. There are certainly plenty of activities to keep the guest occupied; the Royal Oak has a pool room, a skittle alley, quiz nights and darts. There are also netball and football teams run out of the pub, a testament to the owner's community spirit.

The Royal Oak holds an annual beer festival but offers a wide range of beers available all year round and a beer garden to enjoy them in.

69 THE SAXON INN

Gold Hill, Child Okeford, nr Blandford Forum, Dorset DT11 8HD
Tel: 01258 860310
e-mail: peterturner@saxoninn.co.uk
website: www.saxoninn.co.uk

The premises that now comprise the **Saxon Inn** were originally three farm cottages believed to date back some 300 years. There was a small shop in the middle cottage, selling groceries, general supplies and drinks. The Jug & Bottle did not become a hostelry until the early 1950s, when it was known as the New Inn. In 1965 it became the Saxon Inn, one of the most delightful and picturesque country inns you could ever encounter. It nestles under Hambldeon Hill at Gold Hill, by Child Okeford, signposted off the A350 or A357 northwest of Blandford Forum.

The white-painted exterior is adorned with a colourful array of tubs and hanging baskets, and at the back is a lovely garden with trees, shrubs and plants and a Wendy house that will keep the little ones busy and happy. The interior is equally delightful, with horse brasses on old beams, log fires and a warm, welcoming ambience created by hosts Peter and Helen Turner.

The drinks served in the bar include cask-conditioned ales from local breweries and a small, select range of wines from Old and New Worlds. The beers are kept in A1 condition, earning CAMRA approval and quenching the thirsts of walkers, cyclists, motorists and tourists as well as the local community.

The food is another excellent reason for seeking out this marvellous place. A wide choice of traditional pub dishes makes up the à la carte menu, which is supplemented by a daily specials board reflecting the best and freshest of what's in season at the time. Favourite dishes cooked by Helen and the talented kitchen team include cottage pie, steak & ale pie, chicken provençale, cod in batter, salmon with parsley butter and rump, fillet and gammon steaks. Sandwiches and jacket potatoes provide lighter/quicker options. Food is served lunchtime seven days a week and in the evening Monday to Saturday. The Saxon Inn has recently prepared for its continuing success by a major programme to provide more bar and dining space with no loss of the period character and ambience.

The owners have also created four superbly appointed upstairs guest rooms with state-of-the-art en suite facilities: the inn is now not just a place to find outstanding food and drink but a comfortable, civilised base for touring a part of the world that's rich in scenic and historic interest.

70 HALSEY ARMS

Pulham, Dorset DT2 7DZ
Tel: 01258 817 344
e-mail: halseyarms@hotmail.com
website: www.halseyarms.co.uk

In the Lydden Vale of North Dorset lies the village of Pulham, it is here that the **Halsey Arms** is found. Run by Holly Royle, the Halsey Arms is a family-friendly pub which hosts live music and serves good hearty food.

Once a month a special band performs. As well as the live music, once a fortnight there is a karaoke night and every Sunday evening there is a Big Prize Bingo. Food is served from Midday every day with a Sunday carvery being a big attraction, the menu is extremely appetising and represents good value for money.

The pub hosts a large function room which can be hired out, a skittle alley and table football. The public bar has a wide selection of real ales, lagers and ciders that are best enjoyed in the beer garden. The pub itself is a very pretty building situated opposite the town hall in the old village of Pulham, which is mentioned in the Doomsday Book. The website is well worth a visit, as there is a blog set up to inform about news and upcoming events.

71 CAPHAYS HOUSE

Caundle Marsh, Sherborne,
Dorset DT9 5LY
Tel: 01963 23325

Built in 1620, **Caphays House** is the quintessential country property complete with stone walls, an inglenook fireplace and magnificent views of the Blackmore Vale from its extensive grounds. It is the perfect place to stay a night or two as a break from sightseeing, walking or cycling. Situated in the heart of the Blackmore Vale, Caphays House offers excellent access to nearby towns of Sherborne, Dorchester and Sturminster Newton, the area well known for its unspoilt natural beauty and National Trust properties.

Sherborne is a well known tourist attraction, visitors flocking from around the country to view the impressive Sherborne Castle, once the home of Sir Walter Raleigh and Sherborne Abbey, which, back in AD705, was the Mother Cathedral for the whole of southwest England.

Penny, who has lived in the house for 30 years, during which time it has been an active bed and breakfast, welcomes all types of visitors, walkers, cyclists, active retirees and those purely interested in peace and quiet. There are two comfortable rooms available to hire and there is plenty of parking.

72 SCRUPLES COFFEE HOUSE

2A Barnack Walk, Blandford Forum,
Dorset DT11 7AL
Tel: 01258 459157
e-mail: adlinkforum@hotmail.com

The main square of Blandford Forum boasts many shops and retail outlets, but down a secluded walkway into a lovely Georgian building, you can find **Scruples Coffee House**. This well maintained property is full of character and the charm continues inside the coffee house; artwork by a local artist adorns the walls, ready to be snapped up by the discerning customer and the exposed beams are complemented by the pastel colours.

The café is contemporarily decorated and furnished with inviting sofas and quaint coffee tables and has internet access. In finer weather there is an outside dining area and the coffee house is very popular among walkers, cyclists, families, and both locals and tourists. The owner, Adam, takes great pride in the coffee house's homemade dishes; pizzas, jacket potatoes, quiches, soups, pastas, cakes and sandwiches are all made to order with seasonal specialties finding their way into the extensive menu.Vegetarian options are also available. Open for food between 9am and 5pm from Monday to Saturday, Scruples Coffee House offers a great dining experience for all who visit Blandford Forum.

74 THE OLD TEA HOUSE

44 High Street West, Dorchester,
Dorset DT1 1UT
Tel: 01305 263 719

Deborah and Derek bought the premises in January 2008 and have spent 7 months restoring **The Old Tea House** back to its 16th century glory. Magnificent oak beams, panelled walls; featuring Medieval Tapestries, a famous Inglenook fireplace (the Abbots Bible was found in it) and a 'friendly spirit' is said to haunt the place! This is certainly packed full of character, said to be the oldest freestanding building in Dorchester, the exterior is adorned with hanging baskets and white front oak beams, there is a lovely stone walled enclosed garden to explore as well. Situated in the heart of Dorchester, which is famous for Thomas Hardy and its proximity to the glorious Dorset countryside and coastline.

The Old Tea House contains 8 comfortable and cosy rooms, and the place makes a perfect base for tourists looking to explore the surrounding countryside.

Open between 7.30am – 5.30pm for breakfasts, lunches, afternoon teas and high teas, this Tea House is perfect for contemplating the many famous people who have lived and visited the place over the years: Thomas Hardy, William Barne, George Bernard Shaw, Robert Louis Stevenson and the Dorchester Abbot.

73 LUCCOMBE FARM

Luccombe, Milton Abbas,
Blandford Forum, Dorset DT11 0BE
Tel: 01258 880558 Fax: 01258 881384
e-mail: mkayll@aol.com
website: www.luccombeholidays.co.uk

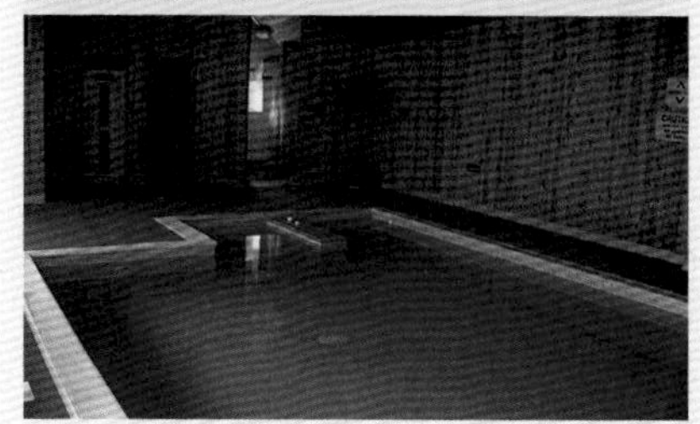

If you are looking for a hidden place this is it.

Luccombe, or 'Leu combe' in Anglo Saxon, means Hidden Valley. **Luccombe**, once part of the great lands of nearby Milton Abbey remains a working farm of some 650 acres teeming with wildlife. It is served by a private lane, making it a truly private place. The six Georgian self catering cottages, surrounded by landscaped grounds and fenced ponds, have been converted over the last 20 years to very high standards, and hold a 4 star Visit Britain award.

You will find fully equipped kitchens and comfortable relaxing chairs in all cottages. Four boast king sized double beds, with dishwashers in all but the little Granary and of course TVs, DVDs and Freeserves are fitted throughout. Linen, towels, complimentary toiletries and a hearty welcome pack await your arrival.

All six cottages are different. The Old Granary on its Staddle Stones is perfect for a couple and the Stables with three bedrooms can sleep 7. The single storied Old Sty once home to Prudence, the first pig, and the Cakehouse have been designed for those with slight disabilities. The Stalls and Tackroom can interlink to provide four bedrooms for sharing families.

The extensive facilities include an indoor heated pool, sauna and a gymnasium to work off those extra pounds. There is the tennis court with a superb view, the games room, a laundry room, and a new out door play area for the young. You can book a ride or a lesson in the riding centre through Amy Stanners, (01258 880057) and, as a guest, ask for a discount. Why not hire mountain bikes or explore the farm on foot and walk to the historic thatched Milton Abbas village with its excellent pub and shop. Meet the menagerie of sheep, alpacas, donkeys and other two and four footed friends. Perhaps later, catch a trout in the ponds and even barbeque it by the summer house, while enjoying the setting sun and sounds of tinkling water in the wishing well. The orchard provides you with fruit in season and the various fowls with rich eggs all year round.

Lying in the centre of Dorset but close to the historic Jurassic coast and aided by good road access Luccombe provides an excellent touring base for all seasons.

"There is truly something for everyone in our hidden valley at Luccombe. Just e-mail or ring us. We are here for you." *Murray and Amanda Kayll*

75 ABBOTS

7 Long Street, Cerne Abbas, Dorset DT2 7JF
Tel: 01300 341 349
e-mail: rl@3lamb.com
website: www.abbotsbedandbreakfast.co.uk

Abbots Kernel is the name given to Cerne Abbas by Thomas Hardy in his works and it is from this that **Abbots** gets its name. Owned and run by Bertie Lamb, Abbots specialises in home cooked food using the best of local West Country suppliers. Open between 10am and 5pm from Tuesday to Sundays, the menu is extensive and caters for every taste, from full English breakfasts to Fish and Chips. There are five rooms available and this bed and breakfast is ideal for touring West Dorset and the Jurassic coastline. All the rooms are very comfortable and offer televisions and tea and coffee making facilities.

Cerne Abbas has been voted Favourite Village by Savills and Country Life and is well known for its Cerne Giant, a chalk outline of a giant etched into a nearby hillside.

For guests staying, the town of Cerne Abbas has ample facilities: 3 pubs, a tea room, a village shop, antiquities shop and a clothes shop. There is also plenty to do, a Heritage trail is an easy walk around the village which takes in the local history, including the 14th Century St. Mary's Church and St. Augustine's Well, said to have been created when the visiting Saint struck the ground with his staff.

76 THE BLUE VINNY

12 The Moor, Puddletown, Dorchester, Dorset DT2 8TE
Tel: 01305 848 228
website: www.thebluevinny.co.uk

Alex Ford and Nicky Boltwood took over this traditional village pub in Puddletown in June 2008. Keeping the very best of the old, they set about combining its warm, friendly country ambience with a cool, airy modern interior – part of a style that is reflected in their approach to the food and hospitality for which the **The Blue Vinny** is rapidly gaining a first-class reputation.

The food is home cooked, and where possible the ingredients are seasonal and sourced locally from the family farm, friends or trusted specialist suppliers. The wines have been chosen to compliment the menu, and there is always a range of excellent guest ales on tap. The menu, too, reflects their very personal tastes, with an international approach to the cooking, a style that owes as much to the hot islands of the Mediterranean as it does to the classic and everyday dishes of Britain and mainland Europe. Having only recently returned to their home county of Dorset, Alex and Nicky are passionate about producing the very best food at accessible prices, as well as extending a warm and friendly welcome to locals and visitors alike.

77 WADHAM GUEST HOUSE

22 East Street, Weymouth,
Dorset DT4 8BN
Tel: 01305 779640

Wadham Guest House is enviably situated right in the heart of old Weymouth, just a few yards from the picturesque and interesting Old Harbour. The spacious Georgian house of around 1776 retains its 18th century character outside while providing all modern conveniences inside. These include an extremely spacious and comfortable TV lounge on the first floor. The accommodation comprises 9 en suite bedrooms, all equipped with colour TV and hair dryer. One of the rooms is on the ground and particularly useful for the elderly or infirm.

78 EDENHURST GUEST HOUSE

122 The Esplanade, Weymouth,
Dorset DT4 7ER
Tel: 01305 771255
website: www.edenhurstweymouth.com

Ideally located on Weymouth's Esplanade, not far from the famous Victorian clock tower you will find **The Edenhurst** is a friendly, family-run guest house offering good food and quality accommodation. The beach is a mere 20 yards from the front door and there are glorious views from the dining room with its large windows. It's just a short walk to the historic harbour, the pier bandstand and the town centre with its many shops, bars, restaurants; the railway and bus stations are also conveniently close if you are travelling by public transport. Parking can be a problem during the summer months but the guest house has a limited number of 'on street' parking permits – these are free and issued on a 'first come, first served' basis.

The guest house has 12 comfortable guest bedrooms, some with sea views and balconies, and all with en suite facilities. All rooms have colour television, radio alarm and tea/coffee-making equipment and an information pack. Hair dryers, high chairs, irons and ironing boards can be provided on request. Please note that smoking is not permitted anywhere in the guest house. Children are welcome.

79 WEYMOUTH SEA LIFE PARK

Lodmoor Park, Weymouth,
Dorset DT4 7SX
Tel: 01305 761070 (bookings)
Tel: 0870 840 5678 (information)
website: www.sealife.co.uk

From seahorses to sharks and seals to stingrays, **Weymouth Sea Life Park** takes every visitor on a fascinating journey to experience a magical world of underwater wildlife. A pair of breeding otters can be seen in their carefully re-created natural habitat, whilst information displays highlight the dangers that many species of otter face in the wild.

A seal sanctuary offers a permanent retirement home for orphaned or injured seals that are not able to be returned to the wild. The Park is also home to a pioneering and highly acclaimed sea horse breeding programme with over five species already successfully reared into adulthood.

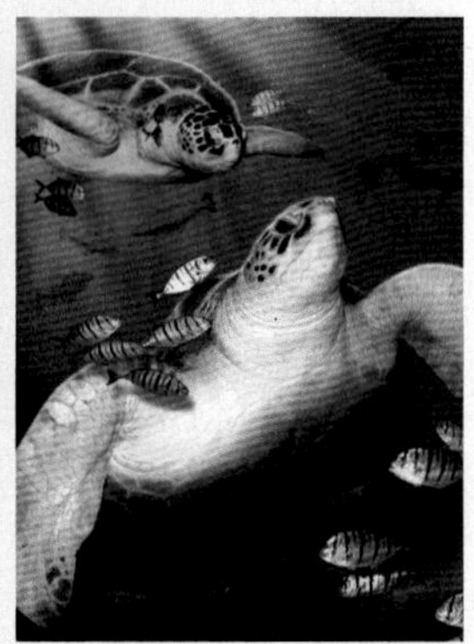

With over thirty displays and a full programme of talks and feeding demonstrations, the Sea Life Park offers a great mix of hands on fun, learning and conservation in one great day out.

Please phone for opening times.

81 SOUTHVILLE GUEST HOUSE

5 Dorchester Road, Weymouth,
Dorset DT4 7JR
Tel: 01305 770382
e-mail: stay@southvilleweymouth.co.uk
website: www.southvilleweymouth.co.uk

Located just 100 yards from Weymouth's award-winning beach and the esplanade, the 3-star **Southville Guest House** is a handsome Victorian building, the home of Rebecca, Tim and family who extend a warm welcome to their guests. They are associate members of the 'Direct from Dorset' organisation which promotes the use of local produce. "We have made it our aim" they say "to use quality Dorset produce wherever possible, from our breakfasts to the complimentary biscuits we leave in your room".

The accommodation at Southville comprises 8 attractively furnished rooms, 5 of which have en suite facilities. All are centrally heated and equipped with TV (some with DVD players), hair dryer and clock radio. Some have king size beds.

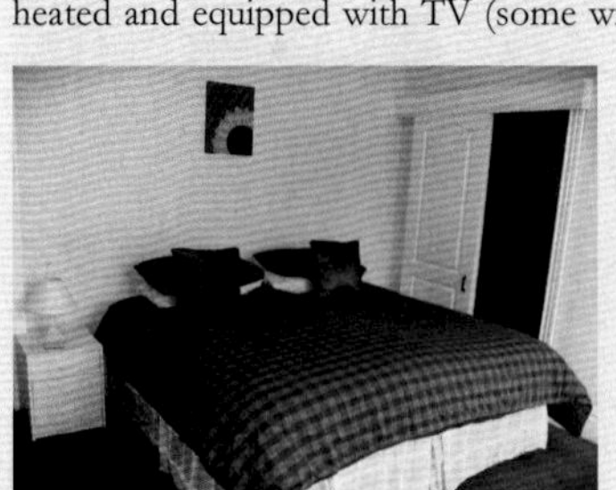

There are good pubs and restaurants within a 5-minute walk, and a much fuller range in Weymouth town centre which is a mere 10-minute walk away. Southville is just 5 minutes from the bus and train stations, and an added bonus is that quite a number of coach excursions in the beautiful Dorset countryside pick up virtually outside the front door.

80 THE WARWICK

9 The Esplanade, Weymouth,
Dorset DT4 8EB
Tel: 01305 785960
e-mail: info@warwickhotelweymouth.co.uk

The Warwick is an impressive 4-storey building dating back to 1810 and with a Grade II* listing. It occupies a splendid position with the beach just 20 metres away and the harbour on the other side. Shops, bars and restaurants are just a few minutes walk away. The Warwick provides the perfect base for coastal walks along the Jurassic Coast, for visiting nature reserves and nearby attractions and for enjoying the wealth of water sports that Weymouth has to offer.

The Warwick has 8 guest bedrooms of which 3 have en suite facilities; with single, twin, double, a triple and a family room. All enjoy superb views of either the beach or the harbour and all rooms are provided with TV and hospitality tray.

The Warwick caters for those on chartered sea angling trips with an early full english breakfast available, plus fridge and freezer facilities to store your days catch and a secure area for tackle. Some local skippers will pick you up at the back of the hotel on the harbourside.

Early breakfasts can also be arranged for Condor Ferry passengers.

Weymouth town itself varies from a rich heritage heartland with historical buildings and Georgian Seafront, to a bustling modern town centre complemented by quaint side streets with traditional pubs and contemporary bars, cafés and restaurants. All of this is connected by more than three miles of level promenade, making access between the areas easy for all. Weymouth's picturesque leisure harbour boasts fishing boats, yachts, catamarans and the high-speed Condor Ferries making day trips to the Channel Islands and St Malo in France.

Frequented over 200 years ago by King George III, Weymouth's Central Beach with its Golden Sands is a consistent winner of the national "Tidy Britain" Seaside Awards and one of the Elite 8 beaches in the UK. In the summer of 2007, records show that Weymouth had more sunshine hours than anywhere else in the UK!

82 TURK'S HEAD INN

6 East Street, Chickerell, Weymouth,
Dorset DT3 4DS
Tel: 01305 778565
e-mail: theturksheadinn@aol.com

A warm stone building that dates back more than 250 years, **The Turk's Head Inn** has long held a prominent position in the village of Chickerell – first as a private dwelling, then as the village bakery and, during World War II, housing a fire engine in its outbuildings. This charming old hostelry retains a wealth of original features and old world character, complementing the warm and friendly atmosphere engendered by mine host, Tim Guarraci, who has been welcoming customers here for more than 20 years.

The inn stands less than a mile from the Fleet and Chesil Beach, and its long association with the sea inspired the name: the Turk's Head knot was used by local fishermen, as depicted on the signboard in the forecourt. The inn has a renowned restaurant offering an extensive range of dishes,

amongst them a wonderful selection of locally caught fish dishes along with grills, salads, lite bites, jacket potatoes, sandwiches, ploughman's lunches and children's meals. To complement your meal, there's a well-chosen wine list of mostly European varieties, all at very reasonable prices. Food is served every lunchtime (12 noon until 2.30pm) and evening (6pm to 9.30pm), Monday to Friday; and from noon until 9.30pm, Saturday and Sunday.

84 LORD NELSON HOTEL

52 East Street, Bridport, Dorset DT6 3LL
Tel: 01308 422 437

Bridport, which in recent years has been featured on television in Hugh Fearnly-Whittingstall's programme River Cottage, is a charming town surrounded by the rolling hills of Dorset countryside. It is here that the **Lord Nelson Hotel** can be found, Sally and her family took over from the previous landlord of 26 years in the summer and have settled in very well.

Built in 1818 and originally called 'The King of Prussia' the Lord Nelson is a traditional local, hosting darts teams, table skittles, a pool table whilst

providing good pub grub, and a roaring fire in the winter. The pub also has a good range Palmers ales produced locally from a friendly family run brewery. The three rooms available are all comfortably furnished and a good size, including a family room for the larger groups wishing to stay. The pub is open from 11am, seven days a week.

The Lord Nelson Hotel is in a perfect location for tourists visiting the area, Bridport is close to Westbay, which hosts the Harbour Life Exhibition, Charmouth and Lyme Regis, both popular sea side resorts.

83 ABBOTSBURY

Abbotsbury Tourism Ltd, West Yard Barn,
West Street, Abbotsbury, Dorset DT3 4JT
Tel: 01305 871130 Fax: 01305 871092
e-mail: info@abbotsbury-tourism.co.uk
website: www.abbotsbury-tourism.co.uk

Surrounded by hills, with the sea close at hand, **Abbotsbury** is one of the county's most popular tourist spots and by any standards one of the loveliest villages in England. Very little remains of the Benedictine Abbey that gives the village its name, but what has survived is the magnificent Great Abbey Barn, a tithe barn almost 250 feet long that was built in the 14th century to house the Abbey's tithes of wool, grain and other produce.

The village's three main attractions, which bring the crowds flocking in their thousands to this lovely part of the world, are the **Swannery**, the **Sub-Tropical Gardens** and the **Tithe Barn Children's Farm**. The most famous of all is Abbotsbury Swannery, which was established many centuries ago, originally to provide food for the monks in the Abbey. For at least 600 years the swannery has been a sanctuary for a huge colony of mute swans. The season for visitors begins in earnest in March, when the swans vie for the best nesting sites. From May to the end of June cygnets hatch by the hundred and from then until October the fluffy chicks grow and gradually gain their wings. Cygnets who have become orphaned are protected in special pens until strong enough to fend for themselves. By the end of October many of the swans move off the site for the winter, while other wildfowl move in. An audio-visual show is run hourly in the old swanherd's cottage, and a few lucky visitors are selected to help out at the spectacular twice-daily feeding sessions. The swans' feed includes eelgrass from the River Fleet. In May of this year the Swanherd, who has looked after the colony for 40 years, Dick Dalley, retired. When he first started the birds were still being raised for the table, but today, the 159 breeding pairs - including 2 black swans - are protected by law. Also on site are a shire horse and cart service, a gift shop and a café housed in a delightful building that was converted from Georgian kennels.

At the western end of the village, Abbotsbury Sub-Tropical Gardens, established by the first Countess of Ilchester as a kitchen garden for her nearby castle, occupy a 20-acre site close to Chesil Beach that's largely protected from the elements by a ring of oak trees. In this micro-climate a huge variety of rare and exotic plants and trees flourish, and the camellia groves and the collections of rhododendrons and hydrangeas are known the world over.

There's a woodland trail, a children's play area, visitor centre, plant nursery, gift shop and restaurant with a veranda overlooking the sunken garden. Most of the younger children will make a beeline for the Tithe Barn Children's Farm, where they can cuddle the rabbits, bottle feed the lambs, race toy tractors, feed the doves and meet the donkeys and horses. The Farm's latest attraction is the Smugglers Barn, where the little ones can learn and play at the same time.

86 THE BRIDGE HOUSE HOTEL

Beaminster, Dorset DT8 3AY
Tel: 01308 862200 Fax: 01308 863700
e-mail: enquiries@bridge-house.co.uk
website: www.bridge-house.co.uk

Set in the heart of this attractive old market town, **The Bridge House Hotel** has a history stretching back to the 13th century when it served as a priest's house. Much of the present fabric is Georgian and the warm stone, oak beams and large fireplaces all evoke a more leisured and elegant age. Owners Mark Donovan, a former documentary film producer and his wife Joanna, have ensured that character has not been sacrificed for comfort – though comfort is there in plenty. All the 14 guest bedrooms have a 3-star rating from the AA and all have their own bathroom, colour television, direct dialling telephones, free wireless broadband and tea/coffee-making facilities. Four of the bedrooms are situated on the ground floor with easy access.

Central to the hotel's hospitality is the food served in its AA rosette rated restaurant. Whether you are taking a light al fresco lunch in the new brasserie overlooking the secluded garden, or eating in the stunning panelled dining room, you will appreciate the rare attention to detail and the use, wherever possible, of fresh organic produce from local farms and fishing ports; individually priced menus are available to both resident and non-residents.

The hotel welcomes dogs by arrangement in the Coach House but they are not allowed in public rooms and must not be left unattended in bedrooms.

The Bridgehouse offers a variety of Getaway Breaks with dinner, bed & breakfast for a minimum of two nights at advantageous rates which include a 4-course table d'hôte dinner and coffee, plus a full multi-choice English or Continental breakfast.

Beaminster itself is a delightful place to explore and is a convenient base for touring, walking or exploring the magnificent West Dorset countryside. Golf, fresh and salt water fishing, diving and shooting are all available locally, and many fine houses and gardens, as well as Dorset's World Heritage site – the Jurassic Coast – are all within easy reach.

85 NEW INN

Mount Lane, Eype, Nr. Bridport,
Dorset DT6 6AP
Tel: 01308 423 254
website: www.new-inn.eype.co.uk

Just 10 minutes from the sea, and offering magnificent views over the Dorset countryside, the **New Inn** is well placed for people admiring the Jurassic coastline, an Area of Outstanding Natural Beauty, or a good home-cooked meal.

The varied menu caters for all tastes; all cooked using locally sourced produce, and on offer are salads, steaks and mouth-watering Sunday roasts, to name just a few options. To accompany the meal, the New Inn hosts a wide range of real ales, wines and spirits, not to mention the friendly service and homely atmosphere. During the summer, the beer garden has to be visited just for the magnificent views over the rolling Dorset hills. Built in 1837, the pub certainly looks the part as well, with a slate roof and hanging baskets adorning the walls, the New Inn is a very welcoming place.

For tourists, the pub is in an ideal location as well: close by to the market town of Bridport and the popular sea side towns of Charmouth and Lyme Regis. The pub is closed on Mondays during the winter, open between 12pm-3pm and 6pm-11pm Tues – Sat and all day Sunday.

88 BLUE SKY B & B

8 Pound Street, Lyme Regis,
Dorset DT7 3HZ
Tel: 01297 442 339
e-mail: stay@bluesky-lymeregis.co.uk
website: www.bluesky-lymeregis.co.uk

Known as the 'Pearl of Dorset', Lyme Regis is a delightful sea side town, attracting people from all over the world due to its position at the heart of the Heritage Coastline, known as the 'Jurassic Coast'. In fact in the early 1800's, a 12 year old girl called Mary Anning discovered the fossil of the first Ichthyosaur in England.

It is among such history that the **Blue Sky B & B** is located and the B & B manages to provide accommodation fitting to the surroundings. The building is a large terrace and has retained many of its original Edwardian features. The six bedrooms are all en-suite and they are very comfortably furnished, one room even has a luxury 4 poster bed! After a relaxing night's sleep, guests are then invited to choose from a smorgasbord of breakfast choices, including the classic full English and a less filling continental. The B & B is open all year round and is offering a very tempting special Christmas deal, the details of which can be found on the website. Ample parking nearby and some disabled access available. B & B from £33 pppn.

87 TALBOT ARMS

Lyme Road, Uplyme, Devon DT7 3TF
Tel: 01297 443136
e-mail: steve@talbotarms.com
website: www.talbotarms.com

The **Talbot Arms** is a free house with adjacent accommodation located in the beautiful village of Uplyme, Devon. Popular with locals for the high quality pub food and warm hospitality, it is also a great hit with those coming from far a field as the riverside accommodation is tastefully decorated and of high quality- the prices are also very reasonable. Landlords Steve and Wendy Gardner have a beautifully traditional, country Inn here and aim to provide the best service they can to their visitors. The free house is traditional, with exposed beams and a modern twist on exposed brickwork and there is a great selection of Beers, Lagers, Ciders, Wines and Spirits to enjoy. As well as the wide range of drinks available, the Talbot Arms also offers superb, home cooked food. Steve has 30 years of experience in catering and he has used this to create a great menu, which always goes down well. Food such as Sautéed King Prawns in garlic butter, Homemade Steak and Ale Pie and Beer Batter Cod and Chips can be found on the menu, as well as Treacle Tart and Apple Crumble for desert. All food served at this establishment is almost entirely sourced locally, making the food taste great. Within the restaurant there are events that take place weekly; Tuesday sees a takeaway night and Thursdays have a Lunch catered for OAP's.

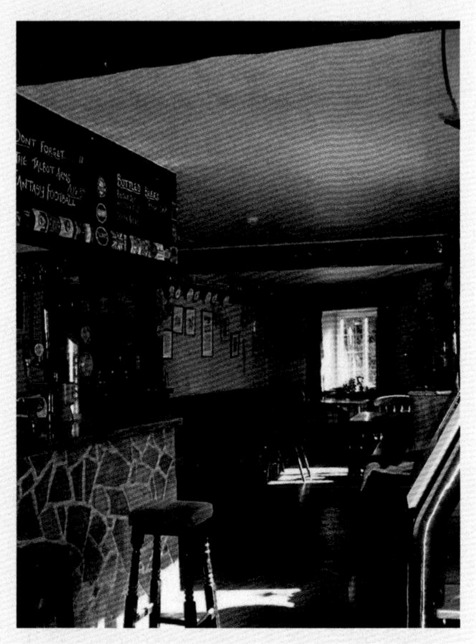

There are also dates to jot down in your diary annually, such as the Beer Festival, which takes place over a weekend in the summer. A great selection of beers and ciders, entertainment and barbeques on Friday and Saturday evening and a Swing band and unbelievable Hog roast on Sunday, making it a weekend not to be missed. The bed and Breakfast available here is fairly new, and has 5 newly built ensuite rooms. There are 4 double rooms and one twin available, all of which are situated in a quiet location by the river Lym- prices start from £60 per night for the room only.

If you come to the Talbot Arms to stay for a weekend, you will not be disappointed. The accommodation has been finished to a very high standard and the local interest close by will ensure you have a memorable stay and want to return again and again.

89 CHARMOUTH HERITAGE COAST CENTRE

Lower Sea Lane, Charmouth,
Dorset DT6 6LL
Tel: 01297 560772
website: www.charmouth.org

Charmouth Heritage Coast Centre is one of the country's leading coastal geological visitor centres. The Centre's displays introduce the visitor to the amazing geology and fossils of the West Dorset coast. There are fossils for you to look at and touch, interactive fossil identification displays and a "fossil beach" to practice fossil hunting.

Two large aquariums house a variety of local marine life, while a computerised display lets you dive into Lyme Bay and discover the secrets of the underwater world. For a small charge you can visit the Jurassic Theatre and discover "Finding Fossils at Charmouth" or "Secrets of the Sea". A wide selection of books, postcards and gifts are on sale.

The Centre is run by three wardens who organise a series of guided walks throughout the season. As well as the popular fossil hunting walks, there are rockpooling sessions and walks in the local countryside. Details are available from the Centre or from the website.

90 BOTTLE INN

Marshwood, Nr Bridport,
Dorset DT6 5QJ
Tel: 01297 678 214
website: www.thebottleinn.co.uk

Proprietors Rory and Toni-Marie have a wealth of experience between them of the trade, having worked in various pubs throughout Dorset and this knowledge has shown through in the **Bottle Inn**. The name came from the pub being the first Inn in the area to sell beer in a bottle sometime in the 18th century. Now the premises are more famous for the internationally acclaimed World Stinging Nettle Eating Championship, held annually; the current world champion is Paul Collins.

The premises were built in 1585, and the beautiful thatched building benefits from a huge beer garden, which is very popular with families and a separate camping field. The Inn offers great food from a well thought out menu, there is something for everybody; tempting choices include Roast Duck with an Orange & Ginger sauce and Medallions of pork Fillet in a Stilton sauce. Following a country theme, the food often boasts local specialities such as in season Game. The bar is well stocked, three real ales and a guest are always available and with many bar games: skittles, pool, darts, there is plenty to keep the guest occupied.

A popular draw to the Bottle Inn is the twice weekly live music on Friday nights and Sunday lunchtimes.

Tourist Information Centres

DORSET

BLANDFORD FORUM

1 Greyhound Yard, Blandford Forum, Dorset DT11 7EB
e-mail: blandfordtic@north-dorset.gov.uk
Tel: 01258 454770

BOURNEMOUTH

Westover Road, Bournemouth, Dorset BH1 2BU
e-mail: info@bournemouth.gov.uk
Tel: 01202 451700

BRIDPORT

47 South Street, Bridport, Dorset DT6 3NY
e-mail: bridport.tic@westdorset-dc.gov.uk
Tel: 01308 424901

CHRISTCHURCH

49 High Street, Christchurch, Dorset BH23 1AS
e-mail: enquiries@christchurchtourism.info
Tel: 01202 471780

DORCHESTER

11 Antelope Walk, Dorchester, Dorset DT1 1BE
e-mail: dorchester.tic@westdorset-dc.gov.uk
Tel: 01305 267992

LYME REGIS

Guildhall Cottage, Church Street, Lyme Regis, Dorset DT7 3BS
e-mail: lymeregis.tic@westdorset-dc.gov.uk
Tel: 01297 442138

POOLE

Enefco House, Poole Quay, Poole, Dorset BH15 1HJ
e-mail: info@poole.gov.uk
Tel: 01202 253253

SHAFTESBURY

8 Bell Street, Shaftesbury, Dorset SP7 8AE
e-mail: tourism@shaftesburydorset.com
Tel: 01747 853514

SHERBORNE

3 Tilton Court, Digby Road, Sherborne, Dorset DT9 3NL
e-mail: sherborne.tic@westdorset-dc.gov.uk
Tel: 01935 815341

SWANAGE

The White House, Shore Road, Swanage, Dorset BH19 1LB
e-mail: mail@swanage.gov.uk
Tel: 01929 422885

WAREHAM

Holy Trinity Church, South Street, Wareham, Dorset BH20 4LU
e-mail: tic@purbeck-dc.gov.uk
Tel: 01929 552740

WEYMOUTH

The King's Statue, The Esplanade, Weymouth, Dorset DT4 7AN
e-mail: tic@weymouth.gov.uk
Tel: 01305 785747

WIMBORNE MINSTER

29 High Street, Wimborne Minster, Dorset BH21 1HR
e-mail: wimbornetic@eastdorset.gov.uk
Tel: 01202 886116

HAMPSHIRE

ALDERSHOT

Prince's Gardens, 2a High Street, Aldershot, Hampshire GU11 1BJ
e-mail: mail@rushmoorvic.com
Tel: 01252 320968

ANDOVER

Andover Museum, 6 Church Close, Andover, Hampshire SP10 1DP
e-mail: andovertic@testvalley.gov.uk
Tel: 01264 324320

FAREHAM

Westbury Manor, 84 West Street, Fareham, Hampshire PO16 0JJ
e-mail: touristinfo@fareham.gov.uk
Tel: 01329 221342

FORDINGBRIDGE

Kings Yard, Salisbury Street, Fordingbridge, Hampshire SP6 1AB
e-mail: fordingbridgetic@tourismse.com
Tel: 01425 654560

GOSPORT

Bus Station Complex, South Street, Gosport,
Hampshire PO12 1EP
e-mail: tourism@gosport.gov.uk
Tel: 023 9252 2944

HAYLING ISLAND

Central Beachlands, Seafront, Hayling Island,
Hampshire PO11 OAG
e-mail: tourism@havant.gov.uk
Tel: 023 9246 7111

LYMINGTON

St Barbe Museum & Visitor Centre, New Street,
Lymington, Hampshire SO41 9BH
e-mail: information@nfdc.gov.uk
Tel: 01590 689000

LYNDHURST & NEW FOREST

New Forest Museum & Visitor Centre, Main Car Park,
Lyndhurst, Hampshire SO43 7NY
e-mail: information@nfdc.gov.uk
Tel: 023 8028 2269

PETERSFIELD

County Library, 27 The Square, Petersfield,
Hampshire GU32 3HH
e-mail: petersfieldinfo@btconnect.com
Tel: 01730 268829

PORTSMOUTH

The Hard, Portsmouth, Hampshire PO1 3QJ
e-mail: vis@portsmouthcc.gov.uk
Tel: 023 9282 6722

PORTSMOUTH

Clarence Esplanade, Southsea, Portsmouth,
Hampshire PO5 3PB
e-mail: vis@portsmouthcc.gov.uk
Tel: 023 9282 6722

RINGWOOD

The Furlong, Ringwood, Hampshire BH24 1AT
e-mail: information@nfdc.gov.uk
Tel: 01425 470896

ROMSEY

Heritage & Visitor Centre, 13 Church Street, Romsey,
Hampshire SO51 8BT
e-mail: romseytic@testvalley.gov.uk
Tel: 01794 512987

SOUTHAMPTON

9 Civic Centre Road, Southampton, Hampshire SO14 7FJ
e-mail: tourist.information@southampton.gov.uk
Tel: 023 80 833 333

WINCHESTER

Winchester Guildhall, High Street, Winchester, Hampshire
SO23 9GH
e-mail: tourism@winchester.gov.uk
Tel: 01962 840500

ISLE OF WIGHT

NEWPORT

The Guildhall, High Street, Newport,
Isle of Wight PO30 1TY
e-mail: info@islandbreaks.co.uk
Tel: 01983 813818

RYDE

81-83 Union Street, Ryde, Isle of Wight PO33 2LW
e-mail: info@islandbreaks.co.uk
Tel: 01983 813818

SANDOWN

8 High Street, Sandown, Isle of Wight PO36 8DG
info@islandbreaks.co.uk
01983 813818

SHANKLIN

67 High Street, Shanklin, Isle of Wight PO37 6JJ
e-mail: info@islandbreaks.co.uk
Tel: 01983 813818

YARMOUTH

The Quay, Yarmouth, Isle of Wight PO41 4PQ
e-mail: info@islandbreaks.co.uk
Tel: 01983 813818

Towns, Villages and Places of Interest

A

B

C

TRAVEL PUBLISHING ORDER FORM

To order any of our publications just fill in the payment details below and complete the order form. For orders of less than 4 copies please add £1.00 per book for postage and packing. Orders over 4 copies are P & P free.

Name:

Address:

Tel no:

Please Complete Either:

I enclose a cheque for £ __________ made payable to Travel Publishing Ltd

Or:

Card No: Expiry Date:

Signature:

Please either send, telephone, fax or e-mail your order to:

Travel Publishing Ltd, Airport Business Centre, 10 Thornbury Road, Estover, Plymouth PL6 7PP

Tel: 01752 697280 Fax: 01752 697299 e-mail: info@travelpublishing.co.uk

	Price	*Quantity*
HIDDEN PLACES REGIONAL TITLES		
Cornwall	£8.99	....
Devon	£8.99	....
Dorset, Hants & Isle of Wight	£8.99	....
East Anglia	£8.99	....
Lake District & Cumbria	£8.99	....
Lancashire & Cheshire	£8.99	....
Northumberland & Durham	£8.99	....
Peak District and Derbyshire	£8.99	....
Yorkshire	£8.99	....
HIDDEN PLACES NATIONAL TITLES		
England	£11.99	....
Ireland	£11.99	....
Scotland	£11.99	....
Wales	£11.99	....
OTHER TITLES		
Off the Motorway	£11.99	....
Garden Centres & Nurseries	£11.99	....

	Price	*Quantity*
COUNTRY LIVING RURAL GUIDES		
East Anglia	£10.99	....
Heart of England	£10.99	....
Ireland	£11.99	....
North East	£10.99	....
North West	£10.99	....
Scotland	£11.99	....
South of England	£10.99	....
South East of England	£10.99	....
Wales	£11.99	....
West Country	£10.99	....

TOTAL QUANTITY:

POST & PACKING:

TOTAL VALUE:

READER REACTION FORM

The *Travel Publishing* research team would like to receive reader's comments on any visitor attractions or places reviewed in the book and also recommendations for suitable entries to be included in the next edition. This will help ensure that the *Hidden Places series of Guides* continues to provide its readers with useful information on the more interesting, unusual or unique features of each attraction or place ensuring that their visit to the local area is an enjoyable and stimulating experience. To provide your comments or recommendations would you please complete the forms below and overleaf as indicated and send to:

The Research Department, Travel Publishing Ltd,
Airport Business Centre, 10 Thornbury Road, Estover, Plymouth PL6 7PP

Your Name:

Your Address:

Your Telephone Number:

Please tick as appropriate:

Comments ☐ Recommendation ☐

Name of Establishment:

Address:

Telephone Number:

Name of Contact:

READER REACTION FORM

COMMENT OR REASON FOR RECOMMENDATION:

....

....

....

....

....

....

....

....

....

....

....

....

....

....

....

....

....

....

....

....

READER REACTION FORM

The *Travel Publishing* research team would like to receive reader's comments on any visitor attractions or places reviewed in the book and also recommendations for suitable entries to be included in the next edition. This will help ensure that the *Hidden Places series of Guides* continues to provide its readers with useful information on the more interesting, unusual or unique features of each attraction or place ensuring that their visit to the local area is an enjoyable and stimulating experience. To provide your comments or recommendations would you please complete the forms below and overleaf as indicated and send to:

The Research Department, Travel Publishing Ltd,
Airport Business Centre, 10 Thornbury Road, Estover, Plymouth PL6 7PP

Your Name:

Your Address:

Your Telephone Number:

Please tick as appropriate:

Comments ☐ Recommendation ☐

Name of Establishment:

Address:

Telephone Number:

Name of Contact:

READER REACTION FORM

COMMENT OR REASON FOR RECOMMENDATION:

READER REACTION FORM

The *Travel Publishing* research team would like to receive reader's comments on any visitor attractions or places reviewed in the book and also recommendations for suitable entries to be included in the next edition. This will help ensure that the *Hidden Places series of Guides* continues to provide its readers with useful information on the more interesting, unusual or unique features of each attraction or place ensuring that their visit to the local area is an enjoyable and stimulating experience. To provide your comments or recommendations would you please complete the forms below and overleaf as indicated and send to:

The Research Department, Travel Publishing Ltd,
Airport Business Centre, 10 Thornbury Road, Estover, Plymouth PL6 7PP

Your Name:

Your Address:

Your Telephone Number:

Please tick as appropriate:

Comments ☐ Recommendation ☐

Name of Establishment:

Address:

Telephone Number:

Name of Contact:

READER REACTION FORM

COMMENT OR REASON FOR RECOMMENDATION:

READER REACTION FORM

The *Travel Publishing* research team would like to receive reader's comments on any visitor attractions or places reviewed in the book and also recommendations for suitable entries to be included in the next edition. This will help ensure that the *Hidden Places series of Guides* continues to provide its readers with useful information on the more interesting, unusual or unique features of each attraction or place ensuring that their visit to the local area is an enjoyable and stimulating experience. To provide your comments or recommendations would you please complete the forms below and overleaf as indicated and send to:

The Research Department, Travel Publishing Ltd,
Airport Business Centre, 10 Thornbury Road, Estover, Plymouth PL6 7PP

Your Name:

Your Address:

Your Telephone Number:

Please tick as appropriate:

Comments ☐ Recommendation ☐

Name of Establishment:

Address:

Telephone Number:

Name of Contact:

READER REACTION FORM

COMMENT OR REASON FOR RECOMMENDATION:

Index of Advertisers

PLACES OF INTEREST